Classroom
Celebrations

The Best of
*Holidays & Seasonal
Celebrations*

Teaching & Learning Company

1204 Buchanan St., P.O. Box 10
Carthage, IL 62321

This book belongs to

_____

Edited and compiled by Donna Borst

Cover illustration by Darcy Tom

Illustrations by:

Janet Armbrust	Gary Mohrman
Pat Biggs	Chris Nye
Cara H. Bradshaw	Becky Radtke
Priscilla Burris	Shelly Rasche
Mary Detring	Luda Stekol
Alex Glikin	Veronica Terrill
David Helton	Darcy Tom
Gary Hoover	Gayle Vella
Teresa Mathis	

Copyright © 1996, Teaching & Learning Company

ISBN No. 1-57310-047-1

Printing No. 987654321

Teaching & Learning Company
1204 Buchanan St., P.O. Box 10
Carthage, IL 62321

Table of Contents

Fall 13

Winter 110

Spring and Summer 226

Dear Teacher or Parent,

When we first thought about publishing a magazine, our staff got together to brainstorm ideas and share the thoughts we had gathered from speaking and listening to teachers. Needless to say, we have gathered much feedback from teachers, parents, homeschoolers and day-care providers.

The most surprising thing about that meeting was how quickly it was over! We were in complete agreement about what we wanted to do and how we wanted to do it. It seems that everyone we had heard from wanted and needed more ideas for holidays and seasons. That gave us our starting point. Each of us had also discovered a dearth of multicultural resources relating to the holidays and seasons and wanted our publication to reflect the diversity in today's classrooms. We felt strongly that this should not only apply to content but should also be reflected in the illustrations. We all wanted the magazine to be environmentally aware and to convey that philosophy with ideas and activities that made good use of recycled materials. Visually, we wanted the magazine to be appealing, ethnically diverse, colorful, filled with art, easy-to-read, easy-to-use, age-appropriate, friendly, fun and professional. Editorially, we wanted it to be different, practical, creative, innovative, classroom-tested, written by teachers and educators, and most importantly, useful to one and all.

The response to our efforts has been incredible. We want to thank all of our writers, illustrators and subscribers for making this first year such a success. We can think of no better way to do that than to compile all those wonderful words and pictures into a single, one-of-a-kind resource. If you love the magazine, you're really going to love this book—320 pages of our very best. If you've never heard of *Holidays & Seasonal Celebrations*, here is a great introduction to what we're all about. The next time you need ideas for a holiday or seasonal celebration, we hope you'll think of us—we're doing this for you and hopefully we're doing it right. Together maybe we can put some fun and energy back into the classroom—and we believe that's a real cause for celebration!

Sincerely,

Donna

Donna Borst

If you would like to contribute to future issues of *Holidays & Seasonal Celebrations*, please direct your submissions to:

> Teaching & Learning Company
> Holidays & Seasonal Celebrations
> 1204 Buchanan St., P.O. Box 10
> Carthage, IL 62321

Mixing Holidays Can Be Fun!

The Easter Bunny

   would feel out of place

at a Halloween parade

   with a mask on his face!

If he dressed as a goblin,

   or the wicked old witch,

his many admirers

   wouldn't like the switch!

The Easter Bunny

   should carry a basket

with brightly colored eggs!

   A tisket! A tasket!

If Valentine's Day,

   the day of old Cupid,

came on St. Patrick's Day,

   it would seem pretty stupid

to see leprechauns,

   who are wearing the green,

delivering valentines

   to your favorite queen!

Choose a funny situation,

   Mix a holiday or two,

and create a combination

   that is comical and new!

by Peggy Cochard

This light verse will stir the imagination of young children and encourage them to create some of their own holiday mixes!

After the children verbalize a variety of situations, they can draw their own holiday mix. Santa Claus might be dressed as a hobo for Halloween or the Easter Bunny may be setting off fireworks on the Fourth of July.

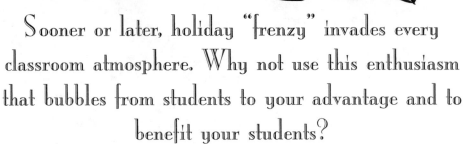

HOLIDAY

Sooner or later, holiday "frenzy" invades every classroom atmosphere. Why not use this enthusiasm that bubbles from students to your advantage and to benefit your students?

The following activities help promote student interaction and group cooperation. When students are in a mood to talk anyway, why not give them something exciting and productive to talk about? I have long noticed that students often receive greater stimulation and motivation from one another than they do from constantly listening to adults speak. With the lessons included in this article, the important process of "brainstorming" is involved. Students collectively share their ideas and use their creative thinking skills for a common goal.

The tasks described here can be adapted to all grade levels and student abilities. Since they do not require hours of preparation on the part of the teacher, they can be used spontaneously or within the framework of a language arts or social studies session. Teachers and students can decide how far they want to take these activities. I have used some of them that developed into elaborate projects involving writing and related artwork, and I have used some of these activities as 15-minute brain stimulators. Flexibility is definitely built into these tasks.

For best results, students should be allowed to work in pairs or groups of three or five, although I have directed some of these activities with the entire class at once. The greater number of ideas generated from any one group, the more original the final products tend to be.

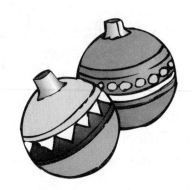

Talk-Abouts

Each group should be given a large blank paper on which one designated "secretary" jots down all of the group's ideas. The word *all* is significant here, because it is important that no editing take place at the beginning of these tasks. Every student's ideas should be recorded. Many times, the ideas from one student can inspire another student. In this way, constant learning from one another is taking place and all students feel they are contributing.

Since group discussion is an important part of these lessons, the noise level in the classroom may seem high at times. Actually, this is a good sign that real thinking is taking place. But for practical purposes, when the discussion seems too loud and interferes with idea sharing, I tell my students that they should speak softly so that their group's ideas are not accidentally overheard and used by another group. When all individual group discussion of a topic is completed, it is extremely important that

time is provided for listening and sharing. This is the crucial time when each group of students gets to share its ideas with the other students in the class. Respect for one another's ideas should be stressed at this time. Positive criticism or suggestions can be made to improve a group's ideas after they are heard, but destructive criticism or ridicule of ideas is emphatically discouraged.

It is important that time limits be set for the idea-generating sessions for a group. Usually, 10 to 20 minutes, depending on the subject, is all that should be allowed.

There are many holidays which children look forward to throughout the year. Each activity provided in this article can be adapted to different holidays with a little creativity. So the next time your classroom is invaded by a bout of holiday spirit, why not try some of these Holiday Talk-Abouts?

by Joanne Coughlin

Activity 1—What Might They Say?

Each group is given an index card with one of these questions written on it.

1. If they could talk, what are some things ornaments hanging on a tree or in a store window might say?
2. What are some things beautiful wrapping paper on a gift might be thinking and saying?
3. What are some things an old toy might say, if it could talk, at a gift-giving time of the year such as Christmas or Hanukkah?
4. What are some things a decorated tree in a department store might be saying or thinking?
5. What are some things a fork might say as it sits on a dining room table after Thanksgiving dinner?
6. What are the types of things a pumpkin might say as a child begins carving it as a jack-o'-lantern?

After students are given ample time to think of and list their answers to the types of questions found above, they may individually or collectively, in a mural-type manner, illustrate their favorite ideas. One-caption cartoons can be successfully created from their thoughts. These in turn can be shared and enjoyed on a bulletin board display or in some type of class book.

Activity 3—Unheard of Holiday Recipes

After a discussion of favorite holiday treats such as pumpkin pie, walnut fudge, or macaroons, students are asked to create NEW recipes that no one has ever heard of before. They must come up with a new name for their concoction and a list of its unique ingredients.

For example, instead of the traditional gingerbread men, students might create a recipe for gingerbread women. Instead of spice drops, ice drops might become a new holiday treat.

For older students, more abstract ideas could be created such as nice drops. A recipe for these might look like the one on the right.

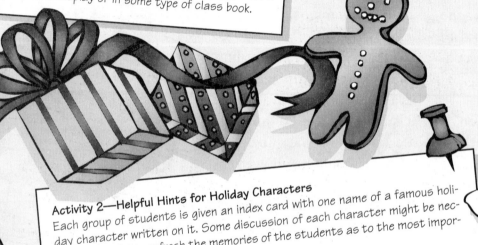

Activity 2—Helpful Hints for Holiday Characters

Each group of students is given an index card with one name of a famous holiday character written on it. Some discussion of each character might be necessary in order to refresh the memories of the students as to the most important aspects of the character's traits.

Examples of Characters:
Frosty the Snowman
Peter Cottontail

Ebeneezer Scrooge
The Grinch

Santa Claus
A Lucky Leprechaun

Students are told to list suggestions or helpful hints they think might be of help to this character.

After the groups' ideas have been shared, students can choose the one or ones they liked best and write friendly letters or advice columns for the characters.

For older students; characters from literature can be used. This activity obviously lends itself to great character analysis.

Nice Drops

Delicious candies that when eaten make someone a nicer person.

Ingredients:

1 ounce of kindness
1 quart of understanding
16 ounces of compassion and caring for others
2 tablespoons of sweetness
4 teaspoons of patience

After each group writes its recipe, they could be compiled into an original class cookbook.

Activity 4—We Rewrite the Songs

After asking students what some of their favorite holiday songs are, and perhaps having a group sing-a-long, students are given index cards with the FIRST line or phrase of a familiar tune written on it.

Samples:

1. "Dashing through the _____.
2. "Here comes Santa Claus; here comes Santa Claus, right down _____.
3. "Up on the housetop reindeer _____.
4. "Rockin' around the _____.
5. "Oh the drums go bang and the cymbals clang and the _____.
6. "Here comes Peter Cottontail, hopping down _____.

The task for students is to finish the familiar tune in a NEW way. The tunes may stay the same, but the lyrics must be original. When the new versions of the songs are completed, students should feel free to sing them and even record them for a class holiday cassette.

Activity 5—Holiday Think-Abouts

There are many questions that promote creative thinking about the holidays. After pondering and discussing them, students could write about and illustrate their ideas. One question per index card could be distributed to students for them to brainstorm and follow through with.

Sample Questions:

1. There are all kinds of gifts to give. Which gifts could you receive or give that DO NOT cost money?
2. What is the best place you can think of to be for the holidays?
3. What is the best gift you ever received?
4. What is the best gift you ever gave someone?
5. If you could afford to give only one person a gift all year, to whom would it be and why?
6. What would you do if it snowed on the Fourth of July?
7. What would you do if it were 90°F (32°C) on New Year's Eve?

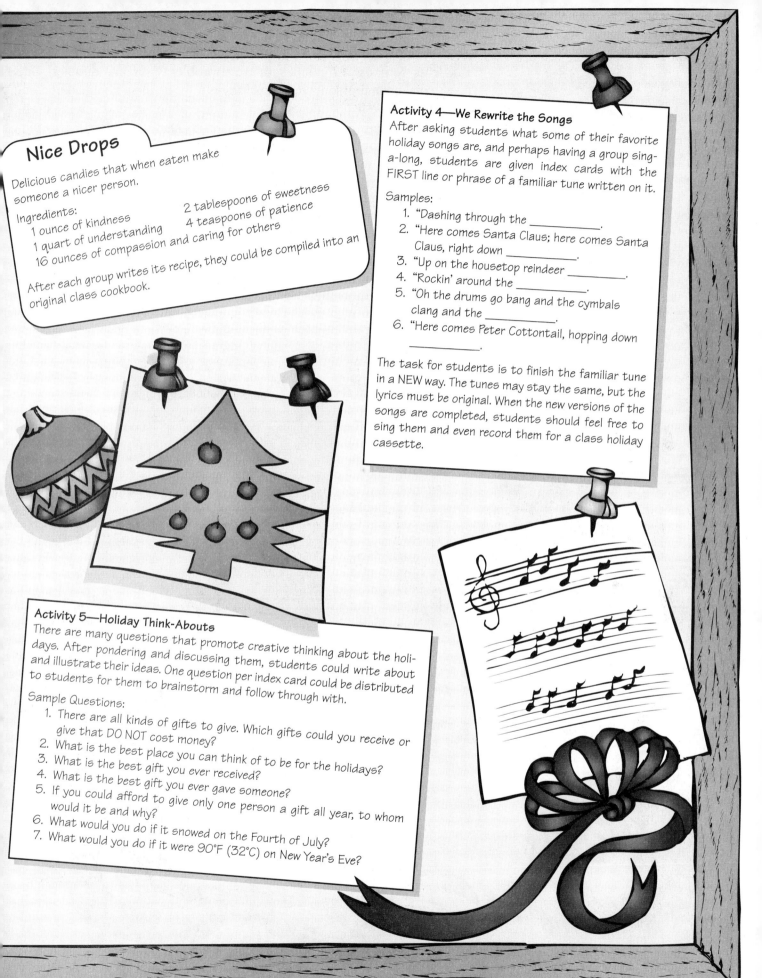

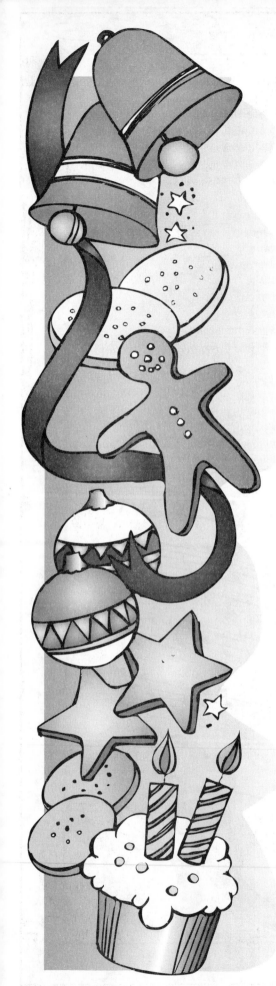

An excellent way to combine math and language skills is to have students compose original math word problems for one another. One way to make the problems more exciting is to write them about an upcoming holiday. I've had students go on and on composing and solving problems about Thanksgiving dinners, Passover feasts and Memorial Day picnics. Students love to solve one another's problems.

I kept a word problem bulletin board in my classroom all year. Once again I used large colored index cards. Students would write their original problem on the front of the card. On the back of the card the problem could be solved by other students. I found students to be so enthusiastic about this that they kept adding to the bulletin board all year long and voluntarily taking the problems home to solve. They were tuning up their math skills as well as their writing and comprehension skills.

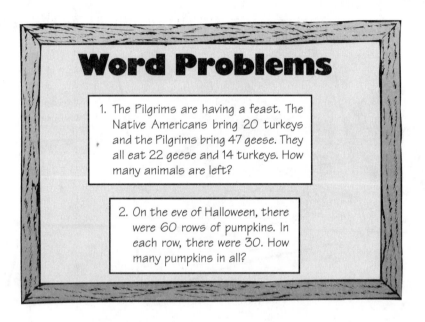

Word Problems

1. The Pilgrims are having a feast. The Native Americans bring 20 turkeys and the Pilgrims bring 47 geese. They all eat 22 geese and 14 turkeys. How many animals are left?

2. On the eve of Halloween, there were 60 rows of pumpkins. In each row, there were 30. How many pumpkins in all?

Flexibility is important with any of these activities. They can be easily geared to your own teaching situation.

I can't emphasize enough that creativity and imagination can flow easily in an atmosphere in which competition and negative criticism are minimized and openness and acceptance are encouraged.

Always enjoy your students' creativity and Happy Holidays!

Hooray for Fall!

Roller skating,
Riding bikes,
Picking apples,
Flying kites,
Carving pumpkins,
Playing ball,
Hooray, hooray . . .
Hooray for fall!

by Rebecca Kai Dotlich

First Day

It's almost time for school
  to start.
This year I'm eight, you see.
My little brother Joe (he's six)
Will walk to school with me.

He's never been to school before;
I know he's kind of scared.
I've told him all the things I know
To show him that I cared.

I'll take him to his room, of course.
He'll meet new friends, I know.
His teacher will be waiting there
To smile and say hello.

I'll tell my brother not to cry
And wipe his tears away.
(I hope he never asks me how
I acted my first day!)

by Jean Conder Soule

As I Go to School

As your students return to school this fall, sing "As I Go to School." (Tune: "The Wheels on the Bus.")

Verse 1:
(Pretend to drive a bus, using steering wheel.)
The driver on the bus says, "Step-right-up, step-right-up, step-right-up."
The driver on the bus says, "Step-right-up"
As I go to school.

Verse 2:
(Jumps up and down to indicate a bell ringing.)
The bell in the school goes, ding-ding-dong, ding-ding-dong, ding-ding-dong.
The bell in the school goes, ding-ding-dong.
As I go to school.

Verse 3:
(Motions to come inside room.)
The teacher in the class says, "Come-right-in, come-right-in, come-right-in."
The teacher in the class says, "Come-right-in."
As I go to school.

Verse 4:
(Motion to come play with hands.)
The children in the room say, "Play with me. Play with me, play with me."
The children in the room say, "Play with me."
When I go to school.

by Carolyn Tomlin

ALL ABOARD!

Letters are made from orange construction paper and laminated.

Yellow construction paper buses are laminated for future use. The windows are cut out and students' names who ride that bus are listed on the background paper.

Light blue background

Use this bulletin board at the beginning of the school year to help students learn their bus numbers. Corresponding name tags can also be made for the students to wear the first few days of school.

Name Tag
Student's name, address and bus number are printed on name tag before laminating. These may be worn as a necklace or pinned on—depending on the age of the child.

by Evelyn Woods

16

White letters are laminated for future use.

Yellow chalkboard

Dark blue background

Use black construction paper for hooks.

This is a bulletin board that can be used at the beginning of the year or anytime using a subject theme. (For example, "You're Sure to Get Hooked on Math.")

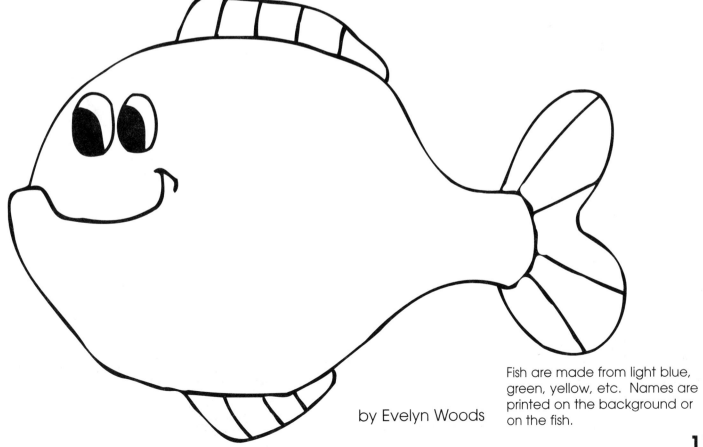

by Evelyn Woods

Fish are made from light blue, green, yellow, etc. Names are printed on the background or on the fish.

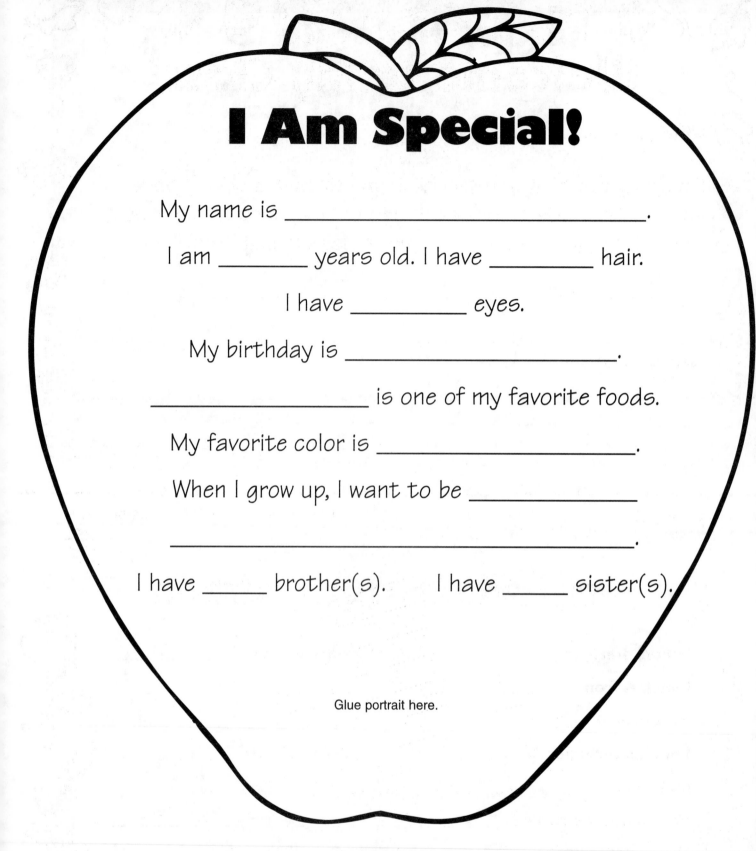

I Am Special!

My name is _____.

I am _____ years old. I have _____ hair.

I have _____ eyes.

My birthday is _____.

_____ is one of my favorite foods.

My favorite color is _____.

When I grow up, I want to be _____

_____.

I have _____ brother(s).   I have _____ sister(s).

Glue portrait here.

To the Teacher: Use this to help students get acquainted at the beginning of the year. Give each student a copy of this apple. Have them fill in the information or let someone else write it in for them. Students can then decorate the apple any way they wish. Display on a bulletin board. You can also use this information as a graphing exercise. Chart how many students have a birthday each month, which color is the most popular, and so on.

Welcome to My Class!

Dear _____,

I'm delighted that you will be in my class this year. I have some great projects planned, and we will have lots of good times together. These are some things we will be doing:

_____

_____

See you soon!

_____
(teacher)

Important Information

School starts at _____. School dismissal is at _____.

Lunch is from _____ to _____.

Recess is at _____.

Lunch money per day is _____, per week is _____.

Milk costs _____.

Your teacher's name is _____.

Your principal's name is _____.

The school's phone number is _____

BUSY FINGERS

FIVE JACK-O'-LANTERNS

Five little jack-o'-lanterns sitting on a gate.
  (Hold up five fingers.)
The first one said, "Oh my, it's getting late."
  (Hold up index finger.)
The second one said, "Let's have some fun."
  (Hold up middle finger.)
The third one said, "Let's run; let's run."
  (Hold up ring finger.)
The fourth one said, "Let's dance; let's prance."
  (Hold up baby finger.)
The fifth one said, "Now is our chance."
  (Hold up thumb.)
When "Whoooo" went the wind,
  (Blow hard.)
And out went the light.
  (Snap fingers.)
And away went the jack-o'-lanterns on
  Halloween night!
  (Run fingers behind back.)

FALLING LEAVES

The leaves are dropping from the trees—
  (Flutter fingers around.)
Yellow, brown and red.
They patter softly like the rain;
  (Tap fingers on the floor.)
One landed on my head!
  (Tap head.)

DRESSING FOR SCHOOL

_____, put your pants on, pants on, pants on.
  (Pretend to step into pants.)

_____, put your pants on, one, two, three.
  (Finish putting on pants, zip up, fasten, etc.)

*(Continue with socks, shoes, shirt, sweater, dress, skirt,
  blouse and whatever else is appropriate. Follow
  actions as rhyme indicates.)*

Now _____ is all dressed, all dressed, all dressed.
  (Clap hands in rhythm.)

Now _____ is all dressed and ready to go to school.

AT PLAY

ROSH HASHANAH

(Throughout the entire rhyme, continue to smile warmly and nod head in all directions.)

Happy New Year! Happy New Year!
May your life be very sweet.
Happy New Year! Happy New Year!
Give yourself a treat.
Hope you're healthy and happy, too
And have a lot of fun!
Do everything you want to do,
And be kind to everyone!
    (Spread out arms to encompass
    everyone.)

AUTUMN WALK

I walked down the road as slowly as could be,
    (Walk slowly.)
And I saw three apples on a big apple tree.
    (Hold up three fingers.)
One, two, three.
    (Show and count each finger.)
One, two, three. (Repeat.)
I saw three apples on an apple tree.
    (Hold up three fingers.)

I walked down the road on a bright, sunny day,
    (Walk a little faster than before.)
And I saw three squirrels that decided to play.
    (Hold out three fingers.)
One, two, three. (Show and count each finger.)
One, two, three. (Repeat.)
I saw three squirrels that decided to play. (Hold
    out three fingers.)

I walked down the road on the way to town
    (Walk normally.)
And I saw three leaves that had turned to brown.
    (Show three fingers.)
One, two, three. (Show and count each finger.)
One, two, three. (Repeat.)
I saw three leaves that had turned to brown.
    (Show three fingers.)

I walked down the road and then, and then,
    (Walk briskly.)
I turned right around and I walked back again.
    (Turn and walk the other way.)
One, two, three.
    (Show and count each finger.)
One, two, three. (Repeat.)
I turned right around and I walked back again.
    (Turn and walk back.)

Labor Day Parade

Organize your own Labor Day parade. Have students dress up in their favorite career costumes and let them march around the school. Some students might wish to carry signs telling about their chosen career.

Many careers and occupations are open for students to choose. Divide your class into small groups. Put the following terms on pieces of paper and ask each group to choose a slip. After doing some research, the groups will be asked to report on that career.

Geophysicist
Zoologist
Braille Translator
Linguist
Nutritionist
Cosmetologist
Audiologist
Game Warden
Forester
Contractor
Orthopedic Surgeon
Oceanographer
Aviator
Psychiatrist

Use one or both of the following paragraphs as writing assignments or discussion starters:

During your lifetime it is possible that you will change jobs several times. Some studies have determined that a person will change jobs seven times during his/her career. Think of several jobs or professions you would like to have. Write the story of your labors.

Many jobs that will be available by the time you get out of school do not even exist now. Use your imagination and think of a new job that might occur in twenty years. Maybe you could be a space station custodian or a farmer on an undersea farm. Write and illustrate your job of the future.

Adler, Larry. *Help Wanted: Riddles About Jobs.* Lerner, 1990.
Ancona, George. *Freighters: Cargo Ships and People Who Work Them.* New York: Crowell, 1985.
Berenstain, Stan and Jan. *Berenstain Bears on the Job.* New York: Random House, 1987.
Berenstain, Stan and Jan. *He Bear She Bear.* New York: Random House, 1974.
Blacker, Terence. *If I Could Work.* New York: Lippincott, 1987.
Brill, Marlene T. *I Can Be a Lawyer.* Chicago: Childrens Press, 1986.
Clinton, Susan. *I Can Be an Architect.* Chicago: Childrens Press, 1986.

To most people, Labor Day signifys the end of summer and the beginning of the school year. Labor Day is actually a national holiday for all federal workers but over time has been adopted by most of the nation. Today, Canada (Labour Day), Puerto Rico and the United States celebrate Labor Day on the first Monday in September.

There is also a Labor Day holiday in Australia called Eight House Day and in Europe Labor Day is celebrated on May 1. No matter where or when the holiday is observed, the day recognizes the hard work and dedication of all workers.

After giving your students an historical background on this holiday, use the study of Labor Day as a springboard for a unit on careers. Here are just a few ideas to get you started.

Using scrap construction paper, aluminum foil, paper plates and glue, have your students design the front of a hat for a special job. Using a 2" (5.08 cm) wide strip of construction paper, measure around the child's head and secure the strip to each side of the hat's front. Ask each student to model their Labor Day hat and explain what job the hat might be for.

Have a study about robots and discuss how robots will be more prominent in the future. Have students design their own robots and tell just exactly what jobs their robots will be capable of.

Gather several examples of simple machines for your students to examine. Display such things as toys, pulleys and string, wedges of wood, a fishing reel, etc., on a table. Post pictures of see-saws, ramps, screwdrivers and other simple machines. Ask students to design a labor-saving device using simple machines to accomplish a job.

"What Can I Be?" bulletin board. In large letters at the bottom center of the board, place the sentence, "What Can I Be?" Ask each student to illustrate a job that they would like to do some day on a cloud-shaped piece of white paper. Place the illustrations around and above the sentence.

Craig, Janet. *What's It Like to Be a . . . Ballet Dancer?* Troll Associates, 1989.
Henderson, Kathy. *I Can Be a Farmer.* Chicago: Childrens Press, 1989.
Jaspersohn, William. *Day in the Life of a Marine Biologist.* New York: Little, 1982.
Lillegard, Dee. *I Can Be a Beautician.* Chicago: Childrens Press, 1987.
Martin, Claire. *I Can Be a Weather Forecaster.* Chicago: Childrens Press, 1987.
Sipiera, Paul. *I Can Be a Chemist.* Chicago: Childrens Press, 1992.

by Terry Healy

Jewish Fall Celebrations

Teacher Background

According to the Jewish calendar, which is 5755 years old, the high holy days of Rosh Hashanah and Yom Kippur fall in September, which is the Jewish month of Elul. It commemorates the time when Moses ascended Mount Sinai to ask God's mercy for those who had sinned. He remained on the mount fasting and praying for 40 days and nights. God then gave Moses the 10 commandments and the people were granted forgiveness and a new beginning.

On the two days of Rosh Hashanah, a shofar (ram's horn trumpet) is blown. It serves as a reminder of the shofar heard on Mount Sinai to summon the peo-ple when the 10 commandments were given and accepted for all time. Each year since that time, Rosh Hashanah has symbolized this new beginning or new year. Lasting for 10 days, it culminates with the Day of Atonement or Yom Kippur. This last day is a time for reflecting on one's actions and attitudes of the previous year. It is a resolve to become a better person for the new year.

Each Rosh Hashanah the commitment to serve God is reaffirmed. Just as on the first Rosh Hashanah, actions and attitudes are reconsidered and reevaluated. Each Yom Kippur, the holiest day of the Jewish year, is a time to atone for sins, to apologize and seek forgiveness. Family and friends are included in prayers if there were any ill feelings which may have arisen during the year. Work of any kind is forbidden and fasting is a major part of the ritual. From sunrise to sunset, special prayers of forgiveness are offered. At sundown, the final shofar notes are sounded marking the end of this holy day.

Throughout the 10 days of Rosh Hashanah and the final day of Yom Kippur, people greet each other and shake hands. The greeting is "L' Shōna Tōva"—may you have a very happy new year!

by Teddy Meister

Sweet foods are eaten to symbolize a sweet year. Honey cake is a main favorite, and the ingredients can be easily gathered for a class cooking activity.

Apples and Honey

6 or 7 apples
12 oz. (354.8 ml) bottle of honey
small paper plates
napkins

Cut and core the apples and slice into sections. The number of apples will depend on the students you have. Put 1 teaspoon (5 ml) of honey on each plate and give to the student. Place apple sections on napkins for each student. Tell the class to dip their apple section into the honey and enjoy. A sweet treat for a sweet year!

Honey Cake

2 eggs, beaten	1/2 cup (120 ml) sugar
1/4 cup (60 ml) coffee	1 T. (15 ml) oil
1 3/4 cup (420 ml) sifted flour	3/4 t. (3.75 ml) baking powder
1/2 tsp. (2.5 ml) baking soda	2 T. (30 ml) warm honey
1/2 cup (120 ml) chopped walnuts	1 standard size loaf pan

Add sugar to eggs, beat until light and fluffy. Mix coffee, honey and oil together and combine with eggs. Sift flour, baking powder and baking soda. Add nuts and egg mixture to batter, stirring constantly. Pour batter into greased loaf pan and bake at 350ºF (175ºC) for 45 minutes. Allow to cool. Cut the honey cake according to how many pieces you will need.

1. Contact a synagogue in your area to find out if anyone is available to present a talk to the class about the shofar and demonstrate how it is blown for the high holy days.

2. Brainstorm with the class about nice things they can do for family members, friends and classmates. Record ideas on a chart or chalkboard and ask the students to take one idea and use it for a day. Then take another idea for the second day and do this for 10 days.

3. Give out art paper with the phrase "I will try to _____" printed at the top. Have students fold the paper into fourths. Ask that they draw a picture in each box showing how they could be nicer to others at home and school.

4. Start a "Smiling Faces" bulletin board. Cut out enough smiling faces for the class to use. Tell students that each time they can say or do something positive for someone else, they can put their name on a smiling face and pin it on to the bulletin board. At the end of 10 days, count the number of good things that were accomplished.

5. Have students pronounce "L' Shōna Tōva" to each other. Practice saying it several times. Let them say it and shake hands with others.

6. A traditional custom is the sending of New Year/Rosh Hashanah cards to Jewish family and friends. Provide art paper and crayons, and have students create an original card. They could be given to Jewish students at school or sent to synagogues in the area.

7. How does Rosh Hashanah compare with the New Year's celebration on December 31? How are they alike? How do they differ? Have students compare and contrast these through a class discussion.

8. Resources might be available from synagogue libraries in the area in the form of storybooks, pictures, films and filmstrips. These can be used to enhance your unit.

Learning with Our *Grandparents*

A Very Special Friendship

Grandparents' Day is celebrated the second Sunday of September each year. Although this is not a national holiday, teachers find ways to honor these special people who are a vital link in the extended family.

Senior adults from your community may serve as substitutes for children who do not have grandparents or who do not have them living nearby.

Add these ideas to your list as you search for activities to help young children celebrate this important occasion.

Adopt-a-Grandparent Program

When teachers involve grandparents or older citizens in their program for young children, everyone benefits. If there are not many grandparents available, use these ideas to adopt grandparents of your own. Carefully select senior adults in the community who express an interest in your school or center. Ask "grandparents" to write how they could contribute to your classroom.

Things to Do with Grandparents

Children receive . . .
- a special friend who has time to listen
- someone who will give them extra attention
- a storyteller
- someone to read to them
- a teacher of life skills
- wisdom and patience from an older adult

Grandparents . . .
- receive a feeling of being needed
- share life's knowledge
- receive a purpose for giving to others

Teachers receive . . .
- extra hands for working with students, such as cutting shapes, working on bulletin boards, etc.
- help with small group time
- help in centers
- individualized help for academic-delayed students

Funny Grandparent Sentences

Developing a sense of humor is an important characteristic for young children. Explain that you will say a silly or funny sentence which tells something a grandparent would not do. This makes it funny. The children will add other sentences. Give several examples.

1. My grandmother and I cooked mud for breakfast.
2. My grannie and I walk to town on our hands.
3. I push my grandpa in my doll buggy.

Foreign Names for Grandparents

Spanish: grandfather–abuelo
grandmother–abuela

French: grandfather–doyen or grand-pére
grandmother–doyenne or grand-mére

German: grandfather–der Grobvater
grandmother–die Grobmutter
German (informal): grandma–oma
grandpa–opa

Other Names for Grandparents

"A rose by any other name is still a rose." So are grandparents. On the chalkboard or large poster, ask children to dictate what they call their grandparents. For example: Nana, Papaw, Grannie, Momma (Jones), Pop, etc.

Make a graph showing the number of times that name was used in your class.

Nana	X	X			
Papaw	X	X	X		
Grannie	X	X			
Mamma	X	X	X	X	X

Teacher Activities

Honor these special people who have grandchildren in your room by helping youngsters participate in the following activities:

- Invite grandparents to school for lunch. Let them eat with the child in the lunchroom.

- Present a short program of songs, poems or original stories of "Why My Grandparents Are Special" or "Why I Love My Grandparents."

- Take Polaroid™ pictures of each child and their guest. Have children design a simple photo holder using bright-colored construction paper and paints.

- Make favors ahead of time to take home.

- Invite grandparents to return to your classroom at a later date.

Picture Gallery

Plan a picture gallery using children's drawings of their grandparents. Cut 1" (2.5 cm) frames from an 8" x 11" (20 x 28 cm) sheet of poster board. Display children's original art in frames. Hang before Grandparents' Day.

Grandparents–Alike and Different

No two people are exactly alike. Even identical twins are different in some ways. So are grandparents! Make a chart listing the words *alike* and *different* on the top. Ask children to tell how their grandparents are alike and different from others. Discuss holidays they celebrate, foods they cook, pets they own or other interesting facts. Stress that we are more alike than different, even though we may belong to different cultures, religions or ethnic groups.

Children's Books Using the Grandparent Theme

You'll find many books for children focusing on grandparents. Several deal with multicultural families. Here are a few:

- Ackerman, Karen. *Song and Dance Man.* Illus. by Stephe Gammell. Knopf, 1988.
  Vaudeville comes alive for three children when they watc their Grandpa perform.
- Aliki. *Two of Them.* Illus. by author. Greenwillow, 1979.
  After a little girl thrives on years of care from her grandfathe she cares for him when he grows old.
- Pederson, Judy. *The Tiny Patient.* Illus. by author. Knopf, 1989
  A tiny sparrow with a broken wing is cared for by a young chil and her grandmother.
- Cooney, Barbara. *Miss Rumphius.* Illus. by author. Penguir 1982.
  When Alice grows up, she carries out her grandfather's wis to plant seeds all over the countryside.
- Daly, Nikki. *Not So Fast Songololo.* Illus. by author. Puffir 1986.
  Grandmother and Malusi learn to respect each other's pac when they visit a village marketplace in South Africa.
- Garza, Carmen Lomas. *Family Pictures/Cuadros de Famili* Illus. by author. Children's Book Press, 1990.
  The author tells about her interesting childhood of being pa of Mexican family celebrations. Text in Spanish and English
- MacLachlan, Patricia. *Three Names.* Illus. by Alexander Per zoff. HarperCollins, 1991.
  The story of a boy and his great-grandfather who owns a do named, Three Names. Tells of how the dog went to scho with him and barked at the sun and clouds.
- Smith, Maggie. *My Grandma's Chair.* Lothrop, 1992.
  When Alex sits in his grandma's old chair, he imagines a kinds of adventures, but the best is sitting there with Grandma
- Stolz, Mary. *Go Fish.* Illus. by Pat Cummings. HarperCollins 1991.
  Thomas and Grandfather enjoy fishing and playing games, b he especially enjoys hearing his grandfather talk about h African roots.

Videos Focusing on Grandparents

- John Burningham. *Granpa.* #IR106, Media Basics Video, 30 mi
  The voice of Peter Ustinov is the voice of Granpa in this ar mated tale about the special relationship between a little g and her Granpa.
- Veryl and Jean Rosenbaum. *Healthy Parenting, Grandpa enting.* #VID101, Media Basics Video, 30 min.
  Grandparents from diverse ethnic backgrounds and ag groups discuss joys and difficulties of grandparenting. Pose hard questions about the role of grandparents for follow-u discussion.

Name _____

Having Fun Together

There are many things you can enjoy with a grandparent.
Color the pictures below. Cut out.
Paste on a separate sheet of construction paper those activities you enjoy with your grandparents.
Place on a bulletin board.

Bonus: Draw a picture of an activity you enjoy with your grandparents. Share with a friend.

Walking with Grandfather

Grandfather and I see many things when we take a walk. Number the squares. Cut out the pictures below. Listen as your teacher tells you in what positions to paste the pictures.

Directions: Paste the bird in the third position, fish—eighth, rabbit—fourth, butterfly—first, ladybug—seventh, cat—fifth, dog—second, snail—sixth.

Fun at the Circus

One day my grandparents took me to the circus. We saw a clown holding balloons. Read, then color the words in each balloon the appropriate color.

Booklet Instructions

page A

1. Duplicate page B on the back of page

page C

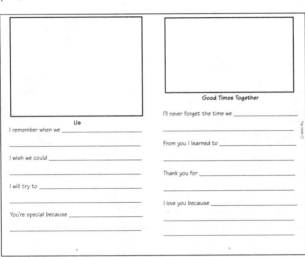

2. Duplicate page D on the back of page

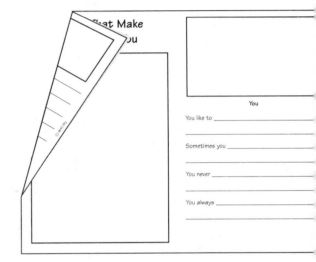

3. Lay page D on top of page B and fold.

page B

62

A
Booklet
for My
Grandparent

To: _____

From: _____

Congratulations

to

_____

Awarded by

_____

You Are
Someone
Special!

I like to _____

_____

Sometimes I _____

_____

I never _____

_____

I will always _____

_____

Me

2

The Gift

I'm more than just a cuddle.
I'm more than an embrace.
I come in cozy sizes
And greet you face-to-face.

I always leave you smiling.
I'm full of love inside.
I'm always waiting for you.
My arms are open wide.

Give or take, I'm still the same.
I hold you warm and snug.
Share me with the ones you love.
I am a great big HUG!

by Charles Ghigna

7

Good Times Together

I'll never forget the time we _____

From you I learned to _____

Thank you for _____

I love you because _____

5

Us

I remember when we _____

I wish we could _____

I will try to _____

You're special because _____

4

Top (side D)

You

You like to _____

Sometimes you _____

You never _____

You always _____

Things That Make
Me Think of You

Listen Up! It's Fall!

Grinning Grandmas

Materials: Reproducible on page 38; pencil; crayons: brown, green
Skills: Listening and looking for details and logic

Look at the page of smiling grandmothers. I will read you some clues to help you figure out which lady is Jasmyne's grandmother. It will help you to know which ones are **not** Jasmyne's grandmother. Put a small *x* above the head of any ladies that you know are not Jasmyne's grandmother. For example, if I told you that Jasmyne's grandmother was wearing striped clothes, you could put an *x* above everyone who is **not** wearing stripes. Here are the clues:

1. Jasmyne's grandma has curly hair.
2. Jasmyne's grandma does not wear glasses.
3. She always wears a dress.
4. Jasmyne's grandma never likes to wear a hat.

Do you think you know which one is Jasmyne's grandma? (Reread clues if necessary.) Now color Jasmyne's grandmother's outfit green. Color her hair brown. Write your name at the top of your paper.

Teacher can play more rounds, selecting clues that will identify a different grandmother each time. (Students can use a different mark for ladies eliminated in each round, such as underlining, drawing a line through their legs, etc.) Here is an additional set of clues that will lead you to Jamal's grandmother:

1. Jamal's granny likes to wear slacks.
2. Jamal's granny has long hair.
3. Jamal's granny likes to wear hats.

When you've found Jamal's grandmother, circle her with your green crayon. Color her hat brown.

Grandparents' Gifts

Materials: Blank paper, pencil
Skills: Critical thinking

Number your paper from 1 to 12. I am going to read you a list of gifts that people might give their grandparents on Grandparents' Day. If the gift is something you would have to **buy** at a store, write *B* by the number on your paper. If the gift is something you could **make** or **give** by yourself, write an *M* on your paper. If you could do **either**—buy or make— write *E*. (You may want to write these choices on the board.) Think carefully about each answer.

1. a cake
2. a card
3. jewelry
4. a hug
5. a book of poems
6. a valuable old coin
7. a new pen
8. a painting
9. a scrapbook of family pictures
10. a helium-filled balloon
11. a bouquet of flowers
12. an afternoon of your time

Write your name under the number 12. On the back of your paper, draw a picture of something you could make for one of your grandparents.

by Ann Richmond Fisher

Grinning Grandmas

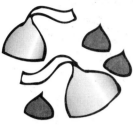

Happy Birthday, Milton Hershey

September 13th

Say a Hands-On "Happy Birthday!" to America's Father of Chocolate

Celebrate with these tasty mathematics activities. Milton Hershey, founder of the Hershey candy empire, was born on this day in 1857.

Turn perimeter into "per-yumeter" by inviting your students to build chocolate fences around a variety of items using Hershey's™ semisweet chocolate morsels. Divide the class into small groups of two to four children. Provide each group with a bowl of morsels and a basket of items to measure. Be sure to include pattern blocks, tangram pieces, a domino, a postage stamp and a playing card. Allow the small groups to work independently, constructing chocolate fences around each item. When the building is completed, list the name of each item on a large piece of chart paper. Choose one item. Ask the children to identify the number of morsels needed to fence each side of

the item as well as the total number of morsels needed to complete the fence. Write the numbers in the form of an equation.

(Example: domino: $5 + 3 + 5 + 3 = 16$. Circle the final number, the sum, and introduce it as the *perimeter*. Repeat these steps for each of the items measured. Invite the children to sample the chocolate morsels as you discuss the results. Ask the children: Which item had the largest perimeter? Which item has the smallest perimeter? Did two different items have the same perimeter? The children will welcome your challenge to measure the perimeter of larger classroom items such as a crayon box, ruler or a favorite book using the same chocolate morsels. For a greater challenge, you may prefer to provide bowls of miniature semisweet chocolate morsels for the children to measure the original items with. Your class is sure to enjoy comparing the perimeters almost as much as sampling the delicious chocolate fences.

How Long Will It Last?

Your class will be eager to answer this tasty question again and again when it involves delicious Hershey Kisses!™ Before beginning this activity, use a stopwatch to demonstrate the length of 30 seconds, 1 minute, 1½ minutes, 2 minutes, 2½ minutes and 3 minutes. Discuss what tasks could be accomplished within one minute (writing their name), two minutes (putting on socks and shoes) and three minutes (singing a popular song). On a piece of chart paper, display the sentence: "In _____ Minutes I Can _____." You'll be delighted with the variety of interesting ideas that are shared. Once the children have an understanding of these lengths of time, it's time to make a tasty challenge. Invite each child to predict whether their Hershey's Kiss™ will last for three minutes when placed in their mouth. Then pass out the foil-wrapped candies, and let the fun begin! You may wish to provide rhythm instruments for the children to play as they wait for the time to pass. Ring a bell and post a sign when each thirty-second period has passed. When the three minutes are up, ask the children to share their results. Did their Kiss™ last the full three minutes? If not, was the length of time closer to 1 minute, 1½ minutes, 2 minutes or 2½ minutes? Repeat this activity, this time inviting the children to estimate the number of times that they will be able to neatly print their first and last names before their Kiss™ melts. Provide a large sheet of lined paper, a pencil and a chocolate Kiss™ for each child and put the estimates to the test. Discuss the results. Using a "thumbs up," "thumbs down" or a flat hand signal, invite the class to communicate whether their estimate was too low, too high or very close. You may wish to take the birthday celebration outside as you challenge the children to estimate the number of times that they can bounce a ball before their Kiss™ disappears. Older children will enjoy using stopwatches to time the melting. For a super challenge, try freezing the Kisses™ and comparing the melting times.

What if everyone measured length with chocolate morsels?

Your class will be delighted at this sweet suggestion. Discuss the delicious advantages and disadvantages of morsel measurement. Provide a bowl of Hershey's™ semisweet chocolate morsels. Invite your class to measure the length of a variety of classroom items such as a pencil, a crayon, an index card and a sheet of paper. Has a clever child mentioned a morsel ruler? Answer this request with a collection of tongue depressors and a tube of colorful frosting. Squeeze a thick stripe of frosting down the center of each tongue depressor. Ask the children to place the chocolate

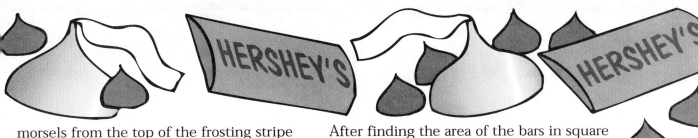

morsels from the top of the frosting stripe to the bottom. The children will enjoy using their rulers to measure larger items. Invite the children to work in small groups. Provide each group with a ball of yarn or string. Challenge the groups to cut a yarn or string piece that measures: 10 morsels long, 13 morsels long, 15 morsels long, 18 morsels long and 20 morsels long. For younger children, you may prefer to make tasty rulers using Hershey Kisses™. The string lengths may be increased or decreased based on the ability levels of your students.

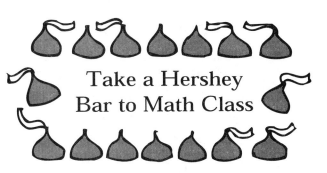

Take a Hershey Bar to Math Class

Surely Milton Hershey would have approved of this scrumptious method of teaching! Invite your class to bring along their favorite Hershey's™ candy bar. Choose from the following list of luscious activities. One of the sweet suggestions is sure to be ideal for your class.

How heavy is your candy bar? Invite the class to answer this question using balance scales, Hershey's™ chocolate morsels and Hershey's Kisses™.

Provide centimeter graph paper for the children to trace their candy bars onto.

After finding the area of the bars in square centimeters, ask the children to fill in the squares using colorful Cuisenaire™ rods. Later, color the squares using crayons that correspond with the rod colors. A crazy new wrapper design perhaps?

Imagine a student's desk covered with Hershey's™ chocolate bars! How many would fit? Challenge each child to find the area of his desktop using their candy bar as a unit of measure.

Using plastic knives, invite the class to cut their candy bar into: halves, then fourths, then eighths.

Your class will enjoy finding the area of their chocolate bars using familiar manipulatives such as Unifix™ cubes or green triangular pattern blocks. For a sweet treat, try this activity using Hershey's Kisses™, semisweet chocolate morsels and semi-sweet mini morsels.

Invite your class to become wrapper readers. They're sure to enjoy creating tally charts showing how often the numerals 0-9 appear on the wrapper.

Challenge the children to locate the longest word, three words with an even number of letters, three words with an odd number of letters, a word with half as many vowels with consonants.

Super Challenge: Which letter appears most often on the wrapper? Ask the children to create a Unifix™ cube train that shows just how often this letter is used.

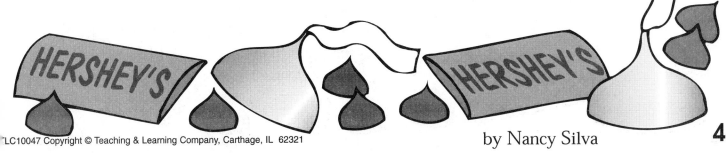

by Nancy Silva

Mexican Independence Day

September 16

It's a Red-Letter Day!

Mexican Independence Day is held on September 16th. This important national holiday celebrates the beginning of the Mexican Revolution in 1810. Mexico's War of Independence began when Father Miguel Hidalgo, a parish priest, rang his church bell. Now, the president of Mexico rings Father Hidalgo's famous Liberty Bell to begin this special holiday, and everyone gives the traditional yell for independence, "Grito!" Fiestas, or festivals, featuring parades, dancing and fireworks are all a part of this big holiday.

by Mary Ellen Switzer

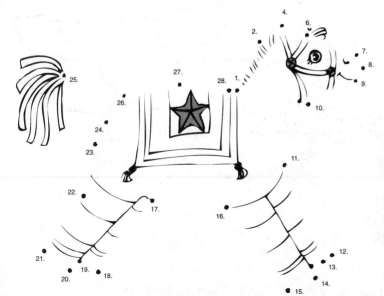

It's Piñata Time

Piñata time is a fun-filled highlight for children at any Mexican celebration. Piñatas are made of papier-mâché or pottery and contain candy, toys or presents. Some piñatas are animal-shaped, while others have seasonal, holiday or other shapes. Children try to smash open the piñatas with a long stick and POW—everyone scatters to pick up the goodies!

Marvelous Map

This page features Mexico. Color the map and draw a circle around Mexico City, the capital of Mexico. Add other cities and important features of Mexico.

Bonus: On the back of this page, write a fact that you have learned about Mexico.

The Magic Suitcase

Calling all tourists! Let's grab our magic suitcase and travel to Mexico.

"Hola" this is the way you would say "hello" if you lived in Mexico! Welcome to Mexico! Mexico is a land of many contrasts, from high mountain ranges to arid deserts. You will even find tropical rain forests there, too. Two large peninsulas are located in Mexico—the Yucatan and Baja Peninsulas. The Baja Peninsula is one of the longest in the world. The capital of Mexico is Mexico City, which is also the largest city in the country.

The Mexicans manufacture many useful products, such as steel, automobiles, cement, paper and textiles. Talented Mexican craftsmen create a wide variety of handicrafts, for example—leather work, rugs, silver jewelry, pottery and carved wooden masks. Some of the food raised in Mexico includes corn, beans, tomatoes, wheat, coffee, rice and sugarcane.

Write or draw a picture of what you would pack in your magic suitcase for your trip to Mexico.

The Color Box

If you were a child in Mexico, the crayons in your color box would read:

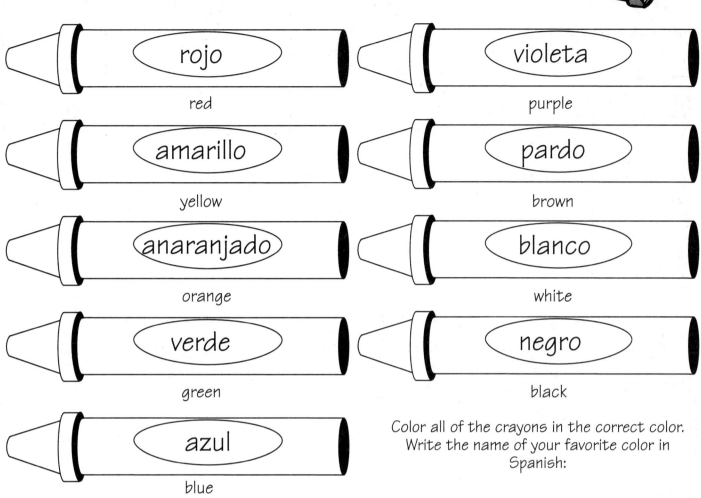

rojo
red

violeta
purple

amarillo
yellow

pardo
brown

anaranjado
orange

blanco
white

verde
green

negro
black

azul
blue

Color all of the crayons in the correct color. Write the name of your favorite color in Spanish:

_____

MEXICAN FLAG

Get your green (verde), white (blanco) and red (rojo) crayons ready—it's time to color the flag of Mexico. The Mexican flag is divided into three parts—from left to right: green, white and red. The colors have special meanings. The green stands for independence, white stands for religion and red stands for union. In the center you see Mexico's coat of arms. The flag was adopted in 1821.

The Legend of

Johnny Appleseed's real name was John Chapman. He was born September 26, 1774, in Leominster, Massachusetts. He was a common man dressed in short ragged trousers, bare feet, a tin pot as a hat and an upper garment of coffee sack material. He moved west from Pennsylvania, where he gathered many of his apple seeds from cider mills, to the Ohio Valley where he planted most of his apple orchards. He showed the Indians and pioneers how to raise apple trees, and they carried this knowledge westward. Many trees today in Ohio, Illinois, Indiana and Pennsylvania are descendants from the trees of Johnny Appleseed. He was also known as a true "man of nature." Appleseed lived and slept mostly outdoors, cared for the animals he loved and was a vegetarian. Following are a few "apple activities" to celebrate the season.

Apple Tree Print

Cut a tree shape from construction paper. Instruct the children to color the trunk brown and the upper tree green. Collect small objects that are round to use for printing apples, such as a small AA battery, a cork, a pencil eraser, etc. Dip these into the red paint and press apples onto the upper tree. You could even use your fingertips, too!

Johnny Appleseed

Apple Oxidation

Cut an apple into slices. Place half on a plate and dip the pieces into lemon juice. Place the other slices onto another plate. What happens to the apples after a short period of time? The apples coated with lemon juice stay white as the others turn brown. The lemon juice is citric acid, protecting the slices from air which turns them brown.

Apple Seed Pictures

Collect seeds from several apples. Provide the children with paper and glue. Let them glue the seeds onto the paper, and then use crayons and markers to enhance their pictures.

Seed Shakers

Give each child two paper plates. Have them color and decorate the bottom side of each plate. After this is finished, place several apple seeds inside the plates and staple around the eggs securely. The children enjoy shaking rhythms, especially to the sound of music!

Apple Textures

This fruit has different flavors, textures and forms.
*Taste different apple slices (many varieties of apples).
*Try eating dried apple slices (sold in stores).
*Make applesauce (recipe below).

Johnny Applesauce

6 apples   1/4 cup (60 ml) honey
cinnamon   1 1/4 cups (300 ml) water

Let children peel, core and slice the apples (supervision needed). Put these slices in a saucepan with the water. Cook until soft. Add the honey and sprinkle on some cinnamon to taste.

Apple Art

Cut an apple crosswise and another one lengthwise. Show the children the star shape inside the apple cut horizontally. Provide containers of red, yellow and green tempera paint. Have the students dip the cut apples into the paint and press designs onto construction paper.

Worm Through the Apple Game

All players stand in a straight line with their feet approximately 18" (45.72 cm) apart. One child is chosen to be the worm, who then wiggles through each child's feet. Choose a new worm and repeat the game.

by Tania K. Cowling

47

A Leaf's Story

Oh, look, I've lost my dress of green;
I'm wearing red instead.
And everywhere I look, I see
Gowns of gold and red.
All my friends upon our tree
Are dressed in scarlet finery.
But some of them it's sad to say,
Are tumbling from the tree.
They're falling, falling, falling,
'Til no one's left but me.
It's sad to be the only one,
No other leaf around.
I can't hang on.
    I must let go.
       I'm going
          down—
            down—
              down.

by Mabel Duch

Autumn in the Great Outdoors

It's autumn and the outdoors is brimming with harvest foods, vibrant colors, earthy scents and creatures readying themselves for winter. Make use of nature's classroom in your Kid Space with these outdoor seasonal activities.

Leaf Crafts

Try some leafy crafts with recently fallen leaves.

Leaf Pile: Rake leaves into a pile. Kids will know where to go from there!

Leaf Hideaway: Use sticks and twine to build a structure large enough to accommodate at least one child. Cover the entire structure with leaves for an autumn hideaway. Discuss animal shelters and camouflage.

Leaf Waxing: Put a leaf between two pieces of waxed paper inside a heavy book for about seven days. Use these waxed leaves to make mobiles, collages or writing paper. Glue small leaves to cardboard to make an autumn wreath or centerpiece.

Bring in the Forest: Cut out a shape of a tree large enough to fill your bulletin board. Students can add their waxed leaves to create a forest on the bulletin board.

Leaf Prints: Choose leaves with interesting shapes to dip into paint, press on a blotter and then gently press onto paper. These leaf prints will make interesting artwork in themselves or for cards, borders, wrapping paper or collages.

by Robynne Eagan

Nature's Colors

Who can resist the colorful leaves of autumn? Collect as many different varieties of leaves as you can. Count, add, subtract, sort and classify your leaves. Provide tree identification guides and identify as many trees and leaves as you can. Talk about the various colors, textures, shapes and smells. Brainstorm for adjectives to describe the leaves, and then write poems or stories.

Corn Maze and Pumpkin Path

If you planned ahead, you could enjoy a deliberate cornfield maze and pumpkin path. Pumpkins can be carved on the vine when they are green. Carefully cutting with a craft knife you can create initials or simple faces that grow with the pumpkin and make for an interesting live pumpkin path.

Kid Space Harvest Celebration and Feast

Reap the benefits of a *Kid Space* garden. Children will love picking, preparing, preserving and eating the crop. Children may prepare foods for canning or freezing to be enjoyed throughout the school year or eat them right away. Classroom soups, stews or vegetable platters will provide hands-on learning opportunities and replace bagged lunches for a while. Host a lunch time corn roast. Boil or barbecue some fresh corn on the cob or baked potatoes with fixings. Tell stories and sing songs that celebrate the harvest.

Musical Vegetables

Choose some interesting-looking gourds and squashes. Poke at least three holes into these using a nail or darning needle. Leave these in a warm, dry location and turn them every day for about 14 days. When completely dry, the seeds will rattle inside and you will have colorful instruments for your harvest celebrations.

Scarecrow

Invite some scarecrows to share the season. Supply frames made from wire, doweling, old broomsticks, 1" x 2" (2.5 x 5 cm) wood pieces or sticks, natural materials and clothing accessories. Make head with stuffed canvas bags, beach balls, pumpkins or other round shapes that can be affixed to a body frame. Scarecrows, a few bales of straw, stalks of wheat or corn and harvest vegetables make a wonderful autumn display that foster an appreciation of the harvest season. Offer your *Kid Space* for school celebrations of Thanksgiving or harvest.

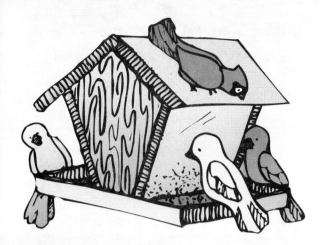

Inukshuk Statues

Inukshuk statues will add atmosphere to your *Kid Space*. The Inuit peoples created these statues to mark the trials of the caribou migrations. *Inukshuk* means "stone in the likeness of a person." Similar rock cairns have been constructed as mystical symbols or as trial markers. These environmentally friendly markers are attractive and functional. Students can create structures to represent something of importance to them. Provide stones of various sizes and shapes. Children will develop an understanding of the science and technique of structure building. Take care that structures are solid and safe. Small structures are just as impressive as the larger ones. Take pictures of your students beside their creations.

Migration Station

Set up a bird-watch station. Supply binoculars, logbook or board and bird identification materials. If birds migrate in your area, you have a lot to watch. Discuss migration as a way for some birds to survive the winter. Students can observe and record the date, time of day, the number of passing flocks, the number of birds if possible, the flying formations, the sounds, the shape of the birds and possible identification.

Don't Forget the Birds

Look ahead to winter in your *Kid Space*. Build and place a bird feeder or several feeders in locations where birds are likely to feast, and if possible you can view from your classroom. Make feeders from plastic jugs, waxed milk cartons, wood or suet and seedcoated pinecones, or leave a live sunflower as a natural bird feeder. Collect pinecones now for winter bird feeder use, and collect sunflower seeds for drying. When the weather turns cold and the snow begins to blow, you can start stocking your feeder.

Think Spring?

Think ahead to spring and plan and plant a bulb garden. The burst of color in the spring will be a welcome addition to any school yard.

Explain that the bulb is a self-contained seed food storage container for the plant within. Rising temperatures tell the bulbs it is time to burst up through the earth and bloom into brilliant color.

Take a trip to the local nursery, and let each child or group choose their own bulbs. Record the name and planting depth on individual bags. Ask a local gardener to assist with the planting or to give a talk about the particular requirements in your area. Bulb planting is quite simple. Dig holes two and a half times the diameter of the bulb, fertilize and place the bulb in the hole, root-side down. Fill the hole with earth and water gently. Students may choose to plant a "spring surprise garden" in which case they scatter their bulbs in a random pattern and wait for a spring surprise. If a more stuctured garden is desired, children can experiment with various colors and design a garden plot with consideration of location of various colors and bulb types. The hard part is waiting for the rainbow of color to bloom in the spring!

Fall Books for Children

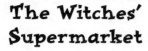

The Witches' Supermarket

Meddaugh, Susan. *The Witches' Supermarket*. Houghton Mifflin.

Helen has a hilarious adventure when she and her dog, Martha, visit the witches' grocery store. If you enjoy these lovable characters, also read the classic *Martha Speaks*.

Scary, Scary Halloween

Bunting, Eve. *Scary, Scary Halloween*. Clarion.

Vibrant illustrations join with a delightful rhyme to engage and surprise the reader. Children will want to hear this book over and over again.

Red Leaf, Yellow Leaf

Ehlert, Lois. *Red Leaf, Yellow Leaf*. Harcourt Brace and Company, 1991.

For the primary child, the simple large print text tells a story about the life of a maple leaf through the leaf's point of view. Illustrated with textured collage, the author ends her book with facts on leaves and trees, as well as information on how to plant a tree.

Why Do Leaves Change Color?

Maestro, Betsy. *Why Do Leaves Change Color?* Illustrated by Loretta Krupinski. HarperCollins Let's–Read–and–Find–Out Science Book.

Bright pictures help the informative text teach children about seasons, trees and leaves. Two art activities conclude the book.

Encounter

Yolen, Jane. *Encounter*. Illustrated by David Shannon. Harcourt Brace and Company, 1992.

Told from the point of view from a Taino boy, the story revolves around his meeting with Columbus. "The stranger made a funny noise with his mouth, not like talking but like the barking of a yellow dog."

He has a frightening dream which fore-shadows the harm that will come to his people. But no one listens to his warnings. The boy is taken on the ship to become a slave, but he escapes by swimming away to an island.

An author's note follows the story, to explain who the Taino people were and where they lived. This compelling book is a good balance to other tales that glorify Columbus. It's illustrated with dramatic paintings.

Autumn Across America

Simon, Seymour. *Autumn Across America*. Hyperion, 1993.

Fall colors burst forth from brilliant photographs. The award–winning author presents information about why seasons change, what makes leaves change color and what happens to animals during fall. This book is a work of visual and written art. Only Simon can make a common milkweed plant a wondrous experience, both through detailed photographs and text:
"Within a milkweed pod are rows of golden brown seeds, each with a tuft of silken threads. Their silken parachutes catch the faintest breeze, and they sail off to unknown destinations."

The Discovery of the Americas

Maestro, Giulio and Betsy. *The Discovery of the Americas*. Lothrop, Lee and Shepard, 1992.

This book contains more than 40 projects for students in the elementary grades. Each activity is illustrated with a color drawing. Skills used are listed under the illustration and students turn the page to read about how they can complete the project. This book is made so the pages can be placed in a three–ring binder for easy accessibility. Projects include Chinese block painting, acting dramatic scenes in history, tracing voyages and planning a trip on an explorer's ship.

by Elizabeth Koehler–Pentacoff

October, Wow, What a Month!

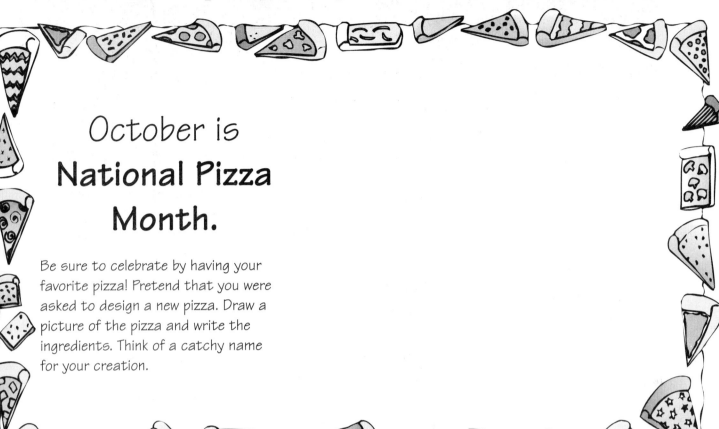

October is National Pizza Month.

Be sure to celebrate by having your favorite pizza! Pretend that you were asked to design a new pizza. Draw a picture of the pizza and write the ingredients. Think of a catchy name for your creation.

October is National Clock Month.

Design a new alarm clock that all your friends will rave about! Draw a picture of your invention and label the parts.

CHRISTOPHER COLUMBUS

Christopher Columbus

In fourteen hundred ninety-two
Columbus sailed the ocean blue.
  (Move hands gently like waves.)
He wanted to show the world was round.
  (Make a large circle with arms.)
And as he travelled, America he found!
Thanks to Columbus, *(Quick, snappy salute.)*
I'm here to say *(Use thumb to point to self.)*
I'm glad that he found the U.S.A.
  (Stand tall and proud and salute.)

by Judy Wolfman

Columbus Day

Country: United States
(Held on the second Monday in October.)

Welcome to the New World, Columbus! The
U.S. celebrates Columbus Day to honor the
famous explorer, Christopher Columbus.
Back in the late 1400s, Columbus believed he
could find a western route to the Indies. In
1492, King Ferdinand and Queen Isabella of
Spain gave him the ships and money for his
voyage. Columbus set sail and later landed in
the Bahamas.

*Congratulations! The time machine you
designed for your science project really
works! Turn the knob back to the year 1492
and travel with Columbus and his crew in
search of a western route to the Indies. Write
a "Dear Diary" page about your most exciting
day on the back of this page.*

by Mary Ellen Switzer

COLUMBUS PUPPET

Color and cut out. Match the dots. Attach arms and legs with brads.

by Carolyn Tomlin

Columbus Day Craft

Here's a quick and easy craft your students can make during the month of October to help celebrate Columbus Day. Each child will need a large, white sheet of construction paper; one half of a paper plate; a sheet of white paper; three craft sticks; one paper fastener; a reproducible Columbus pattern (provided); tape; glue; crayons and scissors. Now just follow the steps below to create a ship that really rocks back and forth!

1. Cut paper plates in half so that each child has one half.
2. To make the ship, color the back side brown. Write *Columbus Day and the year* on it.
3. Cut two squares and a triangle from the sheet of white photocopy paper. Glue each onto a craft stick to make sails.
4. Color and cut out the Columbus pattern.
5. Tape the sails and Columbus onto the back of the ship.
6. Lay the sheet of white construction paper horizontally and color the bottom third to look like the sea. Draw some clouds in the sky.
7. Position the ship onto the sea. Push a paper fastener through the bottom of the ship and the construction paper.
8. Pretend Columbus is sailing on his voyage to America. For added fun, hold the edge of the ship and gently move it up and down.

by Becky Radtke

Important Phone Numbers
Emergency – 911

Fire Dept. _____

Doctor _____

Police _____

Poison Control _____

Ambulance _____

Mom _____

Dad _____

Neighbor _____

Other _____

Rules to Live By

1. **Never** open a door if it feels hot.

2. Get on your hands and knees and crawl.

3. **Never** hide under a bed or in a closet.

4. If your clothes catch fire, do not run. **STOP, DROP and ROLL.**

5. **Never** stop to get pets or toys.

6. Get out of the burning house and stay out!

7. Go to your prearranged meeting place outside your house and stay there.

Fire Prevention Week

Use these handouts to promote fire safety at home. Place this sheet close to each phone in your home. Make copies if necessary.

To the Teacher: Use these worksheets as handouts during Fire Prevention Week, the second week in October.

Fire Safety

Dial 911 or the fire department.

Tell whoever answers that there is a fire.

Tell the dispatcher the following information:

My name is _____ .

My address is _____

_____ .

Do not hang up until the dispatcher tells you to.

This is what a fire fighter might look like when entering a burning building.

Be a fire detective.

Can you find the five (5) fires about to start?
Put an *X* on each. Color the picture.

Name _____

CELEBRATE THE WORLD

On October 24, 1995, people all around the world celebrated the 50th anniversary of the founding of the United Nations. Peace and human rights have always been two of the primary goals of the United Nations. This organization is seen intervening to provide a zone of safety in an area of violence, distributing needed serums to wipe out disease, redistributing food to ease an area of famine and working at the headquarters to resolve differences among nations.

The United Nations has accomplished a great deal in its first 50 years, but its chances for success in the next 50 rests on the shoulders of the children in our schools today. Young children may not comprehend the organization or function of the United Nations, but with thoughtful planning we can offer lessons which foster the understanding and respect necessary for peace and human rights. Here are a few ideas to try with your students. Pick and choose what is right for you.

A GLOBAL COMMUNITY

ACTIVITY: Make a bulletin board or display: "There's No Place Like Home." Include **animals' homes** (bird nest, beaver dam, gopher hole, bear cave, caterpillar's cocoon, squirrel hole, doghouse); **people's homes** (cabin, tent, apartment building, log cabin, tepee, longhouse, igloo, stilt home, grass hut, farm, miscellaneous national styles); **everyone's home** (view of planet from outer space).

DISCUSSION: Every living creature needs a home. A home protects you and gives you a place to rest and someplace to raise a family. Different creatures need different kinds of homes. A home needs to be a safe place to live. Sometimes we live alone, sometimes in groups, but we all live together in our biggest home . . . the Earth.

FOLLOW-UP: Take some time to discuss other similarities between our personal homes and our global home. Talk about who cleans up, sharing chores and responsibilities, helping each other, etc. Be sure to tie your discussion to specific recycling and environmental activities in your school and town.

Just Imagine

Our school day is already full and overflowing with wonderful and important things to do. Each day the news is full of problems we have not yet solved. But here is a chance to celebrate the dream for successful solutions and an organization which has worked for 50 years toward that dream. These lessons are small. They take very little time, but the concepts have incredible power. Picture, if you can, a global community, with open communication, working for peace, respecting diversity and sharing resources. We may not be able to single-handedly change the world. But if we can teach the children . . . just imagine!

OPENING COMMUNICATION

ACTIVITY: Choose the languages and activities depending on the resources available in your school and community. Teach the class how to say courtesy phrases (for example, hello, please and thank you) in several languages. Use them all day long as you speak to each other in class. Label things in your room with signs in different languages (the flag, the door, the window, etc.). Prepare a coloring sheet with the color key in a different language. Practice counting from one to ten in different languages.

DISCUSSION: Explain different languages in the world, that the United Nations uses French and English for official business. Tell about the many of languages found at the United Nations, the headphone interpreters, etc.

FOLLOW-UP: Create your own mini mix of languages by having students do activity with some speaking English, some French, some Spanish, etc. (For example, try counting to 10 in unison three times with three or more languages being spoken at once.) Talk about what that was like. Explain that many countries belong to the United Nations. Ask children to imagine how it must sound in the cafeteria and hallways of the United Nations.

WORKING FOR PEACE

ACTIVITY: Make a bulletin board or easel display: "What do you do when it's not fair?" (Cut out pictures, use silhouettes, stick figures, cartoons, whatever is easiest for you.) 1—a house with a parent talking to two small children, 2—a schoolroom with the teacher settling a dispute, 3—a group of children settling a disagreement (for example, dividing something or taking turns), 4—a courtroom with a judge and jury, 5—the world with the United Nations.

DISCUSSION: How do we settle fights or disagreements? The people involved sit down together, explain the problem and (either by themselves or with the help of someone else) devise a solution. Talk about how the different people shown on the bulletin board do the same things. Explain how the United Nations does the same thing for countries that disagree. (Include the vocabulary words *peacemaking* and *peacekeeping*.)

FOLLOW-UP: After the discussion, make a conscious effort to use the terms *peacemaking* and *peacekeeping* as you encourage and praise your students for their individual efforts. Point out how much nicer it is when the atmosphere is peaceful.

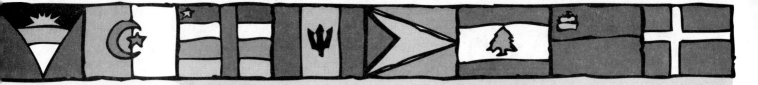

RESPECTING DIVERSITY

ACTIVITY: Have the class sit in a circle. Introduce the idea of differences. Talk about the ways we compare people (height, family size, hair length or color, age, glasses, hobbies, etc.). Go around the circle and have each person say one way he and the person next to him are different. Go around the circle again, and this time each person says one way he and the person next to him are the same.

DISCUSSION: Talk about the ways the class is alike and different. Talk about the ways we can group people. Explain that all day long the class will line up differently to see how many ways they can be grouped. Discuss how much fun it is to have variety. Ask students if they like variety and what it would be like without it. (Ideas: uniforms or choosing clothes, M & M's™ all one color or a mix, a band of all one instrument or typical band, a baseball team of all pitchers or mix, dinner of only one food or a variety.)

FOLLOW-UP: Each time the class goes somewhere have them line up using a different criteria to group them (for example, only children in front, then those with one brother or sister, then two, etc.; those with pets in front, those without next, etc.). Have everyone wearing blue clothes sit in the front, red clothes in the middle, etc. Brainstorm a list of things in our lives that are better with a mix.

SHARING RESOURCES

ACTIVITY: Snack time! Pass out popcorn. One large bowl to every four or five children on one side of the room (A), one small plastic bag for every four or five children on the other side (B).

DISCUSSION: Talk about how the students feel ("It's not FAIR!"). Is it B's "fault" that they don't have as much popcorn? (No, it's just the luck of where one "lives.") What could we do to keep the kids on side B from getting hungry? (Share.) Divide the popcorn more equally. Talk about the United Nations' work to help places without enough food. Talk about local efforts to feed the hungry, like food banks and soup kitchens. Find out if anyone has ever gone trick-or-treating for UNICEF.

FOLLOW-UP: Discuss what other kinds of things are resources (explain the word). Talk about energy (what do students do to recycle or reduce use?), medicine (talk about shots at the doctors office—immunizations) and maybe even education or knowledge as a resource (there are some countries where children can't go to school and never learn to read).

Fall Fun in the

Candy Corn Count

Preparation: On a sheet of paper (one for each team) draw large circles, giving each circle a number. Have a bowl of candy corn for each team.

Game: Seat teammates next to each other. Have each player choose a circle on the paper and write his name above it. The first player begins by putting a corresponding number of candy pieces  in his numbered circle. He then slides the paper and candy bowl to his teammate who finds his circle and fills it with the proper number of candies and so on down the line. Check papers for accuracy to determine a winning team.

Pumpkin Story Pass-Along

Preparation: Have ready one small pumpkin.

Game: As you hold the pumpkin, begin making up a Halloween story. Stop and pass the pumpkin to the person beside you, who then must continue the story. The pumpkin is passed, and the story goes on until each student has had a chance to contribute.

Straw and Leaf Game

Preparation: Divide children into teams. Give each child a plastic drinking straw. At the opposite end of the playing area set up a table with leaf cut-outs (a color for each team, a leaf for each child).

Game: First child on each team runs to the table and using his breath, sucks a leaf of his team's color onto the end of his straw. Without using his hands, he keeps the leaf on his straw and runs back to his team. The next child in line does the same. The first team to collect all their leaves wins.

Classroom

Acorn Race

Preparation: Divide children into teams. Give the first child in each line a tablespoon or teaspoon and the second child a paper cup. At the opposite end of the playing area set up a table with a large bowl filled with acorns.

Game: The first child in each line runs to the bowl, scoops up acorns in his spoon and runs back to the team where the acorns are deposited into the paper cup. Then the cup is handed to the third child in line, and the second child takes the spoon and goes for acorns. If the acorns spill from the spoon, the player must go back and get more. The first team to get all the acorns in the cup wins.

Variation: For more fun (and spills), use large cooking spoons.

Squirrel Hunt

Preparation: This game is best played outdoors. Have a large supply of acorns in a bowl. Tell the children that they are squirrels preparing for a long, hard winter. Give each child a small paper bag.

Game: Toss the acorns high in the air and have children start collecting them. The child who has the most acorns after several minutes is a "well-fed squirrel."

Variation: Paint one acorn a special color. The finder of that acorn wins a special prize.

by Donna Stringfellow

Falling Leaves

Preparation: Give each child a leaf cut-out. Each cut-out should have a different number on it. Have corresponding numbers of folded pieces of paper in a cup or bowl nearby.

Game: Have children line up or separate them in such a way as to make a "tree," some children form the trunk while others branch off from the trunk to form limbs. Have children hold their leaf cut-outs over their heads, waving gently in the breeze.

Begin drawing numbers from the bowl. As each child hears her number called, she drops her leaf to the floor. The child holding the last leaf is the winner. (It's fun to give the children a turn at calling the numbers. That way they can watch the "tree" slowly losing its leaves.)

A pumpkin is a vegetable which grows on a coarse, prickly running vine. The big orange-colored pumpkin was cultivated and perfected by the Native Americans even before America was settled by the Europeans. *Pumpkin* comes from the Greek word *pepon* which means "a large melon." At one time, the early settlers hollowed out a pumpkin, turned it upside down, put it on a person's head and used it as a guide to cutting the hair around the edges. That's how the expression "pumpkin head" originated. Americans eat pumpkins because they are rich in calcium, phosphorous, iron and vitamins A and C.

Today, pumpkins are a favorite during the fall as pie and jack-o'-lanterns. Below are pumpkin activities for the whole class to enjoy.

Pumpkin Stories

Fill a plastic pumpkin with story starters written on slips of paper. The children can reach inside and pull out a story starter. Younger students can work together to recite a group story, whereas, older ones can write individual fiction. Use such topics as "Down in the Pumpkin Patch," "Jamie's Jack-O'-Lantern" or "Pumpkin Surprise."

Mother Goose's Pumpkin

Teach the rhyme "Peter, Peter Pumpkin Eater." Give each student orange construction paper to make a pumpkin shape. Inside the pumpkin shell, have the kids draw their favorite items. Peter kept his wife well inside; children might like to keep toys, candy and other possessions in the shell.

Jack-O'-Lantern Catch

Make catch scoops from plastic gallon jugs. Inflate orange balloons and draw jack-o'-lantern features with a black felt-tip pen. Toss the balloons in the air and catch them back and forth with the homemade scoops.

Pumpkin Parade

Collect different types of empty food boxes. Cover them with orange paper. Cut facial features for a jack-o'-lantern from black construction paper. Glue these onto the boxes. Set up your parad using different size boxes with a variety of faces.

Feelings

Jack-o'-lanterns can be used as a tool to express fe ings. Give each child four pieces of paper to draw the f lowing expressions: happy, sad, sleepy, angry. Draw a color jack-o'-lanterns such as these below and discu them with the children.

# of a **PUMPKIN**

Fingerplay (Author Unknown)

Five little jack-o'-lanterns sitting on a gate (Hold up five fingers.)
First one said, "My it's getting late" (Hold up fingers.)
Second one said, "Sh-h-h, I hear a noise."
Third one said, "Oh, it's just some silly boys."
Fourth one said, "They're having Halloween fun."
   Fifth one said, "We'd better run."
      Oooooooo went the wind, out went their lights,
         and away they all scampered on Halloween night.
         (Move fingers behind back as if running.)

Jack-O'-Lantern Art

Cut out four strips from orange construction paper 8" long by 1½" (20.32 by 29.19 cm) wide. Glue the strips, one on top of the other, as in the sketch. Let the glue dry for a short time. Place a drop of glue onto the tip of each strip. Bring up the ends and glue together to form a pumpkin shape. Cut out facial features from black paper and glue on the face. Don't forget a green stem!

Cheesy Pumpkins

Cut rounds of American cheese and place these onto crackers. Decorate the jack-o'-lantern's face with raisins or use the cheese that can be squirted from a can.

Jack-O'-Lantern Pizza

Spread pizza sauce onto a toasted English muffin. Sprinkle with shredded mozzarella cheese. Use pepperoni pieces for facial features. Broil these lightly until the cheese melts. Enjoy!

by Tania Kourempis-Cowling

The Great PUMPKIN

Supplies

1 large pumpkin
paper and pencil
bathroom scale
1 large spoon (tablespoon)
1 large carving knife (use only with adult)
1 ruler, yardstick or meterstick
newspaper
data sheet

Each step of the experiment needs to be recorded using paper and a pencil and the right data. You will need an adult to help cut the pumpkin into four pieces or quarters. With a friend or family member, record two different sets of data. In one column of your paper record your estimated guesses or "guesstimates." In the other column record your actual facts or "data."

Spread a couple sheets of newspaper on a flat surface. Your kitchen table will do nicely. Guess how tall your pumpkin is. Record your guesstimation. Next, take a ruler/yardstick/meterstick and measure from the table to the top of your pumpkin. (You may include the stem if the pumpkin has one.) Record your answer in the data column.

Now guess the girth of the pumpkin or how round it is at its largest point. Record your guesstimation. If you don't have a measuring tape, make one by carefully measuring a yardstick (meterstick) on a paper shopping bag. Cut it out making sure you wrote the measured inches (centimeters) accurately. Now using your paper measuring tape, measure the girth of the pumpkin and record in your data column. How much does the pumpkin weigh?

Write your guesstimation in the proper column. Using a bathroom scale, weigh yourself and record your weight in the data column. Then take the pumpkin and hold it in your arms, and weigh yourself again. Write your answer in the data column. To find out how much the pumpkin weighs, subtract your weight alone from the weight of you and the pumpkin. If you weigh 100 lbs., and you weigh 120 lbs. while holding the pumpkin, then subtract 120 - 100 = 20! The pumpkin weighs 20 pounds. Record the pumpkin's weight in the data column.

Experiment

Cut the top off the pumpkin. Make sure the pumpkin is on the newspaper on the table. Next, have an adult slice the pumpkin in four equal pieces or quarters. In the guesstimation column, record how many seeds you think the whole pumpkin has. Now comes the real work! Taking each quarter (you might want to use your spoon), carefully count the seeds. As you count each quarter carefully, record the numbers in your data column.

Finished? Now add all the numbers together for a grand total of how many seeds the pumpkin has. Was your guesstimation more or less? If your guesstimation number is larger than the actual total, subtract the smaller number from the larger. Record the difference.

Now bake the pumpkin seeds and eat them! Have an adult preheat the oven to 350°F (175°C). Spray a cookie sheet with shortening and spread the seeds on the sheet evenly. Bake for 20 minutes or until golden brown. Salt lightly and enjoy this nutritious treat. Don't forget to clean up the mess!

The Great Pumpkin Experiment Data Sheet

	Guesstimation	Factual Data
Height	_____	_____
Girth	_____	_____
Weight	_____	_____
Seeds		
Slice 1	_____	_____
Slice 2	_____	_____
Slice 3	_____	_____
Slice 4	_____	_____
Total Seeds	_____	_____

Difference between guess and fact = _____

by Carlene Americk

Haunt Your Classroom

Make learning fun with these haunting, disgusting and motivating activities! Disguise math, science and language activities in stimulating learning centers. Put bats in the belfry, ghosts in the closet, slime in the sink and shivers up the spine as you watch active learning happen in your classroom.

Provide research materials and topic suggestions that will encourage students to research and learn about their health (tooth plaque, germs, bacteria, scabies, lice, ringworm), food (bacteria, artificial additives, fertilizer), fungi, mold, dust mites and creepy crawlies (worms, slugs, spiders, insects).

Haunted House: Provide ghastly materials in bowls and makeup appropriate names or have the children do this for one another. Children are blindfolded or materials are placed in touch and feel boxes where they cannot be seen. Try some of these for gross fun:

peeled grapes:	eyeballs
cold spaghetti:	worms
frozen gelatin:	frozen blood
cold oatmeal:	flesh
fake fur:	werewolf skin
shaving cream:	alien slime

Ghoulish Grub

Prepare spooky snacks ahead of time or provide recipes and ingredients so chefs can stir up their own.

Eyeballs: Use peeled grapes or roll up marshmallows and stuff the center with a half grape or pimento olive.

Witches Brew: Pour apple cider or orange drink into a bowl. Add an eerie floating centerpiece made by freezing water in a plastic container and adding more water with rubber spiders, flies, worms, ants or other flavor enhancers. Black licorice with the ends snipped off makes good straws.

Create a Skeleton: Students can learn about the human body as they reproduce bones in clay. For a whiter effect, paint the dried clay with white tempera or acrylic paint. Provide a diagram of the human skeleton. Can your class create the entire skeleton?

Creator's Clay

Add 1¼ cup (310 ml) water to 4 cups (1 L) baking soda and 1 cup (250 ml) cornstarch in a saucepan. Cook over medium heat until the mixture turns into a moist mass. Dump onto a flat surface and cover with a damp cloth. When cool, knead and create. Air dry or bake in a 200-250°F (90-120°C) oven for two to three hours.

Best Books for Haunting

Eagan, Robynne. *Kid Concoctions.* Teaching & Learning Company, 1994.
Elfman, Eric. *Almanac of the Gross, Disgusting and Totally Repulsive.* Illustrated by Ginny Pruitt, Random House, 1994.
Katz, Bobbi. *Ghosts and Goose Bumps, Poems to Chill Your Bones.* Illustrated by Deborah Kogan Ray, Random House PICTUREBACK, 1991.
Lunn, Janet. *The Unseen.* Lester Publishing, 1994.
Martin, Bill Jr., and John Archambault. *The Ghost Eye Tree.* Illustrated by Ted Rand, Henry Holt and Company, New York.
Witkowski, Dan. *How to Haunt a House.* Illustrated by Jack Lindstrom, Random House, New York, 1994.

TLC10047 Copyright © Teaching & Learning Company, Carthage, IL 62

Bat Cut-Outs: Trace a bat design onto black paper or a rubber inner tube. Cut it out and decorate it in a variety of ways. Provide thick black paint (tempera mixed with Ivory Snow™ soap powder), fake fur, strands of black thread, glue-on eyes and other "bataphernalia."

Shadow Center: Provide a bright light or flashlight and a white screen. Dim the lights and experiment with hands and paper cut-outs. A great way to develop spatial abilities, problem solving and creative expression! Try a shadow play.

Creepy Hands: Fill thick rubber gloves with plaster of Paris. Wrap a thick rubber band or string around the ends and hang them from a clothesline or ceiling to dry. When dry, paint or decorate the hands with nail polish, paint, wool and glue-on effects.

Guess the Ghost: Have one child leave the room. Choose one "ghost," cover this child with a sheet. Other children rearrange themselves around the room. The child returns to the room and tries to "guess the ghost."

Dark Tales: Provide bat, ghost or moon-shaped story booklets. Children can follow the classroom writing process to publish their own dark tales.

Dress-Up Costume Center: Provide old clothing, hats, shoes, pillowcases, sheets, white fabric, gauze strips, fabric paints, fabric markers, glue and various recyclable materials. Children can create costumes and make up a skit.

Spooky Spiders: Provide black plasticine, stick- on eyes and black pipe cleaners for legs. Children can shape the bodies, add the eyes and the eight spider legs as they learn a bit about spiders. What do they eat? Where do they live? How many legs does a spider have?

Aaahhh

Gravestone Epitaphs: Create a bulletin board using students creative writing work. Add a full moon, a few bat silhouettes and a bare hill to a background. Provide students with precut cardboard gravestones, or let them make their own from a template. Students can use their math and language arts skills to add witty, humorous epitaphs and dates. Add the gravestones to the bare hill.

Morbid Math: Make some ghostly manipulatives. Paint lima beans with white acrylic paint or spray paint and add black eyes. Shellac the beans when they are dry. Children draw their own haunted house or hill. Do manipulative math as a group, or have children use these to complete the oriented math questions at the Morbid Math center.

Witch, Witch, Ghost: Children sit in a circle. A chosen "ghost" walks around the outside of the circle and taps children on the head while repeating witch. On a particular tap the "ghost" calls "ghost." The child tapped on the call of "ghost" must race the ghost around the circle back to the empty spot. The last child to reach the empty spot is "ghost" for the next round, and the game begins again.

Eerie Atmosphere: Create a haunted atmosphere with the following: cheesecloth webs hanging from the ceiling and door frames, cut-out bats and spiders hanging from your ceiling, subdued lighting and eerie background music.

Pumpkin Monsters: Provide small pumpkins or gourds and black markers or acrylic paints so each child can create his own pumpkin monster.

Mud and Bugs in a Bucket: Crush chocolate cookie wafers into a bucket, add a little chocolate pudding and some gummy worms, stir up and dig in.

Creepy Reading Nook: Drape cloth over and under a box or desk in a quiet corner. Provide reading lights, flashlights and some haunting tales.

Slime: Add 1 cup (250 ml) cornstarch to 1 cup (250 ml) of green colored water and stir up some slime for a gooey center. Include a graffiti chalkboard for students to report descriptions.

Sinister Sound Center: Children can experiment with technical equipment including the cassette player and microphone as they make their own spooky sounds recording. Provide various materials including gravel, water in a cup, straws, cookie sheet, marbles, a squeaky hinge, chains, shoes that shuffle, sandpaper and more.

by Robynne Eagan

Halloween Book Nook

Celebrate the Halloween season with this exciting collection of books. Your students are sure to enjoy the motivating activities that follow each book review.

Start the holiday mood by reading *Halloween* by Gail Gibbons (New York: Holiday House, 1984). This colorful book features the customs and traditions of Halloween.

The Mystery of the Flying Orange Pumpkin

Kellogg, Steven. *The Mystery of the Flying Orange Pumpkin*. New York: Dial Books, 1983.

A friendly neighbor lets a group of children plant a pumpkin in his yard. They plan to use the pumpkin as their jack-o'-lantern on Halloween until a new grouchy owner wants pumpkin pie instead. Thanks to a smiling orange balloon, the children get their jack-o'-lantern, and the new neighbor gets his pie!

Draw a picture of how you think the children's jack-o'-lantern looked.

Do you think Mr. Klug would let the children plant new pumpkin seeds next year? Why?

Congratulations! You have just grown the world's biggest pumpkin in your backyard. Write a news article telling all about your prizewinner. Draw a picture of your pumpkin that would go with the article.

Yummy pumpkin pie! Write directions on how you would make a pumpkin pie!

by **Mary Ellen Switzer**

Big Pumpkin

Silverman, Eric. *Big Pumpkin*. New York: Macmillan Publishing Company, 1992.

A witch discovers the value of teamwork when she enlists the help of some Halloween monsters to pick and move a giant-sized pumpkin. And how does she reward them for their good deed? With a piece of her delicious pumpkin pie, of course!

Think about it! You grow a giant-sized pumpkin in your yard. What would you do with it? Write a paragraph telling your answer.

Be an inventor! Design a state-of-the-art "super sonic pumpkin pie maker." Draw a picture of your invention and label the parts.

Create a picture book entitled *The Smallest Pumpkin in the World*.

Rotten Ralph's Trick or Treat

Gantos, Jack. *Rotten Ralph's Trick or Treat.* Boston: Houghton Mifflin Co., 1986.

Uh oh! Sarah's rotten cat Ralph creates havoc when he attends a Halloween costume party dressed as her. Ralph's zany antics at the party are sure to tickle any reader's "funny bone."

Sarah and Ralph were invited to come to the party as the thing they loved best. If you were invited to a similar party, what would you wear? Draw a picture of your costume.

Party time! Plan a Halloween party that you would like to have. Make a list of the food you would serve and tell what party games you would play.

Design the Halloween party invitation you would use.

Arthur's Halloween

Brown, Marc. *Arthur's Halloween.* Boston: Little, Brown and Company, 1982.

Halloween is here and Arthur is not so sure he likes this scary holiday. Everything frightens him from the bat wing brownies during morning snack to the spooky old house on the hill. Will he be able to enjoy Halloween?

Arthur had special Halloween "treats" for his morning snack at school. Plan a "spook"tacular menu of morning snack treats that you would like to have at your school. Draw a picture of each of the foods and tell what you would name each treat.

Who's your favorite character in this book? Create a bookmark featuring that character.

Write a "Dear Diary" entry that Arthur might have written on that Halloween night.

Harriet's Halloween Candy

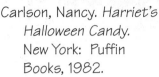

Carlson, Nancy. *Harriet's Halloween Candy.* New York: Puffin Books, 1982.

Harriet has a big problem—she is running out of places to hide her trick-or-treat candy. She soon discovers that sharing is the best answer!

Design a trick-or-treat bag for Harriet. Draw a picture of the bag.

It's trick-or-treat time! Create a poster for Harriet called "How to Have a Safe Halloween."

Think of a new treat for Halloween. Draw a picture of your treat and tell how it is made.

Poems, Please!

Your class will love the lively array of Halloween poems in *Ragged Shadows* (Little, Brown & Co., 1993), poems selected by Lee Bennett Hopkins and *Ghosts and Goose Bumps, Poems to Chill Your Bones* (Random House, 1991), poems selected by Bobbi Katz. Why not have your students create their own poems and have a poetry-reading party with everyone dressed in costumes as they read? Encourage your students to submit their poems to your school or local newspaper for possible publication.

Let's Plan a Party!

Ask your young ghosts and goblins to dress up as their favorite Halloween book characters for a Halloween Book Party. Serve pumpkin treats and orange punch and have your students read some of their holiday creative writing stories from this unit.

To add more excitement to your party, play a Whoooo Are You? guessing game. To make the game, put the names of all the Halloween book characters in a glass bowl. Have someone in the audience come up and choose a character card from the bowl. Next, have the students ask questions with "yes" or "no" answers to try and guess the identity of the mystery character. The student who guesses the correct character can come up and choose a name from the bowl.

Happy Halloween!

A Station Party for Your Classroom

by Diane Retzlaff and Becky Radtke

Are you looking for a unique way to help your youngsters celebrate Halloween? Then a "station" party is the ideal answer! Students are given an opportunity to participate in a variety of games and activities which are held at little stations within the classroom. Consider doubling the fun by putting on a party with another teacher. Children can travel from room to room and enjoy twice as many stations! Prize items can be won and then deposited into nearby individual party bags.

Preparing for the Party

In mid-September, send home a note to students' parents. Explain that you are looking for "helpers" to run games and activities (the stations). Specify the time that you would need them to arrive (plan on 20 minutes before the party begins) and when they can expect to be done. Invite them to wear costumes, if they like! If they are willing to assist, ask that they notify you by October 1. You will need one volunteer for each of the stations, plus an extra to relieve and help others.

In this same note, also ask the parents to donate items that would be suitable for prizes. Give them some examples such as wrapped candy, pencils, stickers, small trinkets, etc. Emphasize that you will need lots! Request that prizes be sent in multiples of however many students are in the class. Lastly, tell them you will need these donated items at least two weeks prior to the party. At that point, you will need to determine which items will be given at which stations. You will also need to take inventory and see if there are enough prizes. Figure it so that every student could visit a station twice and win a prize each time. After the party, tuck away any extra prize items to use for other events throughout the school year.

Two weeks before the party is a good time to start gathering necessary materials for the stations. A week before the party, ask each student to bring a large, brown grocery bag to school. Set aside some classroom time and instruct your children to print their names in large, black crayon letters on either the front or back panel. After doing this, they can use crayons or markers to decorate the rest of the bag in Halloween fashion with pumpkins, ghosts and so on.

When all of the "party bags" are complete, collect them and put them in a safe place. The day of the party, line the bags up where they will be out of the way, yet accessible to students (on a counter or the back of the room).

When only a few days remain before the party, use a fine tipped, black marker to draw a simple outline of a pumpkin onto an 8½" x 11" (22 x 28 cm) sheet of white paper. Photocopy and cut one out for each of your students. Write their names on the backs. Then paper-punch a hole in each pumpkin's stem and thread pieces of yarn through to make necklaces. Students will need to wear these during the party. Each time they visit a station, the volunteer there will stamp their necklace with a rubber stamp. Since each station will have a different stamp, it will be easy to tell if the children have visited all eight.

Explaining the Rules

Encourage students to come dressed in their Halloween costumes the day of the party. Remind them that their costume must allow them to move freely, see well and should not involve face makeup.

Inform the children that the party will last about one hour. Explain that there will be a number of stations throughout the room. At each station there will be a worker who will tell them about the game or activity. When they are finished at a station they will need to have their pumpkin necklace stamped. Tell them that each time they receive a prize they must immediately walk over to their party bag and place the prize inside. Emphasize that they will not be allowed to eat any of the candy or play with any prizes during the party. Explain that students can visit the stations in any order they wish. But make it clear that they cannot visit a station more than twice.

In closing, remind your children that you will expect them to be kind and polite to volunteers and other classmates.

The Stations

If you have done all of the possible preparation for the stations ahead of time, they should only take about 20 minutes to set up before the party actually begins.

Photocopy the directions for all the stations and tape them onto index cards. That way, when a volunteer chooses a station, you simply hand them the corresponding card to read. This will save you the time of explaining everything. In addition to any materials mentioned, each station will keep a supply of prize items, a rubber stamp and an ink pad. Before the child leaves, the volunteer should stamp the child's necklace.

Face Painting

Necessary Preparation: Draw several simple designs (pumpkin, bat, rainbow, etc.) onto a sheet of paper that can be used as patterns for face paintings. Purchase or borrow a face painting set. Fill a few small bowls with water (for rinsing) and place some fine-tipped paint-brushes nearby.

How It Works: The student chooses a design off the sheet. She then stands very still while the volunteer paints this design onto her cheek. Afterwards, the child receives a prize for standing patiently.

Halloween Hop

Necessary Preparation: Draw, color and laminate six large, simple Halloween shapes (witch's hat, haunted house, moon, etc.). Trim the excess lamination material and tape the shapes onto the floor in a circle. Draw the same six shapes in miniature size. Cut them out and place in a coffee can. You will need to have a cassette player and a tape of seasonal music.

How It Works: Up to six children can play at once. They start by standing outside the circle of Halloween shapes. When the volunteer starts the music, the students should hop around the circle of shapes in clockwise order. (To preserve the shapes, don't let the children hop on them.) When the volunteer stops the music, each child stands behind one shape. The volunteer then draws a shape from the coffee can. The child that is standing behind that same shape is the winner and receives a prize item. All other participants can go to the end of the line and try again if they wish.

Bucket Bash Game

Necessary Preparation: Cover three ice cream buckets with orange construction paper. Then use a black marker to draw a different pumpkin face on each. Put a masking tape line onto the floor. Then make a second masking tape line about 7' (2.13 m) away. Place the bucket about 6" (15.24 cm) in front of the second tape line. You will also need to have three beanbags.

How It Works: The volunteer places one prize item in each bucket and puts the covers on tightly. The student stands behind the first tape line and throws three beanbags (one at a time) in an attempt to hit the buckets and pushes them across the second tape line. The child gets to keep whatever prizes are inside the winning buckets. If he did not manage to get any of the buckets over the line, he can go to the end of the line and try again.

Spider Toss Game

Necessary Preparation: Buy a large, reasonably priced, plastic pumpkin and a bag of small spider rings. Make a masking tape line on the floor. Cut the handle off the pumpkin and place it 6' (1.82 m) from the tape line.

How It Works: The student stands behind the tape line and tries three times to toss a spider ring into the pumpkin. If she is successful, she gets to keep the ring. If she was not able to do so, she can go to the end of the line and try again.

Witch's Broom Sweep Game

Necessary Preparation: Use masking tape to make large letter *W* (about 6' [1.82 m] wide) onto the floor. You will need a broom and a watch with a second hand.

How It Works: The child chooses a prize item and place it on the start of the *W*. Then he is given the broom. The child is allowed 10 seconds to try to "sweep" their priz along the entire *W* and off the end. If they do this, they g to keep the prize. If they do not, they can go to the end the line and try again if they wish.

Jack-O'-Lantern Game

Necessary Preparation: Use markers to draw a jack-o'-lantern face on both sides of a heavy paper plate. Paper-punch a hole near the edge and thread a long piece of string through it. Then hang the plate from the ceiling. About 6' (1.82 m) away, make a masking tape line on the floor. You will also need two beanbags.

How It Works: The child is instructed to stand behind the tape line. He then throws the beanbags (one at a time), and tries to hit the hanging plate. If the student does this, they win a prize item. If they were unsuccessful, they can go to the end of the line and try again.

Pumpkin Switch Game

Necessary Preparation: Cut the bottom portions off of three orange two-liter pop bottles to create bowls. Turn them upside down and use a black permanent marker to draw an identical jack-o'-lantern face on each.

How It Works: A student watches as the volunteer places a prize item under one of the three bowls. The child continues watching as the volunteer quickly moves the bowls around for about five seconds. Then she tries to guess which bowl the prize item is under. If they guess incorrectly, they can go to the end of the line and try again.

Witch's Hat Game

Necessary Preparation: Cut three ring shapes from th top, clear portion of a two-liter pop bottle. Construct witch's hat from heavy black tagboard. Make it so th hole in the brim is the same size as the rings. Use tape secure the brim of the hat onto a table or the floor. Als use masking tape to make a line about 6' (1.82 m) fro the hat.

How It Works: The child stands behind the line and given the three rings. She then tries to toss them onto th point of the hat. If she does this with any or all of th rings, she wins a prize. If she misses, she can go to th end of the line and try again.

The Happiest Harvest

Summer, Winter, Spring and Fall
Special seasons, one and all
Yet one gives us the harvest days
With colors of red and brown and maize.

Penny the Pumpkin sat quietly in the September sunshine, listening as the farmer's children sang their happy harvest song. "Everyone is happy, except for me," thought Penny. "All the fruits and vegetables are more beautiful and important than I am." She gave a big sigh.

"Why the big sigh?" asked Penny's neighbor, Yolanda the Yellow Squash. "You sound pitiful!"

"Oh, I surely am pitiful," moaned Penny. You are so smooth and yellow. Every day you become longer and more curved, and the farmer's wife stops by to admire you. She can hardly wait for the Harvest Celebration, to make you into a delicious casserole. You are important."

"That's true," replied Yolanda. "But, I think you need to give yourself a chance, Penny. Every creation is beautiful in its own way."

Repeat verse.

The farmer's children moved down the rows of vegetables, singing their song and looking for weeds and bugs that might spoil the harvest vegetables, so nearly ready for picking. The little boy stopped in front of a tall, proud stalk of corn and admired its bold, yellow color.

"See what I mean?" moaned Penny. "Clarence the Corn Stalk gets so much attention. Not that he does not deserve it. I mean, look how versatile corn can be! He can be ground into meal, mashed into feed or boiled for succotash, and even his stripped-down cob is a treat for deer or squirrels."

"Thanks for the praise," sang out Clarence, "but you're being a little hard on yourself, Penny. Every part of nature has a purpose. You just haven't found your way yet." Clarence finished his speech, and stretched his neck toward the warm fall sun, soaking up a few more rays and becoming even more strong and tall.

by Dr. Linda Karges-Bone

Summer, Winter, Spring and Fall
Special seasons, one and all
Yet one gives us the harvest days
With colors of red and brown and maize.

The farmer's daughter put down her hoe and stooped to gather some of the oak leaves that had blown into the vegetable patch. "These are perfect," she exclaimed. "I'll press them between some waxed paper and make a mobile."

"Do you see what I mean?" called out Penny. "It's not enough that the vegetables get noticed; now even those skinny oak trees are important. Doesn't anyone want a slightly irregular but very loving pumpkin?"

"Rrrreally, Penny," rustled Opal the Oak Tree, as a sudden breeze stirred her colored leaves, "you have a very negative outlook on life. Every part of nature has a place. You just need to think more positively, and you will find yours."

Repeat verse.

The farmer's children sat down at the end of a row of richly colored collard greens and ate their snack. They crunched on the season's first Red Delicious apples and a handful of sunflower seeds, all grown on their farm.

"Children love apples," pointed out Penny, to anyone who would listen to her laments. "But nobody wants me." Andrew the apple tree heard her words, as they were carried across the rows to the orchard, by that same gentle September breeze that had stirred the oak leaves and bent the corn stalks.

"Ohhh my!" cried Andrew, "aren't we feeling sorry for ourselves today. Look at the bright side, Penny. The longer you sit in that pumpkin patch, the bigger and rounder you can become. Don't rush things in nature. They generally work out for the best."

"Fiddle sticks!" retorted Penny. "You don't know how it feels to wait. Folks are beating down the orchard gate to pick the fruit from your branches. Apple cider, applesauce, apple pie, apple cake, candied apples . . . why the list is endless. September is nearly over, and nobody has even looked twice at me."

Repeat verse.

The farmer's children finished their chores and walked toward the house. The sun had begun to shift low in the western sky, and the breeze took on a decidedly chilly tone as evening approached. Penny the Pumpkin watched as the children stopped by a group of autumn mums and chose a nosegay of blooms for their mother. "We can put these in a jelly jar and surprise Mom," said the boy. "Be sure to get a few of that crimson color," added the girl, "she loves those!"

"No matter how scraggly and overgrown they become, folks still love autumn mums," muttered Penny.

"Dear Penny," crooned Christine the Chrysanthemum, "you have so much to offer, but you can't see it. I used to be like you, comparing myself to the velvety roses, or even the delicate lilacs, and I felt so dowdy. But in time I found my own sense of purpose, and saw myself as valuable. You have to believe in yourself. It is right there inside of you."

"You're a good friend, Chris," said Penny, "but I really don't feel very valuable right now. But I'll think about what you said, and perhaps tomorrow things will look brighter."

"Remember my advice, too," called out Yolanda the Yellow Squash.

"Don't forget my words of wisdom," came the voice of Clarence the Corn Stalk.

"Invest some time in my ideas," added Opal the Oak Tree. "Things work out for the best," sang Andrew the Apple Tree. "Thank you all," answered Penny, and she settled down for the night.

Summer, Winter, Spring
and Fall
Special seasons, one and all
Yet one gives us the harvest days
With colors of red and brown
and maize.

The next day, the farmer's children walked down the gravel road, to wait for the school bus. They were singing their song. Penny woke up and recalled the words of advice from her friends.

She decided to change her attitude, and think positively. Just the idea made her sit up straighter in the pumpkin patch.

"Look at that pumpkin in the middle," said the boy as he noticed Penny's proud posture. "That might be just the one for our Harvest Celebration."

We can put it in the center of the table for a decoration," added his sister, as they boarded the yellow bus.

Penny smiled in the warm sunshine, and it made her once pale complexion glow with health and happiness. "What a lovely pumpkin," remarked the farmer's wife, as she unwound the hose to water the garden. "It might be just the one for my Harvest Celebration pie."

It suddenly seemed that everyone wanted Penny. She felt good about herself and spread her trailing green vines triumphantly around the patch, as if to hug the whole world.

"That's just about a perfect pumpkin," said the farmer, as he stopped to give his wife a hug before moving on to the barn. "It would take a prize for sure, if we entered it in the Harvest Fair."

Penny felt so good that she almost burst with happiness. Her friends had been right all along. Things did work out. Every part of nature did have a purpose. Each part of nature was special. But you had to believe it for yourself. That was the secret of it all, and for Penny, the reason for the happiest harvest of all.

The End

Science and Social Studies

1. Give each child a small bag for "collecting specimens," and go out into the park or playground on a nature walk. Point out the changes that autumn brings. Encourage children to collect leaves, acorns or flowers that represent the changing season.

2. Put a squirrel feeder or bird feeder outside your classroom door or window. Spend a few minutes each day watching for birds and squirrels. Talk about their behavior and feeding patterns.

3. Make a comparison chart, showing the differences between how people dress during summer and autumn. Talk about why it is important to dress appropriately during each season.

4. Use a globe and flashlight to demonstrate the changing seasons. Introduce the term *rotation,* and explain how seasons change according to where one lives on the Earth, and as the Earth tilts toward the sun on its axis.

Sample Comparison Chart

	Size of Kernels	Color	Texture
White Corn			
Indian Corn			
Yellow Corn			
Field Corn			

5. Ask parents to bring in special dishes for a Harvest celebration: pumpkin pie, squash casserole, collard greens, corn bread or corn pudding and apple juice. Use this lesson as a lead-in to a health unit on vitamins and vegetables. Encourage the children to try a taste of everything and to make a recipe book for their families.

6. Bring in several different varieties of corn, including field corn, Indian corn, white corn, yellow corn. Let children husk the corn and make a comparison chart examining the differences between the different kinds of corn.

7. Take a field trip to a local produce stand (best option) a well-stocked produce section at a grocery store. Ask the grocer or farmer to describe the autumn harvest vegetables.

8. Be sure to bring in a pot or two of chrysanthemums for the children to observe. Show children how to care for the plants. Many of the children may not have the opportunity to enjoy flowers on a daily basis.

Language Arts

1. Create a bulletin board that teaches a wide variety of color words such as *yellow, gold, maize, crimson, red, brown* and *rust.* Use Velcro™ to make a participative board, where children match the color words (printed on tagboard) to leaves cut out of wallpaper samples or cloth.

2. Extend the children's memory for language by turning the verse in the story into a fingerplay. Make finger puppets out of bath tissue rolls, colored in autumn shades. Recite the verse in a chorus. Patterns can be found on page 82.

3. Make the story into a "big book" by printing all or part of it on sheets of poster board, cut in half and hold together with shower curtain rings. Read the book aloud, and then encourage children to "read" it for themselves.

4. Write a whole group "chart story" about the season of autumn. Use colored markers in shades of brown and red.
Note: This is an excellent follow-up to the nature walk.

5. Publish individual books with the title: "I Am Special Because . . . ." Children can write or dictate their responses after reflecting on how Penny the Pumpkin learned to value herself.

Mathematics

1. Use a pumpkin for a wide variety of mathematics lessons.
   a. Estimate the weight of the pumpkin and record the responses.
   b. Use a string to estimate the diameter of the pumpkin and record the responses.
   c. Compare the estimates to the actual weight and circumference of the pumpkin.

   Use this as the introduction to a corresponding unit on weights and measures.

2. Graph the students' favorite season of the year. Use a yellow sun for summer, an orange pumpkin for fall, a purple flower for spring and a blue mitten for winter. Students can cut out their pattern of choice as a fine-motor activity, and attach it to a large poster board that reads "My Favorite Season."

3. Cook homemade applesauce. Use this activity to discover how matter changes from a solid to a liquid and how heat affects matter. Take note of the changes in volume as the apples cook.

My Favorite Season

Name	spring	summer	fall	winter
Opal	🌷			
Yolanda			🎃	
Penny			🎃	
Andrew		☀		
Clarence				🧤

Creative Arts

1. Use autumn leaves collected on the nature walk to make mobiles for the classroom. Press large, unusual leaves between sheets of waxed paper with a hot iron until they are sealed. Make sure that the work area is safe and well-secured, and that an adult is in charge at all times. Suspend the mobiles from the ceiling using fishing line.

2. Set up the easel with bold autumn colors: red, brown and yellow. Use brushes or sponges cut in the shapes of leaves.

3. Collect scarves or strips of cloth in bold autumn colors, and play some classical music for a background as students dance in the breeze.

4. Make vegetable prints with pieces of corn cob, sweet potatoes and even leaves. Dip the cut pieces into thick tempera and apply to heavy paper. For a really neat idea: use the prints to design book covers for the stories described in the language arts section.

5. Call a local doll collector and invite him or her to visit the classroom and show pictures or examples of dolls made from cornhusks, corn cobs or apples.

Patterns for "The Happiest Harvest"

82

How to Have the Best
Open House

Open House is usually a celebration of American Education Week in November. It is no longer a time to review student progress but a time to strengthen relationships with parents, students and teachers. Use it as a time to show your community the positive atmosphere you provide for students. The event takes place in your classroom so remember . . . you are the host.

Step One: Send invitations home with your class. A sample of a "Polite Invite" is included in this lesson, as well as a response card that will be returned to you.

Step Two: The room should be a gallery of the children's work. Divide your room into subject sections. A spelling display, a reading corner, an area to display science projects and posters. Make a picture gallery and a clothesline exhibit. Also write on the chalkboard your daily schedule Monday through Friday. Let parents know how busy you are.

Step Three: Cover a table with a bright tablecloth. (We like to add one or two helium balloons or a centerpiece using a plant.) Serve punch and cookies to show your hospitality. Tape a big piece of paper on the floor by your front door. Write *Welcome* on it and make footprint designs. Write students' names in the feet.

Step Four: The starting point and main attraction is always the child's desk, so be certain it has a bright name card. On it will be an envelope that says "Open, Mom and Dad." In it will be a puzzle they will need to put together. When solved, it will tell them what to do next. This lesson includes a sample of the puzzle.

Step Five: If they follow the directions, they will have found a cassette tape in the desk. (Have tape player available.) The message for the cassette is included, also. This taped message is a great way to encourage conversation and participation by your "guest." Add whatever complements your teaching style. It is prerecorded by your students so it can be informative, funny or serious. This tape becomes a keepsake.

Step Six: The tape instructs parents to stop by the "You Did Us a Favor by Being Here" bulletin board. Have a guest book there. (Sheets of paper stapled together with a cover "Open House Guests.") The bulletin board need not be fancy. Just a sign or letters "You Did Us a Favor . . . We Made One for You." Each person will take with them a child-made bookmark as a memento of this memorable event.

Step Seven: If you wish, add background music to the evening. Children's or patriotic songs are appropriate.

At the end of the evening you will have instilled a sense of school pride in your community. You will have also demonstrated a welcoming atmosphere to your students and their guardians.

by Jo Jo Cavalline and Jo Anne O'Donnell

A Polite Invite for You

Please return enclosure card ASAP.

Please Come!!

————————————————
Signature

———— people will be with us.
———— Sorry, we cannot attend.
———— Yes, we will attend.

Dear _____,

You are cordially invited to attend an Open House at the

_____ on _____, 19___.

We are planning many activities for you.

We look forward to sharing this celebration with you.

It begins at _____ p.m.

_____
(child)

_____
(teacher)

Directions: Fold picture in half horizontally, with art showing. Fold in half again to make invitation.

Use a marker to write out the message. Use heavy paper. Cut into puzzle pieces. Guide students in writing and cutting.

Dear _____ and _____,
Welcome to my classroom. Please look inside my desk for a cassette tape. Go to the tape player and play it. Follow the directions. Thanks for being here with me.

Love, _____

Messages for Tapes

(prerecorded by individual students.

Hi, _____ and _____. This is _____. I am so glad you came to our Open House. Isn't our room beautiful? Please introduce yourself to our teacher, _____. Be sure to ask her (him) about (the field trip, our reading contest, other special events, portfolios). Stop and look for my work in every display. I am really proud of my _____ in the _____ corner. Many of these papers will be in my portfolio this year. Have some punch and cookies while you are looking around. If you have any questions, just ask. My daily schedule is on the board, so you can see how busy we are. There is a list of things we can use in our room by the computer. We need magazines, old greeting cards, baby food jars, etc. Before you leave, look for the bulletin board that says "You Did Us a Favor by Being Here." On it is a favor for you. Please take one of the bookmarks we made for each of you.

Thanks again for sharing this night with me. I hope you had as much fun as we have had getting ready for your arrival. Add personal ending.)

I visited my child's school, and I think my child is really COOL.

Another Bookmark Idea

My child has class...
and I saw it.
Put name of school and date.

WORLD HELLO DAY

Materials: map, crayons, construction paper, glitter, markers

World Hello Day is celebrated in November. Students can read the following story about how to say "hello" in different languages and then locate the different countries on a map. They can design their own greeting card using *hello* in one or many of the different languages in the story. Cards can be given to fellow students or hung to decorate your bulletin board.

HOW DO YOU SAY "HELLO"?

There are many children in school who come from different far-away places. And they speak different languages . . .

In the United States, they say HELLO. How do you say HELLO?

My name is Maria. I'm from Mexico. I say HOLA. It means HELLO.

My name is Jacques. I'm from France. I say BONJOUR. It means HELLO.

My name is Han Juang. I'm from China. I say NIHOW. It means HELLO.

My name is Johanne. I'm from Ghana. I say JAMBO. It means HELLO.

My name is Nilam. I'm from India. I say NAMASTE. It means HELLO.

My name is Raisa. I'm from Russia. I say ZDRASTVOUKEE. It means HELLO.

My name is Raiki. I'm from Japan. I say OHIO. It means HELLO.

My name is Benjamin. I'm from Israel. I say SHALOM. It means HELLO.

My name is Giuseppe. I'm from Italy. I say CIAO. It means HELLO.

My name is Jung. I'm from Korea. I say YOBOSEYO. It means HELLO.

And we all go to school in the United States.

We are learning English.

GOOD-BYE!

KEY FOR "HELLO"

(O-la)—hola
(BONE-zhoor)—bonjour
(KNEE-how)—nihow
(JAHM-bō)—jambo
(na-MAS-te)—namaste
(sdras-VO-key)—zdrastvoukee
(o-HI-o)—ohio
(sha-LOHM)—shalom
(chow)—ciao
(yo-bo-SAY-yo)—yoboseyo

Diwali in India

Diwali is a festival celebrated in November by the people of India. It is one of the most beautiful holidays because in the evening people light oil lamps, and fireworks light up the sky. Celebrate Diwali by making kulfi, Indian ice cream.

1 cup evaporated milk
1 cup condensed milk
1 cup heavy cream
10 almonds
pinch of saffron
1 tsp. sugar

Blend all ingredients together. Freeze for four hours. Enjoy!

by Donna L. Clovis

Veterans Day in the United States

Every year on November 11th, Veterans Day, the United States honors the men and women who have served in the armed forces. Parades, speeches and other special ceremonies are all part of the celebration. Services are also held at the Tomb of the Unknown Soldier in Arlington, Virginia.

Hooray for veterans! Design a trophy to honor United States' veterans.

by Mary Ellen Switzer

SHICHI-GO-SAN
IN JAPAN

Did you know that there is a holiday especially for children who are seven, five and three years old? Every year in Japan, there is a special festival for seven-year-old girls, five-year-old boys and both girls and boys who are three years old. The holiday, Shichi-Go-San, is celebrated on November 15th. The children dress in their finest kimonos and visit Shinto Shrines with their parents. Later parties are held in the children's honor.

Let's celebrate! Plan a new holiday to honor children. What would you name this holiday? How would you celebrate? Design a greeting card for your new holiday.

by Mary Ellen Switzer

The First Thanksgiving

by Patricia O'Brien

Introduction

The Pilgrims worked hard to prepare for the feast. They were celebrating a fine harvest at the end of their first year at Plymouth Colony. The men and boys gathered the crops from the fields. They hunted deer, turkeys and ducks. They caught fish. The women and girls prepared and cooked the food. Their friends, the Indians, who had helped them so much, were invited to share in the celebration. They had much to be thankful for.

The Pilgrims

The year before, as they started on their journey, no one could know how it would turn out. Aboard the *Mayflower,* a three-mast ship, were the Separatists, who were looking for a place where they could freely practice their religious beliefs. There were adventurers on board, also. They were looking for new beginnings in the New World. Both groups came to be known as Pilgrims.

The Mayflower

After many delays, the *Mayflower* finally set sail from Plymouth, England, on September 6, 1620. The ship was small and overcrowded. It carried 102 passengers and a crew of 25. Stored in the hold were food for the trip and supplies for the colony. They brought building and gardening tools, as well as seeds. In case of unfriendly neighbors, they had cannons, muskets and gunpowder to protect themselves.

During the 66 days crossing the Atlantic Ocean, they had calm, clear days and days of raging storms. One passenger died. A boy was born. He was named Oceanus. The ship reached the coast of Cape Cod on November 11, 1620.

Plymouth Colony

The Pilgrims were happy to reach land. By now the weather had turned cold and winter was near. They would quickly have to find a suitable place to build their houses. Men in small boats, led by Miles Standish, scouted along the shore. They would need fresh water for drinking, trees to build their houses and fields to plant their crops. They needed a protected harbor so they could anchor their ship. They also hoped more ships would come from England with supplies and other settlers to join them. The scouts were able to find a good location. Later they learned a group of Indians had lived there. They had cleared the land for planting before they all became sick and died. They named their new home Plymouth after the port they had sailed from in England.

The First Winter

The first winter was very hard for the Pilgrims. They had arrived too late to complete the building of the houses. Most remained aboard the *Mayflower*, while a small boat took workers to and from the site. Cold, damp weather, combined with a lack of fresh fruits and vegetables contributed to the deaths of half the colonists. In the spring, the remaining Pilgrims faced the task of unloading cargo from the ship and planting crops. There was much to do, and although they didn't know it, much to learn about their new land.

The Indians

In the early spring, an Indian came to Plymouth Colony. Samoset was the first Indian the Pilgrims met. He later introduced them to Massasoit, chief of the Wampanoag. Massasoit was an important leader among the other tribes in the area. He smoked a peace pipe with the Pilgrim leaders, and together they agreed to help each other.

Among the warriors traveling with Massasoit was Squanto. He had been to England and spoke English. He stayed on in Plymouth to act as an interpreter for the Pilgrims and their Indian neighbors. But Squanto did much more. He taught the Pilgrims many things that helped them the first year in a new country.

Life in the Colony

If the Indians had not helped during that first spring, the Pilgrims would not have survived. The seeds they had brought didn't grow well in the soil and climate of Plymouth. The Indians taught them how to plant and care for corn, squash and beans. Without Squanto's help, they would not have known the practice of burying fish with the corn kernels as they were planted. They were shown which wild plants were good to eat. They might have eaten plants that were not good for them and gotten sick. They might also have missed out on some delicious treats. That spring and summer, the Pilgrims worked hard sowing seeds and tending plants. They fished in the sea and streams and hunted in the woods.

The Feast

As autumn approached, the Pilgrims knew the harvest would be good. To celebrate, they decided to have a Thanksgiving feast. They invited the Indians who had taught them about the new land. Together they ate, danced and played games for three days.

The Pilgrims remembered the hard times they had endured. They were thankful for the harvest. They hoped for continued peace and prosperity.

Questions to Discuss

1. Why did the Pilgrims leave England?
2. What special thing would you pack to take with you to a new home?
3. If you had been on the ship, what would you have disliked the most?
4. As they neared land, what were their hopes and dreams for the future?
5. What do you think was the hardest thing the Pilgrims had to face in the new country?
6. What kinds of things would the Pilgrims have to know to be able to survive in their new home?
7. In what ways did the Indians help the colonists?
8. Why did the Pilgrims and Indians get along so well at Plymouth?
9. Why did they decide to have a feast?
10. What part of the celebration would you have liked best?

References

Anderson, Joan. *The First Thanksgiving Feast.* Clarion Books, 1984.
Gibbons, Gail. *Thanksgiving Day.* Holiday House, 1983.
Kroll, Steven. *Oh, What a Thanksgiving.* Scholastic, 1988.
San Souci, Robert. *N.C. Wyeth's Pilgrims.* Chronicle Books, 1991.

Activities

1. Make a time line to show events of the trip and the first year in a new home.
2. Each student will need copies of calendar pages for three months. Cross off the days to show how long the Pilgrims were at sea. Decorate the margins with scenes from the trip.
3. The captain of a ship keeps a daily record of the events of the journey in the ship's log. Write an imaginary page in the log telling about something that happened during your time at sea.
4. Draw a map of Plymouth Colony. Show the village, fields and woods. Indicate where they caught fish, clams and eels.
5. Plan a mural showing Plymouth. Paint a background and add individual pieces to it as more is learned about the colony.
6. Write a letter to an imaginary friend or relative back in England. Tell them about some of the things that happened since you last saw them.
7. Write a name poem featuring one of the Indians. Use each letter in his name to begin a word or phrase that tells about him.
8. Explain to someone how to plant corn the Indian way.
9. Use kernels of Indian corn to make a necklace. Remove the kernels from the cob. Soak them in water overnight to soften them. Use a needle to string them on dental floss or heavy thread.
10. Write a diamante to compare Pilgrims and Indians.
11. The following sentences summarize the events leading up to and including the first Thanksgiving. They may be copied and illustrated for a class book.
    * Long ago the Pilgrims sailed on the *Mayflower* to the New World.
    * They found a place to build their homes and plant their crops.
    * The winter was long and cold at Plymouth Colony.
    * Squanto taught the Pilgrims how to plant corn.
    * Everyone had work to do.
    * The boys and girls did chores and played games.
    * They were all thankful for the wonderful harvest.
    * The Pilgrims and Indians shared a great feast.

A Thanksgiving Giving Tree

*H*ere is a class project that can be initiated just before Thanksgiving and continued all through the holiday season. This is a class project, so all students are encouraged to participate. As they do this project, students will be exercising their language and communication skills, and they will also be developing a sensitivity to the needs and wants of other people around them.

*F*irst find a two- or three-foot branch from a real tree, clean it, trim it and anchor it in a large clump of clay or a large block of Styrofoam™ so that it stands up.

*T*o motivate students to think about and discuss the idea of what it means to "give" something to someone, discuss one or several of the following topics:

1. How does it make you feel when you give a gift?

2. How does it make you feel when you receive a gift?

3. What does it mean to be thankful for something?

4. Is it possible for you to give or receive a gift that cannot be bought in a store? For example, is giving someone a compliment a type of gift?

5. Read Shel Silverstein's *The Giving Tree* and discuss its theme.

6. Why would you want to give someone a gift?

7. To whom would you want to give a gift right now?

by Joanne Coughlin

*N*ow that students are excited about the idea of giving, receiving and being thankful to one another, have each pick a blank cut-out of a package and write (or dictate) a gift they would like to give someone. The recipient could be someone in class, at home or anywhere in the world.

*A*fter all students have their "gift" hung on the "giving tree," have them share their ideas. The other class members will then try to guess to whom the students would like to give their specified gifts. For example, one student might have written, "I would like to give a hug to _____ for helping me with my homework last night." The class would guess to whom this student would want to give the hug: Mom? Dad? Sister or brother? Another student might write, "I would like to give a coat to _____." Students in the class might guess that this person would like to give this gift to all the children in the world who do not have a coat to keep them warm.

*A*fter all the ideas have been shared, the class could organize their ideas. For instance, place these categories across the chalkboard or bulletin board:

Material Gifts
Gifts of Love
Things People Need

Now, decide which gifts from the "giving tree" belong in each category. This is a great exercise for critical analysis, as well as the development of organization skills.

It is never too soon to teach young children the importance of being generous, and thankful as well. Isn't the holiday season the perfect time to begin to do so in your classroom?

Thanksgiving Book Nook

Thanksgiving is coming and have we got a "feast" for you! Enjoy this special collection of seasonal books with your class.

Put your budding young actors and actresses to work performing in Thanksgiving plays. "Pilgrim Parting" and "Thanks to Butter-Fingers" are two one-act holiday plays that are sure to spark up your holiday season and can be found in *Special Plays for Holidays* by Helen Louise Miller (Boston: Plays, Inc., 1986). The book *Feast of Thanksgiving* by June Behrens (Chicago: Childrens Press, 1974) is in drama form, telling how the Pilgrims celebrated the first Thanksgiving. "Meow and Arf, a Play for Thanksgiving," a short play for two actors, can be found in *Small Plays for Special Days* by Sue Alexander (New York: Clarion Books, 1977).

by Mary Ellen Switzer

Little Bear's Thanksgiving

Brustlein, Janice. *Little Bear's Thanksgiving*. New York: Lothrop, Lee & Shepard Co., 1967.

Little Bear has a problem. He is invited to Thanksgiving dinner but will be in his deep winter sleep when the holiday rolls around. Will his friends be able to awaken him in time for the Thanksgiving feast?

* Give Little Bear a great wake-up call! Invent a new state-of-the-art clock to wake him up for Thanksgiving dinner. Draw a picture of your invention and label the parts.

* Design a billboard to advertise your new clock.

* Create a comic strip about "How to Wake a Bear for Thanksgiving."

* Make a list of all the animals you can think of that hibernate in winter.

One Tough Turkey: A Thanksgiving Story

Kroll, Steven. *One Tough Turkey: A Thanksgiving Story*. New York: Holiday House, 1982.

So you think you know the real story of the Pilgrims' first Thanksgiving feast? Now hear Steven Kroll's version of the historical event! You'll chuckle at the antics of "one tough turkey" named Solomon who plots to save the turkeys from being the main course at the Pilgrims' first Thanksgiving dinner.

* Think of another plan the clever turkey Solomon might have used in the story. Write your idea and draw a picture showing what happened.

* No Ham for Thanksgiving! Write a story telling about a clever pig who escapes being part of Thanksgiving dinner.

* Gobble . . . gobble . . . gone! Write a story about a turkey who escapes being eaten by blasting off in a spaceship.

Silly Tilly's Thanksgiving Dinner

ban, Lillian. *Silly Tilly's Thanksgiving Dinner.* New York: Harper & Row, 1990.

oh! It's Thanksgiving morning and for-ful Silly Tilly Mole is trying to make anksgiving dinner for her friends. But ere are the invitations? What about her ipes? See how her friends come to her scue and make this the best anksgiving ever!

Pop . . . Pop . . . Popcorn. Mr. Turkey made popcorn in the story. Make a list of all the words you can think of that describe popcorn.

Design a Thanksgiving place mat that Silly Tilly could have used for her dinner party.

Be a mole detective! Use an encyclopedia or reference book to find out all about moles. Create a picture book called *Moles Are Mammals.* Write a sentence about moles on each page, and draw a picture about each fact.

Squanto, the Indian Who Saved the Pilgrims

thaus, James R. *Squanto, the Indian Who Saved the Pilgrims.* Mankato, Minnesota: Creative Education, Inc., 1988.

t a fascinating look at the life and les of Squanto—the Indian friend of the grims who was a valuable helper in tablishing Plymouth Colony. After riending the Pilgrims, he taught them v to grow corn and where to fish and at. Squanto joined the settlers to cele-te their bountiful harvest at the first anksgiving.

Make a time line to include the impor-tant events in Squanto's life.

Create a "Thank You, Squanto" picture book, showing how Squanto helped the Pilgrims.

Don't Eat Too Much Turkey

Cohen, Miriam. *Don't Eat Too Much Turkey.* New York: Greenwillow Books, 1987.

Anna Maria's first grade classmates are getting annoyed at her for being too bossy to everyone as they prepare for Thanksgiving. She soon learns that shar-ing can be fun as her class celebrates the holiday season.

- Gobble . . . gobble! Create a turkey! The first grade class made a giant turkey out of a cardboard box, a bag, a funnel, red felt and socks. Draw a picture of what their turkey looked like.

- Sharing is caring! Write about a time that you shared something with a friend.

Thanksgiving at the Tappletons

Spinelli, Eileen. *Thanksgiving at the Tappletons.* HarperCollins, 1982.

Thanksgiving Day is becoming a nightmare for the Tappleton family. The turkey slides down a slippery hill, the mashed potatoes are ruined and the bakery runs out of pies. Grandmother comes to the rescue, and the family learns the real meaning of Thanksgiving.

- What was your favorite part of the story? Draw a picture of the event.

- Be an author! Write a story called "Thanksgiving at My House."

Video Selection

Give your class an entertaining history les-son about the Pilgrims' journey aboard the *Mayflower* by showing them *Mouse on the Mayflower* (written by Romeo Muller, Family Home Entertainment, time: approx., 48 minutes). This delightful animated video tells the Pilgrims' story from a tiny, lovable mouse's point of view. Young viewers will get a glimpse of the difficult problems the Pilgrims faced in building a new colony and relive the first Thanksgiving celebration.

Name ______________________________

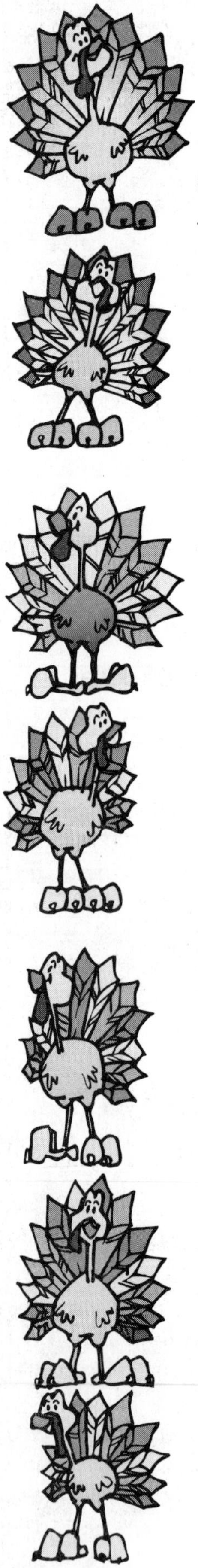

Turkey Chit Chat

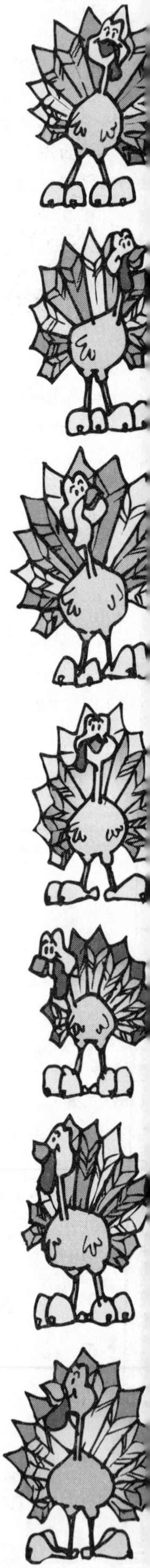

Calling all book fans! Write a review about a Thanksgiving book that you enjoyed and would recommend to others.

Name of book: ______________________________

Author: ______________________________

Summary of book:

____

____

____

____

____

____

What I liked best about this book:

____

____

____

Bonus: Create a bookmark featuring a character in the book.

Thanksgiving Fingerplays

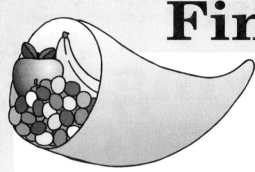

Thanksgiving Day

Thanksgiving Day will soon be here.
It comes around but once a year.
(Show one finger.)

If I could only have my way,
I'd have Thanksgiving every day.
(Rub circles over tummy.)

When Thanksgiving Comes

When we eat our dinner
Our table is small,
(Interlace fingers as tightly together as possible; thumbs point down for legs.)

Just room for our family
And that is all.
(Point to each finger of left hand.)

But when Thanksgiving comes,
What a surprise . . .

That very same table stretches
To nearly this size.
(Expand hands as far as possible; keep fingertips touching.)

Indians and Pilgrims

This little Pilgrim went for a walk.
(Put up forefinger of right hand.)
This little Indian wanted to talk.
(Put up forefinger of left hand.)
This little Pilgrim said, "How do you do?"
(Put up middle finger of right hand.)
This little Indian said, "So, how do you do?"
(Put up middle finger of left hand.)
They looked at each other as if to say,
"I'm glad you're here. Happy Thanksgiving Day!"
(Wiggle all four fingers as if in conversation.)

Mr. Turkey

Run, Mr. Turkey, far away
Wobble, wobble, wobble.
(Tuck hands under armpits; run in small circles in place.)
Or on Thanksgiving Day
I'll gobble, gobble, gobble.
(Pretend to eat, using both hands.)

Five Little Turkeys

Five little turkeys are we.
(Show five fingers on one hand.)
We slept all night in a tree.
(Press palms of hands together and place cheek on top, with head slightly bent to side as if sleeping.)
When the cook came around,
(Place one hand over brow as if looking.)
We couldn't be found,
(Shrug shoulders with hands out.)
And that's why we're here, you see.
(Hands on hips, nod head affirmatively.)

We Celebrate Thanksgiving
Teacher Crafts and Activities

Spice up your seasonal activities this Thanksgiving with these ideas. Your students will learn more about celebrating this national holiday as they practice curriculum skills and following directions.

Brown Bag Turkeys

For a prewriting activity, encourage students to tell stories about a turkey who escapes Thanksgiving dinner. Turn large brown grocery bags into a "turkey." Each child can take a turn wearing the turkey costume. Planning a beginning, middle and end to a tale is an excellent way to teach sequence in storytelling.

Pinecone Turkey

Collect pinecones of different sizes and shapes. If cones are wet, allow to dry. This will open the petals. Cut colored paper into feather shapes and glue between several petals. Make a head from brown paper. Color the wattle red.

Thanksgiving Graph

Harvest Jar

Collect small narrow jars, such as olive jars, for each child. Purchase dried soup beans with a variety of colors and shapes. Fill one jar. Let the children guess how many beans are in the jar. Provide time for each student to layer colors and shapes in their own creation. These can be given to a special older friend before Thanksgiving.

Graphing

Using a large sheet of paper, make a Thanksgiving graph showing what children will have for Thanksgiving dinner. On the left, list each child's name. (Do not insist any child participate, as some children will not observe this celebration.) Across the top, list the items as children call them out. Point out that a graph is a quick way to add numbers. Another time, make a graph listing favorite foods, desserts, sandwiches, etc.

by Carolyn Tomlin

Thanksgiving Table Decorations

Involve children in their family's celebration. Combine a seasonal craft as students practice skills of cutting and pasting. Make a place mat from a long sheet of seasonal-colored construction paper. Supply felt-tip markers for drawing turkeys or other November pictures. Laminate for durability.

For a napkin holder, cut an empty paper towel tube into 1 ½" sections. Glue a strip of felt in seasonal colors around each piece.

For napkins, purchase loosely woven fabric in brown or orange. Every 18" pull a thread to get a perfect square. Cut on this line. Show children how to fringe a 1" border around all four sides. One yard, 36" wide, makes four napkins.

Thanksgiving Mosaic Design

Use the lid from a plastic container, such as sour cream or sandwich spread. Cut and glue a piece of brown felt to fit inside the lid. Make a design using dried corn, noodles and beans to form a mosaic design. Punch a hole near the top. Add a brown or orange ribbon or cord for hanging.

Thanksgiving Celebrations

Show students several pictures of Thanksgiving celebrations. Encourage children to talk about unique family celebrations they observe in their homes during this season.

Secret Spices

Spices have long been associated with the Thanksgiving season. What would pumpkin pie be like without them? Introduce your students to a variety of spices by having them use their sense of smell for identification. Collect clear 35 mm film canisters. Place small amounts of cinnamon, nutmeg, allspice, cloves, ginger or other familiar spices in each container. Observe each color, as well as smell.

Cranberry Relish

Cranberries may be a new food item for some of your students. Find out where cranberries are grown. Point out the location on a map.

    1 pound cranberries, uncooked
    2 large oranges, with peeling
    2 cups sugar

Carefully supervise a hand-turned food grinder. Allow children to drop cranberries and orange pieces into the grinder. Add sugar. Enjoy this traditional Thanksgiving favorite.

Turkey Maze

This turkey is lost. Can you help him find the others? Color the pictures.

Finish

Start

Pie Match

raw a line from the group of children to the same number of pumpkin pies on the right.

 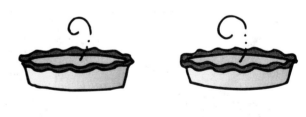

Tail Feather Game

Preparation: Divide children into teams. Have a copy of the turkey for each team and one tail feather (cut from construction paper) for each child.

Instructions: The first child on each team quickly glues his feather onto the rear of the turkey, then passes it to the next child who does the same. If any feathers fall off, they must be glued back on before the team can finish. The first team to get all the feathers on their turkey is the winner. (The larger the team, the better this game is.)

Preschool Learning Version: Give each child a turkey and tail feathers that have been numbered from one to ten (or whatever number the children are familiar with). Each child glues the feathers to the turkey in numbered order.

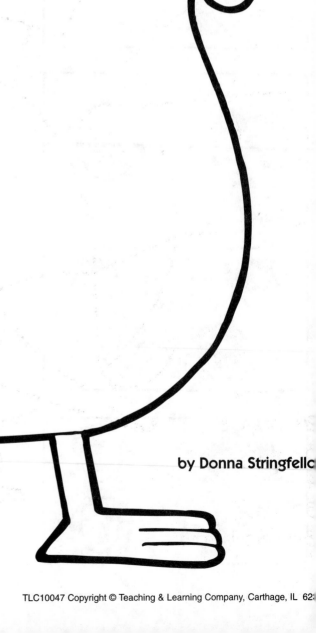

by Donna Stringfello

Turkey Teamwork

structions: Make up teams of six children. Give each team a copy of the turkey and tell them to get crayons ready.
ayer 1 starts by coloring the number one spaces, player 2 does the number two spaces, etc. Any missed spaces
ust be completed by the person with that number. The team who finishes first and has colored the turkey properly
the winner.

1 – yellow
2 – orange
3 – dark brown
4 – red
5 – black
6 – light brown

by Donna Stringfellow

Turkey Feast Name Card

Reproduce the patterns below on heavy paper. Color and cut out. Add child's name. Wrap the turkey body around a 5-oz. paper cup. Glue the tail to the back of the cup.

Glue here.

Glue here.

Cut

Cut

Name

Chelsea

by Veronica Terrill

Thanksgiving Day

Country: United States

Since the day of the Pilgrims, Thanksgiving has been a special holiday to give thanks. Families and friends usually gather together for a big meal. Some people attend church for special services to give thanks. In 1941, Congress voted that Thanksgiving would be a legal holiday, to be celebrated the fourth Thursday in November.

Think about it! What are you thankful for? Draw a picture of the things you are most thankful for.

Uh oh! It's Thanksgiving morning, and your family's prize turkey is getting worried—dinner time is quickly approaching. The clever bird decides to get a disguise from the family's Halloween costume box. Draw a "wanted" poster of what your turkey looks like in its costume.

by Mary Ellen Switzer

WANTED!

Welcome Back!

eraser

abc

Welcome Back

Clip Art for Fall

Happy Halloween!

Classroom Decorations

Ways to Use This Page

Stationery: Using the borders provided, this page can be used as a form for newsletters, annoucements, invitations or any other form of communication. Simply place a sheet of white paper over this text before reproducing.

Door Decoration: Use this border or the clip art on page 106 to create a back-to-school door decoration. Enlarge the patterns, cut out and decorate as desired. Place around the classroom door for an instant back-to-school welcome for your students. If you wish, wait and let your students color the patterns.

Bulletin Board Border: Following the instructions for the door decoration, use these patterns to brighten up a back-to-school bulletin board.

Name Tags/Desk Tags: Enlarge, color and decorate the chosen pattern; add each child's name and laminate.

My New Year

I'm so glad the year is new.
I'll learn to skip and tie my shoe;

Write my names: first and last;
Count by tens to a hundred, fast;

I'll balance on my two-wheel bike,
Instead of riding on my trike;

Hula Hoop™, play ball, skip rope,
Even use the microscope!

I'm so glad the year is new.
These are the things I'm going to do!

by Jeanene Engelhardt

Winter in the Great Outdoors

Winter Kid Space is a place of frosty frolic, adventure, excitement and creative learning in nature's classroom. Let the wintry outdoors bring you and your class to your senses! Look, listen, smell, feel, investigate and have fun in your surroundings.

Snow Wonders

Have you ever really looked at snow? It is a wonder to behold! Encourage your students to look at snow up close and from afar, to feel it, to smell it and to record their findings. Is there a difference between fresh snow and snow that is a few days old? What temperature is snow?

Take a bowl of snow indoors and observe what happens. Take it back outdoors and watch for another change. Time this change.

Melt snow in a coffee filter. What do students see on the filter? Investigate their findings.

by Robynne Eagan

The Snowflake Man

From the time he was 15 years old, Wilson Bentley studied snowflakes under a microscope. "Snowflake" Bentley spent 48 years catching snowflakes and photographing them through a microscope. He photographed over 5,000 snowflakes and studied many more. He found that each snowflake was at least a little different from another.

What Is a Snowflake?

A snowflake is a bunch of tiny six-sided ice crystals stuck together. Two to six miles up in the sky, a droplet of water freezes around a speck of dust, bacteria or another ice crystal. As this crystal falls through the sky, its shape is affected by changes in air temperature, moisture or breeze. Snowflakes occur in an infinite variety of shapes, and no one has ever found two the same.

Catch a Snowflake?

Put a square of black tagboard or felt outside (away from the sunshine) or in the freezer until it is cold. Take the black squares outside on a snowy day and catch a snowflake. Encourage students to observe and discuss the many snowflake patterns. Look at the snowflake with a magnifying glass or a microscope. Compare the shapes of two flakes. How many different shapes can your students find? Repeat this another day when the weather has changed. Are the flakes affected by the different weather conditions?

Snow Fact
Ten inches of freshly fallen snow is considered to be equivalent to 1" of rain. Melt some snow and find out if this is true. Results will vary with the type of snow.

Snow Fact
The odds of two ice crystals being exactly alike are estimated to be one in 105,000,000.

Winter Weather Station

How cold is the temperature? Measure the temperature with a thermometer. How much snow has fallen? Use an ordinary ruler to measure the accumulative snowfall and the newest snowfall. Make a few measurements, and then take an average to compensate for drifting snow.

When fresh snow has fallen on old snow, gently dig a hole until you can see a line dividing the two layers of snowfall. Measure the newest layer. Make a snow gauge out of a large, wide-mouthed plastic container. Adhere a piece of masking tape about 6" (15 cm) long down the outside of the container. Measure and mark the tape at 1/2" (1.25 cm) intervals with a permanent felt marker. Place the gauge in an open area and measure the snowfalls.

Frosty Frolics

~ake a School Yard Skating Rink
~inter, water, a little work and you can have a
~onderful winter wonderland!

~u Need:
~water
~natural rubber hose
~snowshoes or skis
~snow shovel or scraper
~12-14 hours of your time

Optional: 1' x 6' lumber (new or reclaimed), 3"
nails for the corners (or brackets and screws)
and 2' x 4's for strong backs to anchor the
boards from the rear

1. Plan the location and dimensions of your
   rink.
2. Pack the snow down in the designated
   area by wearing snowshoes, skis or big
   boots! Attempt to make the area as
   smooth and flat as possible.
3. Shape the surrounding snow to form
   banks. Optional: Place 1' x 6's around the
   border to act as boards. Nail the corners
   with scrap wood nailed to the back side.
   Build up the snow to anchor the boards.
4. Add the essential ingredient—water! Spray
   a light application of water and let it
   freeze. Repeat this process three or four
   times until you have a solid base.*
5. Flood the ice heavily once the base is built
   up. Build up the low areas until you have a
   smooth, uniform surface.
6. Maintain a bump-free surface with a light
   application of water once a week or so,
   depending on the usage of the rink.
7. Clear the rink after snowfalls using a simple
   snow shovel.

Too much water can create a thin cavity.
Break the thin layer on these cavities, and
pack the hole with slushy snow and water.

Icicle Watch: Observe an icicle dripping
on a warm day. Hang one outside the
classroom window where children can
watch it carefully throughout the day.

Sledding Party

Plan a sledding party for your class.
Walk or arrange transportation to an
exciting hill for sledding fun. Count and
compare the various sleds and tobog-
gans. Back in the class after the fun,
ask students to design a better sled.

Back in the Classroom
Stir up some hot chocolate and talk
about keeping warm. Discuss
hypothermia, winter survival techniques and the layering of winter
clothing. Study the history of winter
wear: boots, zippers, fur coats, waterproof fabrics, ice skates and ski equipment.

Challenge: Can your students make
snow last indoors? Can they keep a
hot potato warm outside in the cold?
Provide various insulating materials.
Consider foil, wool or a thermos.

Sculpt the Snow

Get creative and venture beyond the simple snowman.

You Need:

- snow (slushy snow works best, especially on a warm day after a snowfall)
- waterproof gloves
- shaping, smoothing and carving tools: containers, sticks, shovels, kitchen utensils
- coloring: I cup water with 8 drops food coloring in a spray bottle
- decorations: cranberries, carrots, twigs, raisins, nuts, balls, stones or recycled materials
- props: clothing, footwear, toys, sports equipment, flags

Process:

1. Choose a snowy location.
2. Plan for a wide, sturdy base to the sculpture.
3. Roll a snowball along the ground and watch it get larger and larger. You can shape the snowball by alternating the side it is rolled on.
4. Stack, shape and combine various balls until you have a basic shape. (It is best to begin with simple shapes like snowpeople, bunnies, whales, bears, cars, etc.)
5. Smooth, carve and sculpt with carving tools.
6. Add details, color and decorations.

Try This:

Choose a theme: the manger scene or farmyard (add straw, overalls, feathers, brown eggs), the zoo or circus (give a human figure a clown nose, a seal with a ball, a zebra with black stripes) or dinosaurs (spray them green and make some giant dinosaur eggs). Host a Snow Show. Take photographs and admire your work.

Snowball Math
Put students to work making math manipulatives out of snow. Count the snowballs. Add some more. Take some away. Group them. Estimate size. Measure circumference. Weigh the snowballs. Make comparisons.

Tracks in the Snow

Look for tracks in the snow and try to identify them.

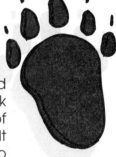

Track Casting

Place a cardboard tube or plastic cylinder collar around an animal or human footprint in the snow. Spray the track with a gentle mist of water to harden it. Mix plaster of Paris to smooth consistency. Add 1 teaspoon (5 ml) of salt to make the plaster harden faster. Pour the plaster into the collar over the track. After about 15 minutes the plaster will harden, and you can remove the surrounding collar and casting. The casting can be sanded gently with sandpaper and painted.

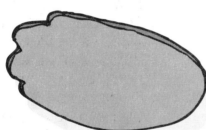

Critter Care

Leave treats for the winter birds and critters who might visit your Kid Space. If possible, locate these where your class can observe the wildlife.

Make a Snowman for the Birds: Decorate the snowman with birdseed, peanut butter seed balls, bread cubes, peanuts in their shells and berries.

String Some Edibles: String cotton thread with cranberries or other red edible berries, apple rings, kiwi fruit or oranges and hang from poles or branches.

Bird Balls: Roll suet balls in birdseed and hang from trees.

Bird Cones: Spread peanut butter on pinecones, sprinkle with birdseed and hang these out for the birds.

Fingerplays

SLIDING FUN

Put on your scarf,
   your mittens, caps,
Snow boots, extra coats,
   perhaps.
   *(Pretend to put on wraps
   as indicated.)*
Please do hurry—run, run,
   run!
   (Move fingers quickly.)
Sliding, sliding
   *(Place hands together,
   make sliding motion.)*
Is fun, fun, fun!
   (Clap hands.)

JANUARY

January's a very cold month,
Shiver, shiver, shiver,
   *(Hug yourself and pretend to
   shiver.)*
Button up and cover your ears,
   *(Pretend to button coat; cover
   ears with hands.)*
Or quiver, quiver, quiver.
   (Make yourself shake all over.)

GEORGE WASHINGTON

I cannot tell a lie, sir,
I'm sorry as can be.
   (Open eyes wide, have a sorry look on face.)
It was my little hatchet that
Chopped down the cherry tree.
   (Pretend to chop down a tree.)

SNOWMAN

Let's roll a tiny snowball
   (Make a small circle with hands.)
Till it gets big and round.
   (Make a large circle.)
Let's roll it through the snowdrifts;
   (Pretend to push through snow.)
It doesn't make a sound!
   (Whisper these words.)
Give Snow Man head and eyes,
   (Point to head and eyes.)
A broom for him to hold,
   (Pretend to hold broom.)
A mouth, a nose and coat,
   (Point to each.)
So Snow Man won't get cold!
   (Pretend to shiver.)

READY FOR PURIM

Oh, Purim time's the time for fun
For you and me and everyone!
   (Point appropriately.)
We go to hear Megillah read,
   (Pretend to hold book and read.)
And each time Haman's name is said
We stamp and clap and all make noise.
   (Stamp feet; clap hands.)
It's lots of fun for girls and boys.
Hamantaschen's what we eat,
   (Pretend to hold a cake and eat it.)
Ummmm, yummy! It's such a treat!
   (Rub circles over tummy with hand.)

for Winter

WINTER WEATHER

Let's put on our mittens
 (Put on mittens.)
And button up our coat.
 (Button coat.)
Wrap a scarf snugly
Around our throat.
 (Throw scarf around neck.)
Pull on our boots,
 (Pull on boots with both hands.)
Fasten the straps
 (Fasten straps with fingers.)
And tie on tightly
Our warm winter caps.
 (Pull on cap with both hands and tie.)
Then open the door . . .
And out we go
 (Turn imaginary doorknob, pull door open, and step through.)
Into the soft and feathery snow.
 (Hold out both hands to catch snow and look up.)

DANGLING ICICLES

When icicles dangle in straight, glistening rows,
 (Dangle fingers down.)
Cover your body from your head to your toes!
 (Pretend to button, zip, and pull on boots.)
You must wear your mittens, scarf and hat,
 (Pretend to put on mittens, scarf and hat.)
Or you'll start sneezing just like that!
 (Pretend to sneeze—ah choo!)

by Judy Wolfman

ABRAHAM LINCOLN

Before Abe Lincoln was great,
He was a child like me.
(Point to self.)
He did some special things,
Like letting slaves go free.
(Make fists and touch wrists together, then pull them apart on "free.")

WIND TRICKS

The wind is full of tricks today—
 (Make sweeping motion with one hand for wind.)
He blew my daddy's hat away.
 (Pretend to sweep hat off head.)
He chased our paper down the street.
 (One hand chases other around.)
He almost blew us off our feet.
 (Almost fall.)
He makes the trees and bushes dance.
 (With raised arms, make dancing motions.)
Just listen to him howl and prance.
 (Cup hand to ear.)

FINGER HEART

See my fingers
Far apart?
(Hold up thumb and index finger on both hands.)
I'll put them together
And make a heart.
(Tips of thumbs touch; curve index fingers slightly with tips touching to form a heart.)

Hanukkah Toys

Toys! Toys! Hanukkah toys!
Some for girls and some for boys.
(Point to girls and boys.)
The pretty doll can smile and dance;
(With arms in "dance position," smile and dance.)
The horse here can step and prance;
(High steps in place.)
Our soldier dolls are Maccabees;
(March in place and salute.)
And the dreidel spins around with ease.
(Spin around in place.)

Hanukkah Candles

It's very bright at home tonight
The houses all have extra
light.
One, two, three, four candles
there,
*(Put up a finger of the
right hand with each num-
ber.)*
Five, six, seven, eight candles
where?
*(Put up a finger of the left
hand with each number.)*
Look at the lamp—the
Hanukkah lamp.
*(Hold all eight fingers in
front of you.)*
There's no more night;
*(Shake head back and
forth for "no.")*
All the world is full of light.
*(Gently wiggle the eight
fingers as a flickering
flame.)*

Santa's Elves

In Santa's workshop far away,
Ten little elves work night and day.
(Show ten fingers.)
This little elf makes candy canes;
(Show one finger.)
This little elf builds super planes;
(Show another finger.)
This little elf paints dolls for girls;
(Show third finger.)
This little elf puts on their curls;
(Show fourth finger.)
This little elf makes lollipops;
(Show fifth finger.)
This little elf packs the jack-in-the-box;
(Show sixth finger.)
This little elf makes books for boys;
(Show seventh finger.)
This little elf checks off the toys;
(Show eighth finger.)
This little elf packs Santa's sleigh.
(Show ninth finger.)
Now they're ready for you on Christmas Day!
(Point to a friend.)

NOTE: Instead of showing fingers, each line
can be pantomimed.

Spinning Dreidel

Top, top, Hanukkah top,
Do not ever stop, stop.
Spin all night; spin all day.
I like to see you spin that way.
*(Sit on floor and spin around on your
bottom.)*

118

Fingerplays

Christmas Bells

Five little bells,
Hanging in a row.
*(Turn one hand upside down,
letting fingers point toward the floor.)*
The first one said, "Ring me slow."
(Slowly wiggle forefinger back and forth.)
The second one said, "Ring me fast."
(Quickly wiggle middle finger back and forth.)
The third one said, "Ring me last."
(Wiggle ring finger back and forth.)
The fourth one said, "I'm like a chime."
(Wiggle pinky finger.)
The fifth one said, "Ring me at Christmastime."
(Wiggle thumb.)

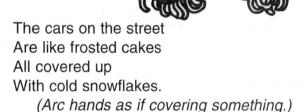

Winter

The cars on the street
Are like frosted cakes
All covered up
With cold snowflakes.
(Arc hands as if covering something.)

The sounds of footsteps
Scrunch on the street,
(Walk in place.)
And people's eyelashes
Are white with sleet.
(Lightly run forefingers up eyelashes.)

And everywhere that
You want to go,
Your face is tickled
By the snow.
(Turn face upwards and laugh.)

Snowflakes

The snowflakes are whirling
Around and around.
The snowflakes are whirling
All over the ground.
(Whirl around in small circles.)

The Peppermint Stick

Oh, I took a lick
Of my peppermint stick,
And I thought it tasted yummy.
(Pretend to lick a peppermint stick.)
Oh, it used to be
On the Christmas tree,
(Point to tree.)
But I like it better in my tummy!
(Rub hand in circles over tummy.)

Christmas Morning

Bright and early Christmas morning,
(Stretch and yawn.)
When they see our shiny toys,
(Open eyes wide.)
We'll be happy that we shared them
With other girls and boys.
(Smile broadly.)

Sinterklaas

December 5 is a very special day celebrated by the Dutch in the Netherlands. This grand day is called Sinterklaas Avond or St. Nicholas Eve. Seventeen centuries ago, a young boy named Nicholas was the "boy Bishop of Myra." His deeds of kindness and generosity are legendary.

The story is told that the young girl of a very poor family did not have a dowry to bring into her marriage, so she was prepared to sell herself into slavery. The money that saved this young girl turned up in the stockings she had hung on the chimney to dry.

The grand celebration starts with the arrival of St. Nicholas in Amsterdam, arriving by ship three weeks before his birthday. St. Nicholas then rides on horseback, dressed in his bishop's finery. He proceeds down the gangplank to be greeted by the Lord Mayor Dignitaries, a brass band and thousands of excited youngsters. The parade goes down the main street to be received by the Royal Family.

Sinterklaas is always accompanied by Zwarte Piet, or Black Pete. Black Pete is a prankster dressed in embroidered finery with puffed velvet breeches and a plumed hat of sixteenth century Spanish courtiers. Both gentlemen winter somewhere in Spain and carry some very special items.

One is large red ledger, carried to record the behavior of all the Dutch children for the year, and the second is a bunch of birch rods to tame any child who chooses to be bad. Black Pete also carries a large bag of goodies—fruits, nuts, candies and cookies to reward those children that are in Sinterklaas's favor.

by Carlene Americk

Throughout the celebration, children fill their shoes at night with carrots and straw to feed Sinterklaas's horse if he decides to visit a household by coming down the chimney. The family draws pictures and sings songs to attract the special pair and are happy when they find little gifts of candy in their shoes.

A special part of the feasting is a pastry called Letterblankets. These edible letters are a flaky puff pastry filled with almond paste. Letterblankets are put at each individual guest's place at the feasting table. A giant M might be in the mother's place or might even be used as the centerpiece. Each guest's first name initial marks their special place at the table. Following is a recipe you and family members can make for your Christmas table.

Letterblankets

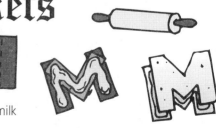

1 cup almond paste
1/4 cup granulated sugar
1 large egg
pastry for two 9" pie crusts
1 egg lightly beaten with 1 tablespoon milk

Heat oven to 375° F. In a small bowl, stir almond paste, sugar and egg. Chill while rolling pastry. Roll out half of the pastry about 1/4" thick into a square. Cut into 2" wide strips. On lightly greased baking sheet, lay strips to form letter M approximately 10" high and 10" wide. Press marzipan on top of letter, leaving a 1/2" border on all sides. Roll remaining pastry in similar fashion. Brush border of M with egg glaze, and place second layer of strips over marzipan. Press edges together. Brush surface with egg glaze. Bake 35 minutes until evenly browned.

121

Foil Cupcake Liners

Make a great Christmas tree bulletin board with foil cupcake liners. Staple liners in place. Put colored circles in some for ornaments. Centers are also a good place for photos of students.

by Mary Maurer

Wreath the World

Have your students trace their hands on pieces of green and red paper. On each handprint, help your students record their wishes for peace or for the holidays. Place these wishes around a picture of the world on the bulletin board.

by Terry Healy

Sparkle Tree

This is as simple as can be but lots of fun! Make a simple tree outline for each child.

Let them fill in the branches with gummed stars. It takes time to lick the stars. This is great for developing manual dexterity. It also makes a great Christmas card.

by Mary Maurer

Nature Tree

In early winter, place an artificial Christmas tree in your room or in the hall just outside your door for everyone to enjoy. The students then add decorations such as pinecones, leaves, pebbles (small), seed pods (for under the tree), cattails, cornstalks, feathers, milkweed (dried) or goldenrod (dried).

On December 1, have the students add holly, dried gypsum (to look like snow), cardinals made from recycled paper, apples, etc., to add a holiday look. (We added stuffed squirrels, birds and rabbits to add a special nature look.)

by Jo Jo Cavalline and Jo Anne O'Donnell

St. Lucia Day

December 13

December 13th is a special day in Sweden—it's St. Lucia Day, or the Festival of Light, which is named after a young saint named Lucia. Early in the morning on December 13th, the oldest daughter dresses as St. Lucia in a long white gown with a red sash and puts on a crown of candles. She then serves her parents coffee, saffron buns and ginger cookies. Many schools and offices have St. Lucia parties and events. St. Lucia "girls" lead processions of children who sing traditional carols and songs.

by Mary Ellen Switzer

St. Lucia Crown

Connect the dots in the picture to make a St. Lucia crown.

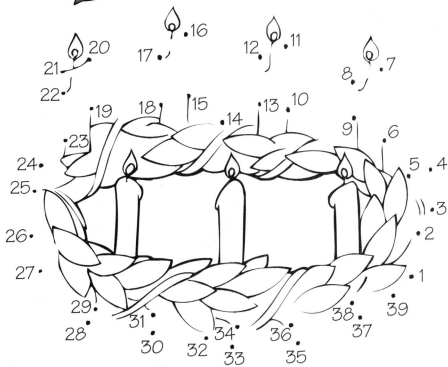

Marvelous Map

This page features the beautiful country of Sweden. Use crayons or pens to color the map. Find Lake Vanern on the map and color it blue. Draw a circle around Stockholm, the capital of Sweden. Label other major cities of your choice.

Bonus: On the back of this page, write three facts that you have learned about Sweden.

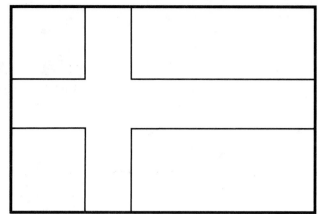

Swedish Flag

Now it's time to color the Swedish flag! The flag has a golden yellow cross on a bright blue background. Although used in the mid-1400s, the flag became official in 1663.

The Magic Suitcase

Attention all tourists! Let's grab our magic suitcase and travel to Sweden.

"God dag" or "Hello." Welcome to Sweden, the fourth largest country in Europe. Sweden is located in the eastern part of the Scandinavian Peninsula. This beautiful country has a varied landscape which includes snowcapped mountains, colorful forests and plains. There are about 100,000 lakes in Sweden, and the largest is called Lake Vanern.

Some important exports in Sweden are wood products, paper, machinery, glass, cars, iron ore and steel. Swedish crystal, textiles and furniture are well-known worldwide for their quality and style.

Sweden's chief agricultural products include barley, wheat, sugar beets and potatoes.

Sweden's capital and largest city is Stockholm. This popular city with its islands and waterfront is called "The Venice of the North."

Write or draw a picture of what you would pack in your magic suitcase for your trip to Sweden.

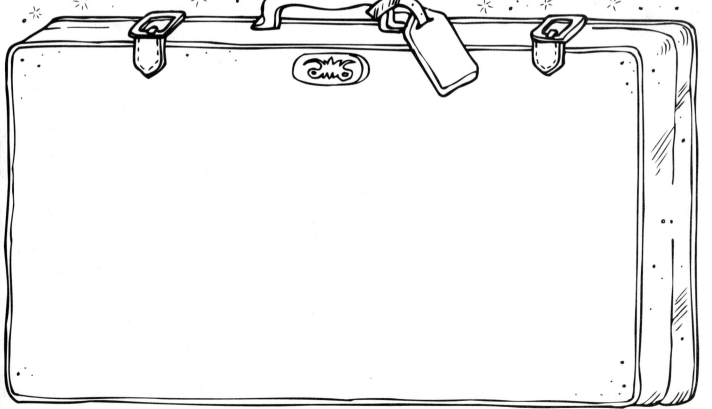

HANUKKAH

HANUKKAH, known as the Festival of Lights, is celebrated for eight days beginning on the twenty-fifth day of KISLEV (the Hebrew month on the calendar). This holiday honors an event which took place over 2000 years ago, when a small band of heroic Jewish men fought a victorious battle for religious freedom. In the year 165 BC, after three years of fighting, the Jewish army (the Maccabees) recaptured their temple from the enemy. When it came time to light the sacred temple lamp, only one night's oil was to be found. But miraculously, the lamp continued to burn for eight full days.

Today, Jewish families reenact this miracle in the temple by lighting one candle for each of the eight days of Hanukkah. A special candle holder called a menorah is used. An extra candle (the tall one) called the shamash (or servant) is also lit each night and then used to light the other candles. Houses are decorated in blue and white and also with the Star of David. Gifts are exchanged among family members for the eight days to spread light and joy. Many children receive a toy piece called a dreidel to play a traditional Hanukkah game.

Food is likewise a favorite part of this celebration. The Jewish people prepare and enjoy delicious potato latkes (pancakes) served with sour cream and applesauce. Cooking these pancakes in oil is a remembrance of the temple's miracle of the lamp.

COUNTDOWN CALENDAR

This can be an individual project to make and take home, keeping one to display in the classroom.

Have the children cut two triangles out of construction paper, as well as eight strips of paper to make chains. The colors of Israel are blue and white.

Glue the two triangles together, one point up and one point down to form a Star of David. Use the strips to make circles, attaching each to form a chain. Assemble all these pieces together to form this countdown calendar.

Let the students take this calendar home, instructing them to remove one link each night of Hanukkah until the holiday is over.

by Tania Kourempis-Cowling

FOIL PICTURES

Cut two triangles from aluminum foil. Glue these onto a sheet of construction paper to form a Star of David. Prepare glue paint in cups by adding drops of food coloring to white glue. Let the children paint designs on the foil stars using small paintbrushes or cotton swabs. Every picture is creative and unique. Display these around the classroom.

HANUKKAH WISH BOOK

ke a construction paper book with eight pages to present the eight days of Hanukkah. Let the children through pages of toy catalogs and magazines to cut pictures of their desires. Glue a "wish to have" pre-t on each page representing one gift each night.

PASS THE DREIDEL (GAME)

ve all children sit on the floor in a circle. With sic playing, start passing a toy dreidel around m child to child. When the music stops, the child holding the dreidel has a chance to spin it on the floor. "Round and round it goes!" Continue playing the music and game so all students can have a turn.

LAND THE LATKE

tato pancakes (called latkes) are a traditional food Hanukkah. Make a fun game using a small paper te, a craft stick and a two-foot length of string.

e kids are going to make a pretend frying pan and p the latke" in the pan. Glue one end of the craft ck to the paper plate (this is the pan). Decorate frying pan with Hanukkah symbols, using yons and markers. Poke a hole near the opposite ge of the plate, and tie the string through it.

ke a "latke" by cutting a 2" circle out of card-ard. Poke a hole through the edge of the latke and ach it to the string also.

to flip the latke in the pan. See how many times u can do it in a minute's time.

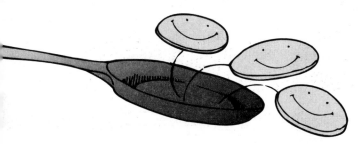

DREIDEL GREETING CARD

Materials:
- paper (construction, drawing or typing)
- crayons or markers
- scissors

What You Will Do:
1. Fold the paper in half.
2. Draw a dreidel on it, with one side of it touching the fold.
3. Cut out the dreidel through both pieces of paper. Do not cut through the fold.
4. Color or decorate the dreidel.
5. Write a message inside. Sign it.
6. Give it to a friend.

HOMEMADE PUZZLES

Mount pictures relating to the Hanukkah holiday (pre-printed or drawn by the children) to poster board. Laminate or use clear adhesive paper over-lay. Cut into puzzle pieces. The number of pieces will depend upon the child's age and skill.

MONEY HUNT

During Hanukkah, games are played and gelt is given as rewards. *Gelt* is the Hebrew word for *money*. Make a fake coin by covering a 4" round piece of cardboard with aluminum foil. Hide the gelt in the classroom, and invite the children to find it. Send the children out of the room; then hide the gelt again!

PAPER MENORAH

Materials:
- construction paper—9" x 12"
- scissors
- crayons, markers or paint
- glue
- glitter

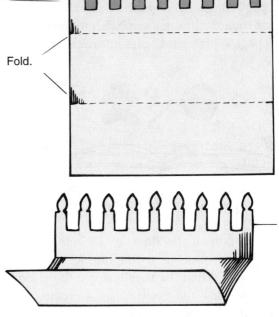

Measure and draw nine candles.

Fold.

What You Will Do:
1. Cut the construction paper to measure 10³/₄" x 9".
2. Fold the paper in thirds lengthwise.
3. Rule off nine candles on one of the outside folded sections, each measuring 1" wide. Leave ¹/₄" space between each candle.
4. Draw a flame on top of each candle.
5. Cut the background construction paper away from the top half of each candle.
6. On the back of the standing-up flap, color or paint the word *Hanukkah* or *Menorah*.
7. Color the candles different colors.
8. Put a dab of glue on each flame. Sprinkle with glitter.
9. Bend back the cut-out part of each candle. When the holiday starts, "light" each candle by bending it upright again.
10. Display on a windowsill or shelf.

Glue on glitter.

MENORAH

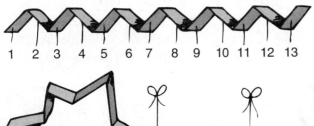

1 2 3 4 5 6 7 8 9 10 11 12 13

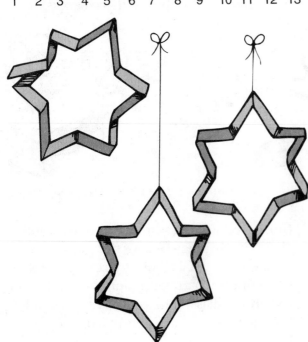

STAR OF DAVID CHAIN

Materials:
- construction paper strips, each 11" x 1"
- clear cellophane tape
- needle and thread

What You Will Do:
1. Fold each strip as you would a fan (one section forwa[rd] and one section back) to make 13 sections.
2. Shape the folded strip into a six-pointed star.
3. Tape the top of one end to the bottom of the other e[nd].
4. Make several stars in different colors.
5. String the stars together with a needle and thread.
6. Tape the ends of the thread to a wall or across the ed[ge] of a table or shelf.

BY JUDY WOLFM[AN]

128

EGG CARTON MENORAH

Materials:

- 1 egg carton (foam or cardboard)
- heavy-duty aluminum foil
- scissors
- thumbtacks
- white craft cement
- Hanukkah candles

What You Will Do:

1. Cut off the lid from the egg carton. Tear apart each cup.

2. Cut off the points from the tops of nine cups. This will leave a rounded top.

3. Cover the entire lid of the carton with foil. Cover each of the nine cups with foil.

4. Push a thumbtack up through the bottom of each foil-covered cup.

5. To make the shamash, get another cup from the egg carton. Do NOT cut off the points. Cut other points on the sides that are straight. Cover this cup with foil, molding the foil down between each point. Glue the bottom of this cup to the bottom of one of the other cups.

6. Glue each cup to the foil-lined lid. The shamash can be at one end, or in the middle, and will be higher.

7. Before putting the candles on the tacks, hold the bottom of each candle over a flame. This will soften the wax and keep it from cracking. The foil makes the menorah safe to use for lighting the candles.

How to Use the Menorah

1. The menorah will be used for eight nights to remember the miracle of the oil that burned for eight days.

2. Each night the shamash is lit and used to light the other candles. *Shamash* means "servant."

3. On the first night, one candle is lit. On the second night, two candles are lit. Each night another candle is added, until on the eighth night, all of the candles are lit.

4. The candles burn until they are gone. Do not blow them out.

5. Place the menorah in a safe place. A small table in front of a window lets others enjoy it.

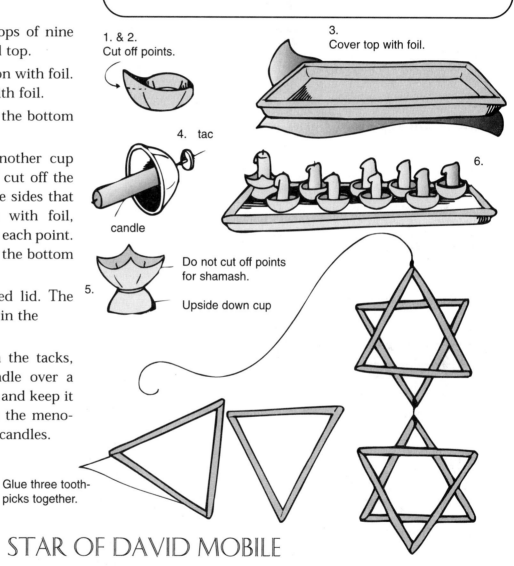

1. & 2. Cut off points.

3. Cover top with foil.

4. tac
candle

5. Do not cut off points for shamash.

Upside down cup

6.

Glue three toothpicks together.

STAR OF DAVID MOBILE

Materials:

- waxed paper
- toothpicks
- white glue
- thread

What You Will Do:

1. Spread out the waxed paper to work on.

2. Put glue on the tips of three toothpicks, and glue them together to form a triangle.

3. Make another triangle the same way.

4. Glue the second triangle upside down on top of the first one. Let dry.

5. Make as many stars as you want.

6. Loop the thread through the top point of one of the stars. Hang the second star from the first and so on until the mobile is as long as you want.

7. Instead of looping the stars together, you could hang each one (at different lengths) from a hanger or stick.

Christmas Sense

(A Choral Speaking Piece for Five Children)

What do I *hear* on this Christmas Day?
The sweet sound of carols, bells of a sleigh;
Greetings of shoppers as homeward they go
And laughter of children who play in the snow.

When I look around me, what do I *see*?
The star at the top of my Christmas tree;
Wreaths in the windows, candles alight,
Holly and pine—a most wonderful sight!

What do I *smell* at this time of the year?
All sorts of scents that bring good cheer—
Cookies and candy and fresh spicy cake—
Yes, all good things a baker can make.

What do I *taste* when Christmas comes?
Gingerbread boys and plump sugar plums;
Turkey and stuffing and pumpkin pies
And bright candy canes—a delicious surprise.

What do I *feel* in December's glow?
The sharpness of tinsel, the softness of snow,
Tickle of pine needles trimming a tree,
An icy north wind blowing cold and free.

All of our senses are tuned to this season,
And Christmas, of course, is the wonderful reason!

(All five children together for the last two lines.)

by Jean Conder Soule

International
HOLIDAY CELEBRATIONS

The United States is often called a "melting pot." Do your students know what this means? It refers to the long history of immigration on this continent. Families immigrate for numerous reasons. Some come for better working conditions, others to be close to their extended family, while some come for educational purposes.

How can we, as teachers, reach out to children in our classrooms who speak English as a second language? How can we turn different cultures into an enrichment for all students? Teachers have many opportunities to learn from people with different life-styles. This holiday season, focus on what people all over the world have in common!

Christmas in Many Lands

The word *holiday* comes from two words, *holi* and *day* or *holy day*. Many years ago, all holidays were considered holy days. Now we celebrate holidays for worship, fun and play.

The special way people in different countries celebrate a holiday is called a custom. This is something done over and over in your family or community. It may go back many generations. Customs include the way you dress, the food you eat and other parts of your life.

Plan a book display of Christmas and other seasonal events in a reading center. Students may research specific customs, foods and other observances from various countries. Share these customs with your students.

by Carolyn Ross Tomlin

NORWAY—ST. NICHOLAS DAY

Wooden shoes are placed by the window on December 5th by boys and girls. However, they don't lea[ve] treats for Santa—but for his horse. Hay and carrots are favorites. The food is gone by morning, and th[e] shoes are filled with presents.

EUROPE—THE YULE LOG

The day before Christmas is an important time in many parts of Europe. A family will walk to a nearby woods or forest, find a large log and bring it home. This dates back to ancient times when light and warmth were a triumph over darkness and cold—thus adding warmth and light to the holiday season. It's considered good luck to burn the yule log during the 12 days of Christmas. Still more good luck follows if you save a portion to start the next Christmas fire.

Also, the evergreen or "plants that do not die" are decorated with bangles and lights. This is a reminder of the ancients' belief that green plants must contain some of the sun god's special powers, and the sun would return to warm the Earth.

Activity: Collect a variety of evergreens grown in your area. Identify each. Use caution, as some evergreen berries are poisonous. Mistletoe berries can be fatal if eaten. Holly berries can cause stomach distress and mouth burning.

HANUKKAH—THE FESTIVAL OF LIGHTS

Hanukkah is a Jewish holiday lasting eight days. On the Roman calendar, it begins on the twenty-fifth day of the Hebrew month of Kislev. Usually Hanukkah comes near the end of November but sometimes in December. This is a joyous occasion for the Jewish family. Each night the family gathers together to light special candles and repeat special prayers. A candle holder, called a menorah, holds the eight candles. A candle is lit nightly until the festival is over. A ninth cup holds the shamash candle, which is used to light the candles ea[ch] night. (*Shamash* means "servant" in Hebrew.) Children join in singing with their family.

anukkah remembers the Hebrew victory over Syria's oppressive King Antiochus, when the Maccabees captured the temple of Jerusalem. Later, the people built a new temple. Legend says that only enough remained to light a fire for one day. However, the oil lasted for eight days. Today the festival is one ay of remembering the victory. Children play games and receive presents on each day of the lebration.

The symbols and customs of the holiday can be found in *Hanukkah* by Norma Simon, illustrated by Symeon Shimin (Crowell, 1966) and *The Hanukkah Story*, written and illustrated by Marilyn Hirsh (Bonim, 1977).

MEXICO–FELIZ NAVIDAD

Christmas Eve, or La Nochebuena, is the traditional time to break the piñata. A piñata is a jar or papier-mâché container filled with small candies and gifts which hangs from the ceiling. Children are blindfolded and given a big stick; then they swing at the piñata. When it's broken, everyone rushes to get the candy and gifts.

SWITZERLAND–SANTA CLAUS NIGHT

Parading around town with lighted candles in hats is one way children and grown-ups celebrate Santa Claus Night on December 6. When wearing one of these, you are called a Klause. In Switzerland, Santa Claus wears the clothing of a bishop, which is a long white robe. A tall, pointed hat, called a miter, completes his costume.

SWEDEN–SAINT LUCIA DAY

A young girl in Sweden is called a Lucia Queen when she wears a crown containing lighted candles. On December 13, girls place the crowns on their heads, and wake up their parents, brothers and sisters with songs and special food for breakfast.

A sudden open door at night could mean a gift was being thrown in your house during the holidays. Adults tell children that an old man and woman throw the presents—but no e knows their identity.

TEACHER ACTIVITIES

Bulletin Board

Merry Christmas in Other Languages

Decorate a bulletin board with a world map. Copy the phrases indicating *Merry Christmas* on poster board. Place the terms on one side of the board. Using a thumbtack, attach a red piece of yarn from the country to the word card. Ask parents who speak a second language to help with pronunciations by making a recording. Include this in your study of customs in other countries during the holiday season.

Merry Christmas—English
Aferihia Pa—Ashanti
Glaedelig Jul—Danish
Joyeux Nöel—French
Frohliche Weinachten—German
Kala Christougenna—Greek
Buon Natale—Italian
S Rhozhdyestvom Khristovym—Russian
Feliz Navidad—Spanish

Explore Christmas with Literature

The holidays are a good time to introduce good literature to children. Use these well-known books to teach how other cultures observed this event.

Arrow to the Sun, adapted and illustrated by Gerald McDermott (Viking, 1974), winner of the 1975 Caldecott award, portrays how early Native Americans gave great reverence to the sun as the source of light. In the Northern Hemisphere, ancient people worshiped the sun. As they did not understand why the days grew shorter and colder, they built fires to help the sun god.

This story focuses on a Pueblo Indian legend about a boy who delivers the spirit of the Lord of the Sun, his father, back to the pueblo after he has been transformed into an arrow.

Activity: Read the story. Provide paper and colored markers or pencils for illustrating one specific scene. Arrange in order and display on a bulletin board.

Christmas Feasts and Festivals by Lillie Patterson, illustrated by Clift Schule (Garrard, 1968). In an easy-to-read text, students gain an understanding of Christmas as a time when Christians celebrate the birth of Jesus Christ, nearly 2000 years ago. Information is given on how the holiday is celebrated from family to family and country to country.

Activity: Make a recording, allowing all students in your classroom to tell at least one way their family celebrates Christmas. Suggest they mention food, customs, being with family or other events.

Holly, Reindeer and Colored Lights: The Story of the Christmas Symbols by Edna Barth (Seabury, 1971). Explains the differences between Christmas and earlier pagan feasts.

Activity: Make a reindeer hat to wear during this season. Trace around each student's hands on brown construction paper, cut out and glue to a headband made from a double layer of paper.

Skip Around the Year by Aillen Fisher (Crowell, 1967) and **More Poetry for Holidays,** an anthology selected by Nancy Larrick (Garrard, 1973; Scholastic paperback) are good teacher resources for showing December celebrations as rich and varied holidays.

Activity: Read "Light the Festive Candles," "Suddenly," "First Gifts," "Country Christmas" and "Christmas Candles." Ask students to tell at least one thing they remember from reading the poems. Illustrate the work.

Listen Up! It's Christmas!

Christmas Math

Materials: lined paper, pencil   **Skill:** Sums to 10

Write your name in the top corner of your paper. Number your lines from 1 to 10. For each line I will ask you a math question. Write the answer by the number.

1. Mom wrapped four gifts in the morning and five gifts in the afternoon. How many gifts did Mom wrap altogether?

2. Leroy decorated three dozen cookies. Lisa decorated four dozen cookies. How many dozen did they decorate altogether?

3. According to the song, on the second day of Christmas my true love gave to me two turtle doves. On the fifth day of Christmas my true love gave to me five golden rings. How many gifts in all was I given on those two days?

4. Susie hung seven bells on her family's Christmas tree. Her brother hung three bells. How many bells did they hang altogether?

5. Ling went to two stores to shop for gifts. Her mother went to six more stores. How many stores did they visit altogether?

6. In the Christmas play, five students were shepherds and five were angels. How many shepherds and angels were there in all?

7. On Christmas Day, Sandy's family will drive four miles to her Uncle Ned's house and then drive four more miles to her grandma's house. How many miles will they drive in all?

8. On Christmas Day, two guests will arrive at Maria's house at noon. Later, seven more guests will arrive. How many guests will come altogether?

9. Julia set six places at the table for Christmas dinner. Luke added four more places. How many places were at the table in all?

10. Brent's parents put two gifts under their Christmas tree. Santa added eight more. How many presents were there in all?

by Ann Richmond Fisher

Yuletide Clues

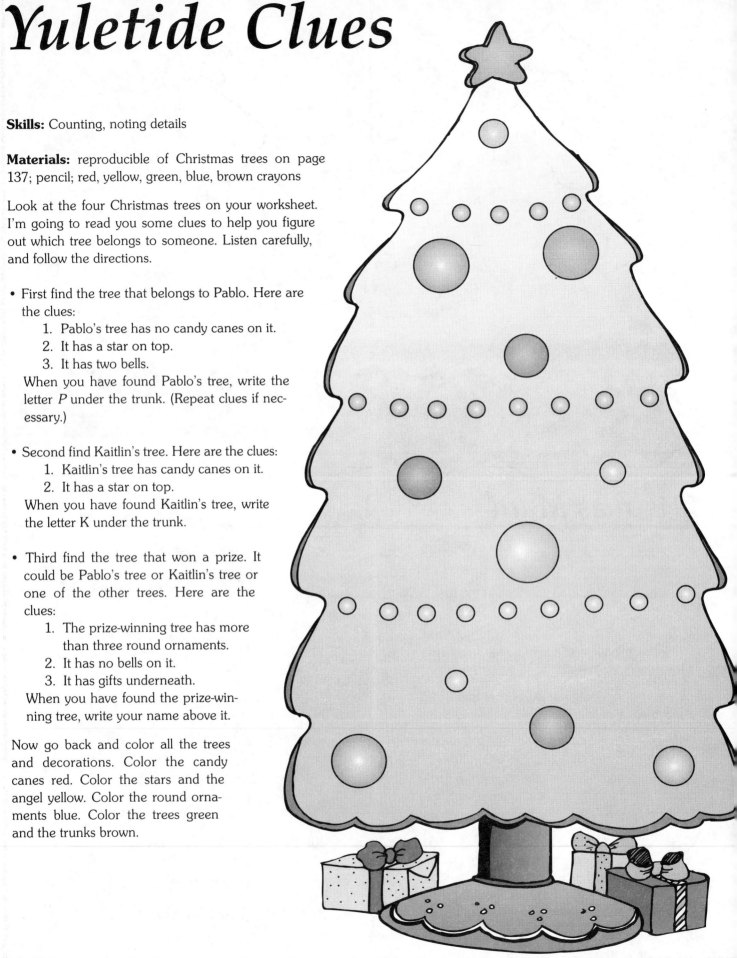

Skills: Counting, noting details

Materials: reproducible of Christmas trees on page 137; pencil; red, yellow, green, blue, brown crayons

Look at the four Christmas trees on your worksheet. I'm going to read you some clues to help you figure out which tree belongs to someone. Listen carefully, and follow the directions.

• First find the tree that belongs to Pablo. Here are the clues:
  1. Pablo's tree has no candy canes on it.
  2. It has a star on top.
  3. It has two bells.
When you have found Pablo's tree, write the letter *P* under the trunk. (Repeat clues if necessary.)

• Second find Kaitlin's tree. Here are the clues:
  1. Kaitlin's tree has candy canes on it.
  2. It has a star on top.
When you have found Kaitlin's tree, write the letter K under the trunk.

• Third find the tree that won a prize. It could be Pablo's tree or Kaitlin's tree or one of the other trees. Here are the clues:
  1. The prize-winning tree has more than three round ornaments.
  2. It has no bells on it.
  3. It has gifts underneath.
When you have found the prize-winning tree, write your name above it.

Now go back and color all the trees and decorations. Color the candy canes red. Color the stars and the angel yellow. Color the round ornaments blue. Color the trees green and the trunks brown.

Incredible Edibles
for the Holidays

Cooking in the classroom is a great participation experience. The holiday season is a time of wonderful smells, colors and tastes. Take time to create some fun treats. Try a few of these below.

Toasted Ornaments

Pour about an inch of milk into several paper cups. Add a few drops of food coloring to the milk to create a deep shade of holiday colors. Give each child a slice of white bread to decorate with this milk paint. Use a cotton swab as a brush to paint circles, zigzags and all sorts of designs on the bread. Toast the slice on a light setting in your toaster. Cut ornament shapes with cookie cutters and serve along with the Festive Eggs.

Rudolph Snack

Ingredients:
1 slice brown bread
creamy peanut butter
1 maraschino cherry
  (cut in half)
2 stick pretzels
2 raisins

Trim the crust from the bread (optional). Lightly spread peanut butter over the bread. Slice the bread diagonally to form two triangles. Insert the two pretzels in the top of the bread slice (antlers). Place the raisins on the bread for eyes.
Place half of a maraschino cherry on the point for the nose. Note: One slice of bread makes two Rudolph snacks.

by Judy Wolfman

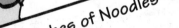

Munchy Bunches of Noodles

Ingredients:
12 ounces of vanilla chips or white chocolate
3 cups crisp chow mein noodles
red and green sugar sprinkles

Put the vanilla chips in a glass bowl. Melt the chips in a microwave for about 2-3 minutes until creamy (stove method can also be used). Fold in the chow mein noodles, mixing carefully to coat. Scoop out little stacks and drop the mounds onto a cookie sheet covered with waxed paper. Sprinkle the mounds with candy sugar and cool in the refrigerator. What a simple and fun treat to make together! Note: Chocolate, butterscotch and peanut butter morsels could also be used.

Festive Eggs

Prepare scrambled eggs, using the amount of eggs that will accommodate your class size. Add diced red and green bell peppers to the mixture before frying. Serve with the toasted ornaments. (See above.)

by Tania Kourempis-Cowling

Holiday Punch

You Will Need:
20 ounces unsweetened frozen strawberries
46 ounces pineapple juice
lime sherbet

Puree the strawberries in a blender. Combine with the pineapple juice in a pitcher. Pour this punch into serving cups and garnish with a dollop of green lime sherbet.

Crunch Christmas Trees

You Will Need:
1/4 cup margarine
1-10 oz. package
(40 large)
or 4 cups miniature
marshmallows
green food coloring
6 cups crispy rice cereal
decorations such as cinnamon red
hots, silver ball candy
sprinkles

In a large saucepan, melt the margarine over low heat. Add the marshmallows and stir until melted. Add drops of food coloring until you reach the desired shade. Remove from the heat.

Add the cereal to the marshmallow mixture. Stir well. To make tree shapes, lightly grease a 1-cup funnel. Pack it with the cereal mixture. When full, turn it upside down and unmold it on a plate. While it's still warm, press in the candies.

Note: This recipe makes five trees. You can increase the ingredients according to your class size.

Christmas Cookies

Make your favorite rolled sugar cookie mixture. Roll out the dough and cut out festive ornaments with cookie cutters. With a plastic drinking straw, make a hole at the top of each cookie. Bake as directed. Now the kids can frost and decorate the cookies. Place ribbon or yarn through the hole to hang the "cookie ornaments" on your classroom tree.

Christmas Cupcakes

Prepare cupcake batter according to package directions. Fold in chopped red and green maraschino cherries. Bake as directed. Use canned vanilla frosting, and make it festive by adding food coloring.

Delicious Dreidel

You Will Need:
1 marshmallow
1 toothpick
1 Hershey's Kiss® (candy)

Poke the toothpick through the marshmallow. Add the Kiss to the end to form a spinning top—a dreidel to spin and to eat, too!

Menorah Sandwich

You Will Need:
1 slice white bread
peanut butter (creamy)
9 pretzel sticks (candles)
9 raisins (flames)

Spread the slice of bread with peanut butter. Place the pretzel sticks in a line across the bread. The middle stick should be raised a little higher than the rest, by adding an extra piece of pretzel or adding two flames instead of one. Place a raisin on top of each stick for the flame.

Snow White Hot Chocolate

After playing in the snow or when celebrating a winter festival, there is nothing more satisfying than a steaming mug of hot chocolate. This recipe offers an aesthetically intriguing twist to an old favorite.

You Will Need:
4 cups of water
large saucepan
(8 ounces) white chocolate baking squares
mini marshmallows, white chocolate shavings or
    whipped cream

12 cups of milk
wire whisk
mugs

Heat the white chocolate and the water over medium heat. Stir constantly until melted. Bring the mixture to a boil and then simmer for two minutes. Add the milk and heat thoroughly, stirring occasionally. Ladle into mugs, top with a fluffy white topping of marshmallows, shavings or whipped cream. Serves 25-30 children.

by Robynne Eagan

The International Christmas Tree

A Multicultural Story About Winter Festivals

by Donna L. Clovis

ool breezes brought winter to the forest. Many ees had already shed their colorful fall leaves, and eir branches looked like arms reaching for the sky. nly a family of evergreens kept their leaves during e winter.

s gentle snowflakes began to fall from the sky, randpa Evergreen knew it was time to share a very nportant message with the family. It would be a essage of celebration and love.

randpa and Grandma Evergreen called the chil-ren, aunts, uncles and cousins together for the amily meeting. The forest was quiet, for even the ther trees were eager to hear the story. Only the nowflakes whispered in the darkness.

"You know," he began, "this is the time of year when we can spread peace and happiness to every part of the Earth. Men will come and take the older Evergreens to homes and schools throughout America. People will dress us in garlands and orna-ments and lights."

The Evergreens listened in amazement to all the things he said.

"I want to go," Little Evergreen said.

"Me, too!" Cousin Evergreen chirped.

"Not yet," Grandpa warned. "I don't think you are big enough. You must grow tall and strong to carry the beautiful lights and ornaments upon your arms and shoulders."

"Will I grow strong and tall like you one day?" Cousin Evergreen asked.

"Yes, you will," he said, hugging the little Evergreens. "And I've heard the trucks in the mountain this morning, so I'd like to say my good-byes to everyone now."

The Evergreens said good-bye and gave hugs to Grandpa. They were very excited for him and his new adventure. They all wanted to go, but they knew someday they too would have a chance to spread good cheer and be dressed in beautiful ornaments. Well, everyone except Little Evergreen. He sat in the corner and began to cry.

"Why are you crying, Little Evergreen?" Grandpa asked.

"Because you're leaving. I love you and I'll miss you. I don't want you to go," he sobbed.

"I will miss you, too, Little Evergreen. You are very special, but there comes a time in the life of older Evergreens when they must leave their families and bring joy to boys and girls in homes and schools throughhout America. It is a family tradition, something we do over and over again with great happiness," Grandpa explained.

"Yes, Little Evergreen, we all will miss Grandpa, but he will always be remembered in our hearts. And he is going to a very nice place. He will be happ there." Grandma added.

Little Evergreen wiped his eyes and hugge Grandpa again. "Will you be happy there?"

"Yes, Little Evergreen. I will be very happy there Grandpa said, giving him a kiss on his head.

The next day, men came for Grandpa and took hi to a beautiful nursery school filled with children. Th children cheered as the men brought Grandp Evergreen through the door and placed him in the center of the room. As the teacher began to speak, the children gathered around the tree.

"Tomorrow we will decorate our tree in a very special way. Since many of you come from different countries, maybe you could bring something special from your country to dress our tree," she said.

142

he next day, the children brought special gifts from their countries for Grandpa Evergreen to wear. Everyone was so excited! And Grandpa Evergreen couldn't wait to see what everyone had for him.

First Martina, who comes from Italy, placed beautiful red candles upon the tree.

And Pascha, from Russia, brought special matrioska dolls.

Gisela added chocolate kisses from the winter festivals of Brazil.

And Lior, from Israel, brought some dreidels.

Doris, from Kenya, placed colorful small masks upon the tree.

And Han-Juang, from China, added small blue fans.

Tome brought kangaroo cookies his mom had made from Australia.

And Olga, from Germany, hung her candy canes.

Mark, from Nigeria, added his small orange and green paper fish.

And when the children were finished, the teacher added the gold garland, colored lights and crowned Grandpa Evergreen with a star.

"Look!" she began. "Our International Christmas Tree! What a wonderful way to celebrate winter festivals!"

The children cheered and began to sing "Let There Be Peace on Earth."

And Grandpa Evergreen sang, too! How happy he was to be bringing joy to others.

Edible Ornaments

When the holidays begin to wind down, what do you do with all the decorations you've created for your class and tree? Do you send them home? Throw them away? Why not eat them?

With edible ornaments, you and your students can decorate for the holidays and enjoy tasty snacks at the same time. The following ideas will give you some unique decorations that will surely tempt your children's creativity (and taste buds). All of these projects are easy, edible and inexpensive. You might want to have some extra ingredients on hand, because some snacking while creating is inevitable.

Gumdrop Ornaments

Materials: one medium-sized Styrofoam™ ball, bag of colored gumdrops, ribbon and a box of toothpicks for each student

Poke a hole in the Styrofoam™ ball and squeeze on a dab of white glue. Double the ribbon to form a loop, pushing the cut ends of the ribbon into the hole in the ball. Stick a toothpick in each gumdrop. Stick the other end of the toothpick into the ball, completely covering the ball with gumdrops.

Candy Playdough Cut-Outs

Materials: margarine, corn syrup, salt, vanilla, food coloring, sugar

Mix together 1/3 cup margarine, 1/3 cup corn syrup, 1/2 teaspoon salt, 1 teaspoon vanilla and food coloring of your choice. Knead in 2 cups of sugar until the mixture is smooth.

Roll out the dough and use cookies cutters to cut out decorations. Be sure to poke a hole in the top of each cutout for hanging. Lay ornaments on waxed paper to harden.

Pretzel Garland

Materials: several bags of pretzels (regular kind—not sticks or braids), red or green ribbon

Slide ribbon through "arms" of first pretzel and staple the loose end so the pretzel doesn't come off. One at a time, slide more pretzels onto the ribbon until your garland is as long as you wish.

by Donna Stringfellow

Christmas Wreaths

Materials: large box of crispy rice cereal, vanilla, green food coloring, margarine, bag of large marshmallows, butter, waxed paper, red cinnamon candies

An adult needs to melt together 1/2 cup of margarine, 30 marshmallows and 1 teaspoon of vanilla in a saucepan. When mixture is creamy, add food coloring. Remove from heat and stir in cereal to make a firm mixture, mixing well.

When the mixture has cooled to the touch, let children butter their fingers and form the cereal into the shape of wreaths. Use the cinnamon candies as berries.

Let the wreaths harden on waxed paper, then tie on a ribbon and hang up.

Cookie Handprints

Materials: your favorite sugar cookie recipe or commercial refrigerated cookie dough, candy decorations like sprinkles, ribbon

Roll out dough to 1/2" thickness on floured waxed paper. Have each child lay his/her hand on the dough and carefully cut out the hand shape. Let children decorate, making sure they poke a hole at the wrist end of the cookie for hanging. Carefully transfer the handprint to a baking sheet and bake according to recipe directions.

Variation: Painted Cookie Handprints: Mix 1 egg yolk with 1/4 teaspoon of water. Divide the mixture into several small cups. Add a different color of food coloring to each cup. (If paint thickens, add a few drops of water.) Use a paintbrush to paint designs on each cookie.

Gingerbread Men Garland

Materials: one package of gingerbread mix, flour, gingerbread man cutter, raisins, red cinnamon candies

Mix gingerbread mix with 1/4 cup warm water. Knead dough on floured surface until smooth. Roll dough to 1/8" thickness and cut out "men" with cutter.

Place "men" on greased baking sheet and decorate with raisins and candies. Be sure to poke a hole in the top of each "man" for hanging. Bake 6 to 8 minutes in 375° oven.

When cool, use ornament hanger or paper clips to hang "men" from a length of pretty ribbon.

Easy Stringing Garland

Materials: 1/4" wide or smaller ribbon, cereal with holes (such as Froot Loops™), LifeSavers™, pretzels, popcorn, cranberries, blunt-ended needles

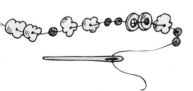

Young children can work entirely with cereal and pretzels; older children will enjoy using the needles to thread popcorn and cranberries, as well as candies and other goodies.

Magic Reindeer Food

A Secret Recipe

Ingredients
1/2 cup dry oatmeal
1/3 cup sparkly glitter
1 heart full of Christmas hope

Before Christmas Eve

Mix oatmeal and glitter together in a bowl. Fold in Christmas hope. Put in a seal-top plastic bag or baggie with a red bow to tie it shut. On Christmas Eve, sprinkle the Magic Reindeer Food on your lawn before bedtime.
(Attach the poem when giving it as a gift.)

Mix ingredients together and on Christmas Eve,
Sprinkle all over your lawn.
The glitter will shine in the moonlight
And lead Santa to your house before dawn.
The smell of oats will lead the reindeer
Directly to your rooftop.
The Christmas hope in the magic food
Guarantees dear Santa will stop!

by Jo Jo Cavalline
and Jo Anne O'Donne

146

This is a fun activity for children and a great way to get the entire family involved.

Using the pattern provided, trace a gingerbread man or woman on a piece of large cardboard—one for each student. Send the cardboard gingerbread person home with the children, along with a note explaining the project.

When the gingerbread creations come back to school, take pictures of each one individually. Put the pictures on pieces of oaktag to form a booklet. Give each child a chance to talk about his/her creation. Then send duplicate pictures and the original creation back home.

The children love having their parents help with the project, and the results are wonderful and varied. It's also a great time to discuss recycling and making "something out of nothing."

A Family
Gingerbread Man

Dear Parents,

We are sending home a gingerbread man/woman shape for the entire family to decorate. Use your imaginations and anything else that you have sitting around the house.

Please return your creation by
_____.

Thank you,

by Linda Threatt

7 ways to recycle old Christmas cards

Christmas Card Frames

Materials:

lightweight cardboard (you could use a cereal box), Christmas cards, white glue, a glue stick and a photograph (3½" x 5" or 4" x 6" works best)

Directions:

Cut the cards into triangles. Cut the cardboard into rectangles about 1" larger than the photo you are using. Have children glue the photo to the center of the cardboard, using a glue stick. At this point, it is helpful to cover the center of the photo with a Post-it™. This protects the photo from glue.

Next, glue the Christmas card triangles all around the photo. Place the flat edge of the triangles against the photo, letting the points stick out. Putting three or four layers of triangles on the frame will make it sturdier and more attractive.

Christmas Napkin Rings

Materials:

cardboard tube from paper towels, Christmas wrapping paper, old Christmas cards

Directions:

Cut the cardboard tube into rings that are about 1¼" wide. Cover the rings with Christmas wrapping paper. Cut out seasonal pictures from old Christmas cards. Glue a picture onto each covered ring.

At Christmas dinner, slip napkins into the napkin rings and put one at each place setting.

by D.A. Woodliff

Collage Tree

This is another great way to use old Christmas cards. Cut the cards into small triangles using the method shown. Don't worry about being exact! Duplicate a simple tree outline for each child. Children then glue triangles on the outline to create a collage tree.

Christmas Weaving

This project provides good exercise for little hands with pretty results. Trim two cards so they are the same size. Cut one into strips and the other into a mat as shown.

by Mary Maureen

Christmas Border

Christmas cards can easily become a decorative accessory in your classroom. One idea is to use old cards to dress up your holiday bulletin board.

Use large cards and trim them so they are all the same size. Then cut the cards as shown to form two triangles.

To make a border, you'll need long strips of paper or poster board. Typing paper or copy paper can be used by cutting each sheet in half horizontally and gluing the sheets together to make one long strip. Assemble cards as shown, and glue on the paper strip for stability. Staple or tack the border to your bulletin board.

Cozy Quilt Bulletin Board

Recycle Christmas cards into an old-fashioned bulletin board. Although you can make this bulletin board yourself, you'll have much more fun letting your students make the squares and assemble the "quilt."

To begin, cut 7" squares of green and red construction paper. Then cut old Christmas cards into triangles.

Glue card triangles to construction paper to form a "quilt square." Assemble squares on bulletin board as shown.

Peek-a-Boo Plates

Materials:

white glue, glitter or poster paint, two paper plates, Christmas card, pipe cleaner or yarn, hole punch, scissors

Directions:

Cut Christmas card picture to fit center of plate. "Scene" cards work best. Card should be big enough to cover most of the center portion of the plate.

Cut Christmas tree, ornament, star or snowman pattern from center of second plate.

Lightly paint reverse side of cut plate, or coat with glue and sprinkle with glitter. Let dry.

Glue cut plate to card plate, centering opening over scene or design on card. Punch hole and use pipe cleaner or yarn to hang.

by Mary Maurer

Holiday Gifts

Children can give their family and friends a Christmas or Hanukkah gift they have made themselves!

Mosaic Picture

Materials:
- piece of cardboard
- colored construction paper, or colorful pages from magazines, or colorful Styrofoam™ trays
- glue
- dark-colored marker
- crayons or markers

Directions:
1. Draw a simple design or shape on a piece of cardboard. Use a dark marker to outline it.
2. Tear or cut the colored paper or trays into small pieces.
3. Glue them inside the outline of the picture or design.
4. Spaces can be filled in with crayon or marker for color.
5. The picture can be framed or hung as is.

Note Holder

Materials:
- 2 paper plates (one cut in half)
- stapler and staples
- yarn or string
- magazine pictures or old greeting cards
- markers or crayons
- glue

Directions:
1. Color the inside of the whole plate and the rounded back of the half piece.
2. Place the half piece over the bottom of the full plate (rounded side up). Staple together.
3. Glue pictures from magazines or greeting cards on the bottom half.
4. Punch a hole on each side of the whole plate (a little over halfway up).
5. Tie yarn or string through the holes.
6. Hang and use. Good for notes, coupons, letters and other important papers.

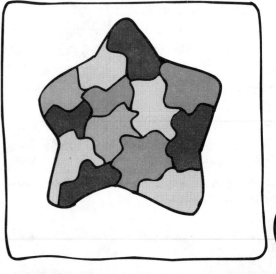

by Judy Wolfman

150

Gift Wrapping Paper

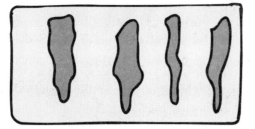

Materials:

- white paper
- poster paints
- brush
- newspapers

Directions:

1. Spread newspaper over your work area.
2. Let a single color of paint drip off the paintbrush onto a sheet of white paper.
3. Hold the paper up so the wet paint will run down the sheet (like raindrops down a window).
4. Add more drops of the same color, and keep turning the paper around so the paint will run in different directions. Let it dry.
5. Repeat the process with other colors. You will have a colorful and interesting design.
6. When dry, wrap your gift in your beautiful paper.

Fancy Necklace

Materials:

- variety of pasta (that can be strung)
- food coloring
- wax paper
- yarn

Directions:

1. In a jar, place 3 tablespoons water and liquid food coloring (enough to give you the color you want).
2. Fill the jar 1/3 full of uncooked pasta.
3. Swirl the jar gently to coat the pasta.
4. Remove pasta with a slotted spoon.
5. Place on wax paper to dry.
6. When dry, tie a length of yarn on one piece of pasta.
7. String the rest of the pasta onto the yarn.
8. You can add buttons and beads to the necklace if you want.
9. When finished, tie the two ends of the yarn together.

Make sure the necklace is long enough to slip over the head.

Bookmark

Materials:

- construction paper, poster board, oaktag or felt
- scissors
- crayons, markers or paint
- glue

Directions:

1. Cut a rectangle, or long design, from the paper, poster board, oaktag or felt.
2. To decorate: You can color your own design, or glue on small bits of paper, felt, ribbon, etc.

Candy Cane Capers

The Christmas season is just around the corner, so treat your class to our festive collection of holiday activities.

Add excitement to your holiday unit by having a Candy Cane Countdown contest. Fill a jar with small candy canes and ask your students to guess the weight of the jar. Give prizes (candy canes, of course!) to the contest winners.

Give your students a firsthand look at an old-fashioned Christmas celebration by reading them *Christmas on the Prairie* by Joan Anderson, photographs by George Ancona (New York: Clarion Books, 1985). This book gives a re-creation of a Christmas holiday in the 1800s with stunning black and white photographs featuring people in costumes amidst an early prairie setting.

Want to know more about the history of Christmas trees? Then *The Family Christmas Tree Book* by Tomie de Paola (New York: Holiday House, 1980) is the perfect book for you! Find out information about the customs surrounding the Christmas tree and other interesting facts about the subject.

My Candy Cane Story

One cold, winter day I was walking in a meadow near my house, when I saw a sign. The sign read "Welcome to Candy Cane Cottage." Finish the story.

Name: _____

_____

_____

_____

_____

_____

_____

_____

_____

by Mary Ellen Switzer

Wow, What a Christmas Stocking!

Design a Christmas stocking for your favorite cartoon character.

What's in the Christmas Stocking?

Follow the dots and find out what gifts are inside the Christmas stocking Notice there are upper and lowercase letters.

Candy Cane Surprises

Calling all kids! Grab your pencils and join in the fun. The activities below are just for you. Color a candy cane for every activity completed.

1. Congratulations! You have just been hired by the *Santa's Sentinel* newspaper. Write a "help wanted" ad for an elf to help make toys for Santa.

2. Write a story using this ending: "Santa and I climbed back into his sleigh and headed for the North Pole."

3. Yum-E Candy Company wants to have some new candy cane flavors this year. Write the names of three new flavors.

4. Be an inventor! Design a new robot who can trim a Christmas tree in just one hour. What would you name your invention? Draw a picture of your robot and label the parts.

5. Write an advertisement to tell the world about your new robot.

6. Design a tree ornament for your favorite sports hero. Draw a picture of your ornament.

7. Calling all detectives! Santa needs your help! One of his reindeer is missing. Write a story telling how you and your friends solve the mystery.

8. Design a "wanted" poster, showing the picture of the reindeer-napper.

9. Pretend someone gave you the perfect gift. What would it be? Draw a picture of the gift.

10. Round up some facts about reindeer. Use an encyclopedia or reference book to help you. Write three facts you have found.

POLAR EXPRESS

A Literature Unit Based on the Book by Chris Van Allsburg

Summary: One Christmas Eve, a young boy took an exciting ride to the North Pole on the *Polar Express*. There he was chosen to receive the first gift of Christmas. He selected a silver bell from a reindeer's harness. The wonderful adventure turned into a terrible disappointment when the boy found he no longer had the bell in his pocket. The next morning, when he opened his last gift, he found the bell with a note from Mr. S. Only those who truly believe can hear the bell ring.

Polar Express received a Caldecott medal for the best illustrated book of 1986. Chris Van Allsburg combined reality and fantasy in his drawings as well as in his narrative.

Introduction: Questions are asked to focus attention, to recall main ideas and to encourage creative thinking. Opportunities are presented to listen, speak, read and write. A variety of activities to extend the story are suggested. They may be completed individually, cooperatively in small groups or with whole class participation.

Questions to Review the Story: Ask the following questions to help the students review the main events of the story.

1. Why did the boy look out his bedroom window?
2. Describe the trip on the *Polar Express*.
3. What three things happened when they arrived at the North Pole?
4. What happened that made everyone feel unhappy?
5. Why did the boy's parents think the bell was broken?
6. What unusual things occurred in the story? What things really could have happened?
7. What was magical about the train?

by Patricia O'Brien

Enrichment Activities

Dear . . .

Discuss the form of a friendly letter. Post a model for easy reference. Have students write letters to the following story characters. They may select from the suggested situations or make up one of their own.

Write a letter to one of the following characters:

a. to the boy to ask him questions about his trip or to tell him you agree or disagree with his choice of a gift.

b. to Santa Claus to apply for a job as an elf or to ask how someone could be picked to receive the first gift of Christmas.

c. to the train company to ask if you could arrange to have the *Polar Express* stop in front of your house.

Note: Letters could be exchanged for other students to write responses.

In Other Words

Compile a class book to retell the events of t story. Together list the scenes from the story (s below) in chronological order. Working individually or in sm groups, have the students select a scene to summarize a illustrate.

Events of the Story

- At the North Pole, there was a huge city filled with t factories.
- They raced passed towns and villages.
- The last package under the tree was from Mr. C. The b was inside.
- Like a roller coaster, they went over mountains and do valleys.
- After the children got back on the train, they discover the bell was missing.
- He looked out the window when he heard the sound o train.
- Santa Claus selected the boy to pick the first gift Christmas.
- The boy waited quietly in bed, listening for ringing bells
- An elf cut a bell from a harness before Santa left.
- Wolves and rabbits roamed and hid in dark forests.

It Makes Sense

Encourage the children to use their five senses they recall the story. Assist them in listing thi that could be perceived through their senses as they take imaginary ride on the Polar Express. Help them to develo rich vocabulary by encouraging them to use words that sou good together and help convey the magical experien Depending on the age and ability of the children, th may use a word or phrase to complete each line.

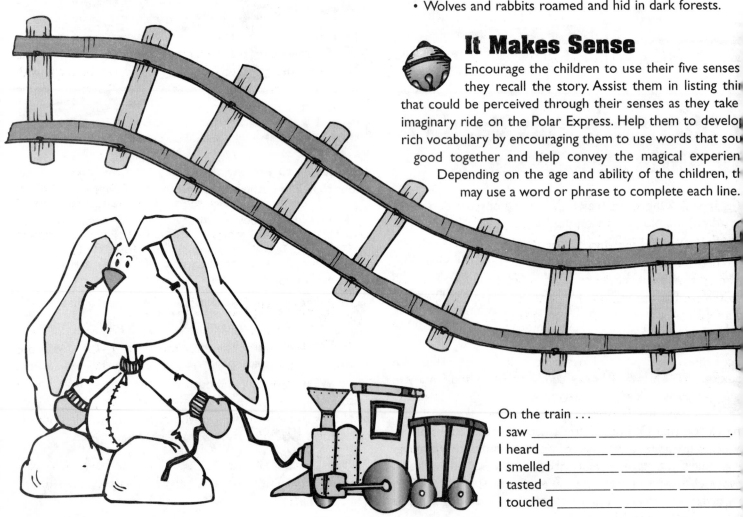

On the train . . .

I saw _____ _____ _____

I heard _____ _____ _____

I smelled _____ _____ _____

I tasted _____ _____ _____

I touched _____ _____ _____

A Dark and Snowy Night

When watercolor or a thinned tempera is [br]ushed over a crayoned pic[tu]re, the paint beads produce an [int]eresting effect.

[Ins]truct the class to select an [ev]ent from the story to illus[tr]ate, using the crayon resist [te]chnique. For best results, [re]mind them to apply the crayon [he]avily or it will not resist the [pa]int. They may try one of the [id]eas below or come up with a [pla]n of their own.

1. Draw a scene from the story using light, bright crayons. It could show a town along the tracks or the city at the North Pole. Brush a dark color over the picture.

2. Try a white wash over darker colors to produce a snowy scene.

From Here to There

Instruct the students to draw a map to show the route of the *Polar Express* from the boy's home to [th]e North Pole. Where might the train have been before it [pic]ked up the boy? Encourage them to use their imaginations [to] complete the activity. You may wish to introduce symbols [an]d a map key, as well as a direction indicator.

Say It with Words

Explain to the children how to transfer their ideas from the creative dramatics activity into writing, [us]ing cartoon strips. Instead of drawing the characters, they [ma]y cut out magazine pictures of children. After the photos [ar]e glued to the page, instruct them to write the dialogue [ab]ove each head and then draw the cartoon bubble around [th]e words.

The Big Picture

Plan a story mural. Discuss ways this may be presented. The children may show scenes from the story, the route of the *Polar Express* and the things that happened along the way, or any related idea. If the pictures are completed on separate sheets of paper, the artwork may then be cut out and glued to assigned areas. This enables more people to engage in the activity. After the mural is assembled, paint may be applied with sponges to quickly cover large background spaces. The artists may then take turns telling about their contributions to the mural.

As I Was Saying . . .

Help the children dramatize scenes from the story. Since there is very little dialogue in the narrative, they will have to ima-gine what the characters might have said. Set the scene with them. Discuss the action and dialogue. Select one of the following scenes to perform:

1. The children are looking out the window as the train speeds through the night. What are they talking about?

2. The boy has just discovered the bell is not in his pocket. What do the other children say to make him feel better?

3. At home on Christmas morning, the boy has just opened the package and is reading the note from Mr. C.

It Looks Like . . .

Help the children plan a three-dimensional scene in a box. Divide the class into small groups. Direct the students to make an imaginative model of Santa's North Pole home and workplace in a carton. Does he have a workshop in a little village or is it more like the huge factory-filled city, or something in between? Those who prefer to work individually could use a shoe box to display their work.

Provide a variety of materials such as small boxes, milk cartons, wood scraps, cardboard, construction paper, felt-tipped pens, paints, etc.

Questions to Extend the Story

Discuss the questions below to give the children an opportunity to respond personally to the tale.

1. If you had been on the *Polar Express*, what would you have enjoyed most about your trip to the North Pole?

2. If you had been chosen to receive the first gift of Christmas, what would you have asked for?

3. When the boy discovered he no longer had the silver bell in his pocket, what thoughts might have gone through his mir
Have you ever experienced a similar misfortune?

4. If you were there, what would you say to make him feel better?

5. Do you think the boy ever told anyone about his visit to the North Pole?

6. What if one day the boy met someone who had also been on the train? What might they talk about?

Additional Activities

1. Read Margaret Wise Brown's *The Important Book*. Brainstorm a list of the important things about snow.

2. Experiment with folding and cutting out snowflakes. Some may be added to the mural and used for other decorations.

3. If you have ever ridden on a train, tell about your experiences.

4. Write a story about Santa Claus. Rewrite the story, replacing some of the words with pictures. Rubber stamps work well for this assignment.

5. Pretend you are on a mysterious journey. You may travel by train, boat, airplane, rocket or any other means of transportation. Write a story about your adventures.

6. Design a Christmas card to send to a children's hospital or convalescent home.

7. Make sugar cookies together. Use Christmas cookie cutters and decorate after baking.

8. Enjoy a thick, rich cup of hot chocolate.

As a special memento, present each child with a bell on a ribbon. Hopefully, they will continue to hear its sound for years to come.

158

Celebrate with a Tree!

The tradition of the Christmas tree is thought to have originated from a pagan ritual dating back to the Roman Saturnalia when a tree was decorated during the mid-winter festival. The first person believed to have decorated a tree for the celebration of Christmas was Martin Luther (1483-1546) of Germany. He was so struck by the vision of stars twinkling behind a tree that he brought a fir tree indoors and decorated it with lighted candles. Queen Victoria's husband, Prince Albert, brought the lighted Christmas tree from Germany to Britain in 1840. This tradition caught on quickly and became well-established throughout Britain and North America.   Bring a tree into your classroom and celebrate in your own way!

Trimming the Tree with Creativity

...hildren create their own tree orna-...ents using their imaginations and ...ms available around the classroom. ...om classic old favorites to trendy ...iginal pieces, this tree will glow ...th creativity. Try these decora-...ns:

...per Chains: Cut out strips of ...il, construction paper or gift ...rap. Glue the ends together to ...rm the links of the chain.

...asonal Shapes: Trace cookie ...tters or use stencils to mark ...apes on construction paper, ...st year's cards or tagboard. ...t out the shape and then ...ver it with tissue, foil or col-...ge materials.

...rn Creatures: Christmas ...aracters or loveable crea-...res can be traced as above ...d cut out of sturdy card-...ard or tagboard and then ...apped in yarn. Try a black ...eep cut-out with chunky ...hite wool, a little green elf ...apped in red and white ...arments," a colorful ...rn-wrapped mitten or a ...ld cardboard star ...apped in white yarn.

Tiny Gifts: Matchboxes or other tiny boxes can be wrapped in colored tissue and adorned with a bow and then hung on a tree.

Snowflakes: Traditional paper snowflakes can be cut from white, silver, gold, red or green paper or doilies.

Edibles: In the period leading up to Christmas, make cookies, candies, popcorn balls, chocolates, dried fruits and other yummy treats to hang on the tree. On the last school day, children may choose and eat a treat from the tree.

Use Your Imagination: Try blown eggs, berries, leaves, shells and wheat sheaf vines, gingerbread cookies, walnuts painted and sprinkled with glitter, converted jewelery, pinecones and "snow," gumdrop garland using fishing line or unlit homemade candles made with glittery pipe cleaner "flames" and rolled beeswax or paper rolls.

Outdoor Live Tree

Children can decorate this tree with natural "treasures" found in the outdoors, reusable lights and decorations or treats for the birds and critters.

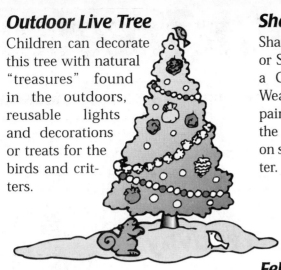

Shape Tree

Shape chicken wire or Styrofoam™ into a Christmas tree. Weave, glue or paint greenery to the frame. Spray on snow or glitter.

The Critter Tree

Decorate a live tree with treats for birds, squirrels and deer. making suet or pea butter pinecones roll in birdseed, popco and berry garlar or hanging co cobs decora with wh sheaves a berries.

A Living Tree

Bring a live tree into your classroom. Live trees can be dug out of the ground and kept alive with a root ball wrapped in burlap. When the celebrations are over, the tree can be kept in a cool place to be planted in the spring. Talk to your local green thumbs or nursery for appropriate instructions for digging up and replanting in your area. Consider donating your tree to a needy park or yard.

Felt Tree

Cut a Christmas tree shape 3-4 feet (1 meter) high out of green felt. Glue or sew 25 pockets to the tree. Fill each pocket with words of wisdom, a festive tale or a seasonal treat. Allow students to retrieve the surprises one day at a time leading up to Christmas.

The Recycler's Tree: Honor the Earth

Decorate this tree with recycled decorations only. Consider handmade ornaments from last year's cards, wrap, ribbons or creative crafts made from recycled items. Recycle this tree when Christmas is over by making it into craft materials, firewood, garden mulch (using a wood chipper) or by setting it in the snow as a bird refuge.

The Celebration Tree

Request that each child make or bring an ornament from home. This ornament should represent an important celebration in the particular child's culture. Each child will present their ornament and explain its significance before placing the decoration on the tree.

The Friendship Tree

Supply small Christmas-shaped paper cut-outs. Throughout the Christmas season, children can write messages of friendship to one another and leave them on the tree. At the end of the day, "friends" take the cheery mes-

Branch Tree

Go for the bare look! Secure a bare branch or evergreen bough in a pot of sand or plaster of Paris. This sturdy branch tree would be appropriate for a three *R*s theme: *reduce, reuse* and *recycle;* or a more traditional "tree" adorned with green lights and traditional tree trimmings.

by Robynne Eag

Winter Fun in the Classroom

Holiday games are great activities to enhance excitement, social skills and even physical development of the child. Use these ideas for a fun daily event or combine several for a planned party in your classroom.

by Donna Stringfellow

Scrambled Letters

Divide the class into two teams. Sit on the floor to play a letter game. In advance, make cardboard squares with the letters H-O-L-I-D-A-Y F-U-N on them (one letter per card). Make at least four sets of these letters and place them in a brown bag. You will need a bag of letters for each team. To play, the children alternate picking a letter. The first team to combine their letters to spell *Holiday Fun* wins.

Christmas Candy Relay

Preparation: Have a pair of mittens for each team and a piece of wrapped Christmas candy for each player.

Instructions: Divide children into two teams and give each player a piece of candy. The first player in line dons the mittens and fumbles about, trying to open the candy. When he succeeds, he pops it in his mouth, removes the mittens and passes them to next player who continues in the same manner. The winner is the team who finishes first.

Hint: Very young children enjoy this game, but you might want to omit the mittens. Use bigger pieces of candy, like candy canes. Hard candies and young children are not a good combination.

Musical Christmas Present Game

Preparation: You will need a Christmas present suitable for any age (like a small box of candy), wrapping paper, tape, ribbon and music.

Instructions: Wrap a present in five or six layers of wrapping paper. Use plenty of tape and ribbon. This game is like musical chairs. Everyone sits in a circle. Someone is in charge of the music. The idea is to unwrap the present without ripping the paper. Each person passes the package until the music stops like musical chairs. If you rip the paper you are out of the game, so be very careful! Whoever holds the completely unwrapped present wins!

by Carlene Americk

Secrets

Place several items in a decorated box. The teacher is to recite this verse and then describe one of the items in the box. The students take turns guessing what's inside. Display the item and then repeat the process again.

Holiday secrets are so much fun!
In this box is a special one.
I'll give you clues to what's inside,
Then try to guess what the box does hide!

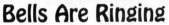

Bells Are Ringing

All the children sit in a circle on the floor. Start passing a bell around the group while holiday music is playing in the background. When the music stops, the child holding the bell rings it according to the teacher's directions. For example, ring the bell three times, ring it with your left hand, ring it above your head, etc.

Elf Exercise

One child is chosen to be the chief elf as he leads t group of elves in a game of Simon Says with a twist. Rec the verse as actions are followed.

All do as I do.
All do as I do.
All do as I do.
Ha, Ha, Ho, Ho, Ho!

Do exercise motions, as well as pretending to make toys or fe reindeer. Take turns being the chief elf.

Stocking Relay Race

Divide your students into several teams. Provide a couple pairs of holiday motif socks. Each child runs across the room, takes a pair of socks, puts on each sock, removes them and then runs back to their teammates. Continue until each child in line takes a turn.

by Tania Kourempis-Cowling

Who Am I?

On separate sheets of paper, write down the name of a holiday character or object such as Santa, ornament, dreidel, North Pole, etc. Tape one sheet onto the back of each student. Let the children mingle, giving clues to each other so they can guess who or what they are. Only three questions can be asked and answered with a *yes* or *no*.

Dress Up a Santa

Set up teams with two people each. Pass out rolls or sheets of crepe paper in red, black and white. At the sound of a signal, one child dresses up the partner to look like Santa. They can only use the paper, no pins, tape, etc. The paper can be torn, stretched and tucked into buttons, loops, belts, etc. When time's up, make a contest decision who's made the best Santa look-alike.

Activity Chain

Cut strips of construction paper to make paper chains. On each strip, write a holiday activity to conduct in class. Put together a long chain. Each child pulls off a link and leads the class in the event. Ideas could include sing a holiday song, read a favorite poem, dance to holiday music, play with holiday balloons, etc.

Kwanzaa, a holiday observed by some African American families, begins on December 26 and lasts for one week. It was created in 1966 by a man named Maulana Karenga. He designed this holiday that is currently celebrated by more than 18 million people in the United States. He wanted to restore African cultural traditions to the African American people.

The seven principles of Kwanzaa are unity, self-determination, working together, cooperative economics, purpose, creativity and faith.

Kwanzaa which means "fresh fruits," commemorates traditional African harvest festivals.

Celebrations of togethe ness include lighting ca dles called Mishumaas ar drinking from a unity cu called the Kikombe at th final feast. Small gifts, us ally homemade, are give each day. The final festiv concludes on New Year Day.

Here are a few ideas f things to make and do celebrate the holiday Kwanzaa in your classroor

Celebrating
Kwanzaa

Kwanzaa Chains

Decorate the classroom walls, ceiling and a small tree or bush with Kwanzaa chains. C strips of red, green and black construction paper. Glue or staple these strips in a circle ar fasten the circles together in a traditional chain-like fashion. Each child could make a sm section to be connected together as a cooperative activity.

African Animal Puppets

Give each child a brown lunch bag and a large circle cut from construction paper. (The c cle should fit and be glued onto the bottom flap.) Have students choose to make a leo ard, zebra or elephant (common animals in Africa).

For the zebra, paint black and white stripes on the circle. The leopard circle should be ye low with black spots sponge-painted onto the face. The elephant circle should be a shad of gray with a gray paper trunk attached (accordion-pleat a strip of paper). On all puppe cut out eyes, nose and ear shapes from construction paper or felt. Glue on these feature Place your hand in the bag and manipulate the animal figures.

by Tania Kourempis-Cowling

Seven Candles: The Mishumaa Saba

On each night of Kwanzaa, the children and their parents light one of seven candles. Then they discuss one of the seven values of African American family life (as discussed on the previous page). You will need three red candles, three green candles and one black candle. Ask the students to bring in candle holders so you can have seven for your holiday table. Draw a picture of a candle holder and candles, colored the correct colors. Glue and sprinkle gold glitter for each flame.

Nutty Bananas

Two favorite African foods are bananas and peanuts. Make this fun snack in your classroom.

Place a craft stick in each banana and freeze on a tray lined with waxed paper. Melt chocolate morsels in a pot. Dip the banana into the chocolate sauce, and then roll it on a plate of finely chopped peanuts. What a yummy treat!

Gifts

Making homemade gifts is part of the Kwanzaa celebration. Ideas for gifts could be place mats in Kwanzaa colors; a plastic cup (unity cup) decorated with permanent markers or paint; fruits and vegetables of harvest such as apples, oranges, corn and sweet potatoes.

Dance to the Beat of Drums

Make homemade drums in the classroom. Collect empty oatmeal containers or coffee cans. Paint these using Kwanzaa colors and decorate the drums with paints, stickers, glitter, sequins, etc. Tap the drums with an unsharpened pencil.

Your library might have selected recordings of African American music. Play this music and tap to the rhythm of the beat.

Winter Books for Children

The Winter Solstice

Jackson, Ellen. *The Winter Solstice*. Illustrated by Jan Davey Ellis. Millbrook Press.

Children learn what the solstice is and how traditional customs vary throughout many different cultures and times. The book includes an experiment with an orange, a flashlight and a toothpick, as well as an adaptation of a Cherokee solstice tale.

Kwanzaa

Chocolate, Deborah M. Newton. *Kwanzaa*. Illustrated by Melody Rosales. Children's Press.

Colorful pictures illustrate this first-person account of the African celebration, and the story contains specific details on how this holiday is observed.

The Reindeer People

Lewin, Ted. *The Reindeer People*. Written and illustrated by Ted Lewin. Macmillan.

Vivid, beautiful paintings portray the life of the Lapland people above the Arctic Circle.

The Legend of the Poinsettia

De Paola, Tomie. *The Legend of the Poinsettia*. Retold and illustrated by Tomie de Paola. G.P. Putnam's Sons.

In this Mexican legend about a girl's gift to baby Jesus, love transforms weeds into la Flor de Nochebuena—The Flower of the Holy Night.

Crafts for Kwanzaa

Ross, Kathy. *Crafts for Kwanzaa*. Illustrated by Sharon Lane Holm. Millbrook Press.

Teachers will find 20 projects using the symbols of Kwanzaa. A valuable book that can be used along with Chocolate's nonfiction story.

Ralph's Frozen Tale

Primavera, Elixe. *Ralph's Frozen Tale*. Written and illustrated by Elise Primavera. G.P. Putnam's Sons.

When Ralph ventures to the North Pole, he meets a lovable polar bear who helps him on his exploration. A lively and humorous story, children will want to hear it again and again.

An Ellis Island Christmas

Leighton, Maxinne Rhea. *An Ellis Island Christmas*. Illustrated by Dennis Nolan. Penguin.

At the turn of the century, a little girl travels with her family from Poland to America. The first-person narrative is warm and insightful. Krysia's experiences, including her first tastes of a banana, help children experience her adventure.

Miracle Meals

ikler Madeline. and Judyth Groner. *Miracle Meals.* Illustrated by Chari Radin. Kar–Ben.

ght Nights of Food 'n' Fun for anukkah, with recipes, parties and mes. Recipe chapters include soups, kes, dairy, meat, desserts and nks.

o! Ho! Ho! The Complete ok of Christmas Words

aham–Barber, Lynda. *Ho Ho Ho! The Complete Book of Christmas Words.* Illustrated by Betsy Lewin. Bradbury Press.

great collection of fun facts, origins words, the story behind Santa aus and how Christmas is cele-ated around the world. Includes a e line of Christmas and a recipe mince pie. An engaging edition to ve in the classroom.

The Reindeer Christmas

Price, Moe. *The Reindeer Christmas.* Illustrated by Atsuko Morozumi. Gulliver Books.

How did Santa's sleigh come to be? Read this delightful original tale to see Santa advertise for applicants to pull his sleigh. Amusing incidents occur when an elephant, a crocodile, huskies and pigs all audition for the position. Morosumi paints gorgeous watercol-ors to accompany the text. This entertaining read–aloud for young children is on my Christmas list!

Other Notable Books:

The Christmas Wreath

Hoffman, James. *The Christmas Wreath.* Illustrated by Jack Stockman. School Zone.

Children will enjoy the story of how a polar bear accidentally changes a scraggly wreath into a dazzling dis-play of wilderness art.

Morris's Disappearing Bag

Wells, Rosemary. *Morris's Disappearing Bag.* Dial.

Humorous picture book with delightful characters.

The Story of Hanukkah

Ehrlich, Amy and. *The Story of Hanukkah.* Illustrated by Ori Sherman. Penguin.

Well–written text is accompanied by strong, bold paintings.

A Newbery Christmas

Greenberg, Martin H., and Charles G. Waugh. *A Newbery Christmas.* Delacorte Press. Fourteen stories by Newbery–winning authors such as Eleanor Estes, Madeleine L'Engle and Beverly Cleary.

The Twelve Days of Christmas

Illustrated by Jan Brett. *The Twelve Days of Christmas.* G.P. Putnam's Sons.

If you teach your students the song, this book will be a colorful compani-ment.

RUSSIA'S WINTER FESTIVALS

New Year's Day is the most important day of the Russian Winter Festival. The festival is held between December 25 and January 5. There are parties, sports and circus performances. Grandfather Frost wears a red suit and a white beard and gives toys to children on this day. Many children receive matrioska dolls as gifts. They can be opened to show smaller dolls inside. Draw faces and clothes on the matrioska dolls below. Use beautiful markers, crayons or glitter.

Ukranians are known for their beautiful eggs. These eggs are called pysanky. They are decorated with mosaics, triangles, waves and ribbons. Decorate your own egg below using crayons, markers and glitter.

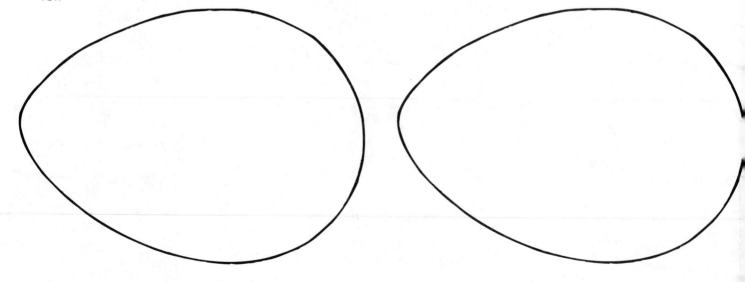

TLC10047 Copyright © Teaching & Learning Company, Carthage, IL 62

A Clean Sweep

In England, people believed an old custom marked the beginning of a new year. Before the arrival of the new year, the English people hired a chimney sweep to clean their chimneys and all the slate on their roofs. This erased all their bad luck so only good luck would prevail in their home. The saying "start with a clean slate" came from this custom.

Discuss chimney sweeps and roof slate with your students. Explain the similarities of roof slate to your classroom chalkboard. We start each school day with a clean slate!

Once this cleaning was done, the English were ready to make their new resolutions. Have your class do the same! Make this broom as a symbol of cleaning your slate roof. Use an empty cardboard tube, like the kind from a roll of paper towels, as the broomstick. Cut paper 1" wide and 5" long. Write your resolutions on each strip of paper. Attach strips to the broom handle with a rubber band. Make a bulletin board with all the brooms titled "Sweep into '97" or "A Clean Sweep to the New Year."

1. Have a chimney sweep visit your class.

2. Draw a map of England for the bulletin board. Use it for the background.

3. Make one big broom for the class resolutions.

by Jo Jo Cavalline and Jo Anne O'Donnell

JANUARY HOLIDAY HAPPENINGS

Hogmanay   Country: Scotland

This important festival in Scotland begins on New Year's Eve (Hogmanay Eve). It is the custom for families to gather for a party to celebrate the new year. Special oatmeal cakes, shortbread and black buns filled with nuts and raisins are favorite party refreshments. After midnight, everyone watches the door to greet the "first-footer" or first person to enter. To ensure good luck, it is believed that the "first-footer" should be a dark-haired man!

Many people in the United States make New Year's resolutions to break old habits or start better ones for the coming year. Write your own New Year's resolution here.

_____

_____

_____

_____

St. Knut's Day   Country: Sweden

Did you know there was a special holiday in Sweden to mark the end of the yuletide season? Every year on January 13th, many Swedes celebrate by taking the decorations off their Christmas trees and having special parties for this occasion. Children enjoy eating the tasty cookie tree ornaments. In earlier times, it was the custom to gather at friends' homes to finish leftover food from the Christmas holidays.

Design your own cookie tree ornament.

by Mary Ellen Switzer

170

EQUAL RIGHTS = EQUALITY

Martin Luther King, Jr. Day   Country: United States

This special national holiday is held to honor the great American leader, Martin Luther King, Jr. Dr. King devoted his life to changing unfair laws and to ensure equal rights for all citizens. In 1964, Dr. King won the Nobel Peace Prize and became the second African American to win this high honor. On this holiday parades, church services and other special events are held all over the country.

If you could plan a special assembly at your school to honor Dr. King, what event would you have? Tell about your ideas below.

_____

_____

_____

_____

EQUALITY = EQUAL RIGHTS

Sapparo Snow Festival   Country: Japan

It's a "winter wonderland" in the city of Sapparo, Japan, every year at the annual Snow Festival. Huge crowds gather to see beautiful sculptures carved from ice and snow. Contests are held for artists to construct these icy masterpieces. The festival has a special theme every year. For example, one year the theme was fairy tales.

Create your own marvelous ice palace. Design an ice castle from your favorite fairy tale.

CHINESE

The Chinese New Year is the most important and festive holiday celebrated by the Chinese people. It is celebrated on the first day of the lunar calendar (with the beginning of the New Moon), anywhere from January 21 to February 19. The color red adorns the houses, a symbol of happiness to the Chinese.

On these pages are several activities you can make with your students to enjoy this festival in the classroom.

LANTERNS

On the fifteenth (last) day of the New Year festival, family members carry a lighted lantern in a parade. The people march alongside friends in a silk and bamboo-covered dragon costume. Make lanterns to decorate the classroom. Fold a 9½" x 11" piece of construction paper in half lengthwise. Draw a line across the paper 1" from the top. Tell the children to cut slits about 1" apart from the fold up to the line. Unfold; curve the lantern around and staple. Attach a paper handle.

PAPER FANS

Cut circles (8" diameter) from poster board. Also, clip small squares of colorful tissue paper. Brush the entire circle with white glue; then place the tissue squares on, overlapping each piece. Make a handle by gluing on two tongue depressors, inserting the circle in between while the glue is wet. It would look nice to decorate both sides of the fan.

BULLETIN BOARD

Cover your board with red construction paper. Write the words GUNG HAY FAT CHOY (Happy New Year). Have the children draw pictures of these animals that correspond with the Chinese zodiac: mouse, cow, tiger, rabbit, dragon, snake, horse, sheep, monkey, rooster, dog and pig.

by Tania Kourempis-Cowling

CHINESE GONG

You will need two disposable aluminum pie pans for each gong. Decorate the pans first with paint, permanent markers or glued-on cut-outs. Ideas for decorations could include Chinese calligraphy, Chinese zodiac animals, dragons or red flowers. Spread a heavy tacky glue all around the plate rims. Place a handful of dried beans or popcorn kernels inside and glue the two pans together. Wait for the glue to dry thoroughly. Poke a hole in the top to thread a ribbon or yarn as a hanger. With the "gong" in hand, walk around the room and hit the metallic chime with the eraser end of a pencil.

DRAGON BAG PUPPET

The Chinese dragon is a symbol of strength and goodness. According to legend, its appearance combines the head of a camel, the horns of a deer, the neck of a snake, the claws of a hawk, the belly of a frog and the scales of a fish. For the young child, an easier version of the dragon would be appropriate as you celebrate this holiday in the classroom.

Make a dragon's face on a brown lunch bag by painting it green, drawing a large red mouth, gluing on large green ears, along with yellow and black eyes. Attach crepe paper streamers in red or orange to the mouth area, representing its fiery breath. Have the child put his hand in the bag to manipulate the puppet's actions.

RED ENVELOPES

Pass out a small white envelope to each child. Have children paint the entire envelope with red tempera paint. Put these away until the class celebration. Place one shiny penny into each child's envelope. Distribute these at the end of the day as a token of good luck.

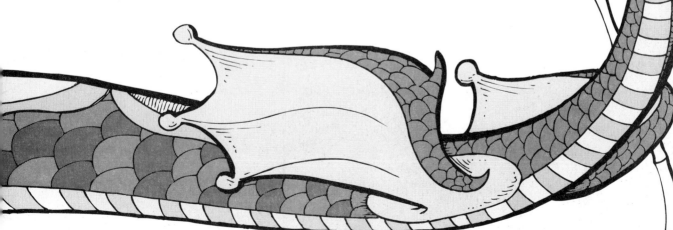

Australia Day

January 26

January 26th is always a special time in Australia—it's Australia Day. This holiday is held to celebrate the anniversary of the arrival of the first British settlers in 1788. On this patriotic day, people gather for special events, including a reenactment of the first landing of settlers. Everyone is proud of their history and culture as they enjoy this holiday. Fireworks light up the night sky as a perfect climax to this exciting day.

Hippity Hop

Connect the dots to make a popular Australian animal.

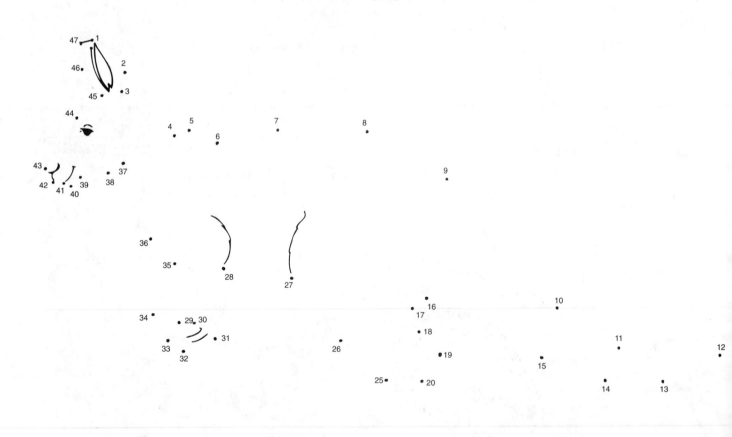

Marvelous Map

This page features Australia. Color the map and draw a circle around Canberra, the capital of Australia.

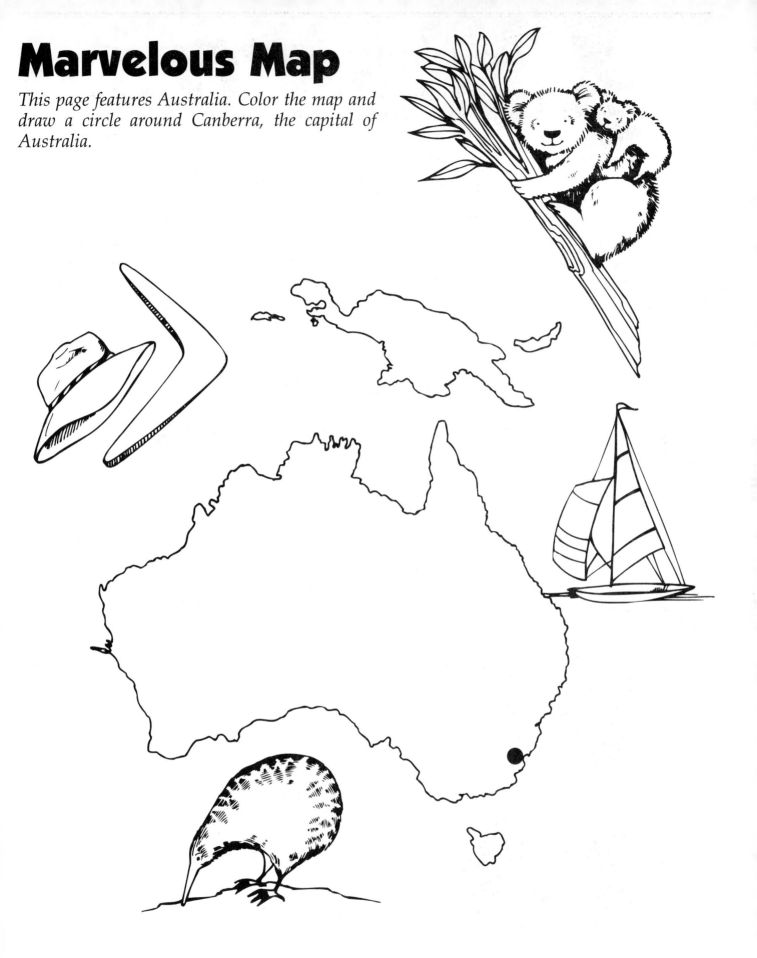

Bonus: On the back of this page, write two facts that you have learned about Australia.

The Magic Suitcase

Calling all tourists! Let's grab our magic suitcase and travel to Australia—the "land down under."

Good day, mates! Today our destination is Australia, home of cuddly koalas and hopping kangaroos. Did you know that Australia is the world's smallest continent, as well as the sixth largest country? There are six states in the Commonwealth of Australia: New South Wales, Victoria, Queensland, South Australia, Western Australia and the island state of Tasmania. Australia is located between the Pacific and the Indian Oceans. The capital of Australia is Canberra.

Some of the useful industries in Australia include textiles, iron, steel, machinery and wood products. Coal, copper, gold and uranium are mined in this country. Food raised in Australia includes wheat, potatoes, rice, apples, grapes, barley and sugarcane.

Write a list or draw pictures of what you would pack in your magic suitcase for a trip to Australia.

Australian Flag

Get your red, white and blue crayons ready. It's time to color the Australian flag. This flag has a dark blue background with the Union Jack located in the upper left-hand corner. The seven-pointed white Commonwealth star appears underneath the Union Jack and five white stars of the Southern Cross constellation are located on the right side of the flag.

Dots and Dashes

Salute Inventor Samuel Morse with Hands-On Mathematics!

The first week in February is National New Idea Week. It's the perfect time for your class to become inventors and to honor great inventors of the past. This year, salute inventor Samuel Morse and the American Morse Code. This code, a system of dots, dashes and spaces, was named for Morse who patented the telegraph in 1840. For many years all telegraph messages and news were sent by Morse code. Although modern methods of communication have replaced the use of the telegraph and the American Morse Code, your class will be delighted to join you on this delightful trip back in time as you re-create Morse code in your mathematics class!

First, display the code on poster board or a large sheet of chart paper. Round, peel-off stickers purchased in a stationery supp[ly] store make ideal dots. Use piec[es] of colorful tape to create dashes, [or] simply draw short, bold lines usi[ng] a thick marker. Explain to yo[ur] class that letters that are used mo[re] frequently in the English langua[ge] were represented by the simple[r] symbols, while more comple[x] combinations represented less po[p]ular letters.

Hands-On Dots and Dashes

Distribute small bowls containing mini marshmallows (dots), 1" pieces of red licorice (dashes) and a few 2" pieces of red licorice (long dashes). Also provide craft sticks to mark where one letter ends and the next letter begins. Now it's time to use the code!

Base 10 Morse Code

Looking for an exciting way to reinforce tens and one[s?] Grab the 10 sticks and unit cubes from your base [10] blocks! Explain to your class that one ten stick will rep[re]sent a short dash, two ten sticks will represent a lo[ng] dash, and one unit cube will represent a dot. Ask t[he] children to form one letter of the alphabet using t[he] base 10 materials and find its value. Together, identi[fy] the letter with the highest value (j:22) and lowest valu[e] (e:1). Send the children on a hunt to find groups of le[t]ters with the same value: b/q/x (13), a/n (11), g/k/[v] (21), i/o/l (2), c/r/s (3), d/f/u (12), j/y/z (4).

Name	Letters	Dots	Dashes
Nancy	5	10	3

Comparing Letters: Invite the children to create one of the letters having: the fewest number of symbols (e, t, l); the greatest number of symbols (p); more dots than dashes (b, d, u, v, x); fewer dots than dashes (g, k, w,); more dashes than dots (g, k, w); fewer dashes than dots (b, d, f, u, v, x); an equal number of dots and dashes (a, j, n); an odd number of dots (a, b, c, e, g, k, n, p, q, r, s, v, w, x); an even number of dots (d, h, i, j, o, u, y, z); an odd number of dashes (a, b, d, f, n, q, t, u, v, x); an even number of dashes (g, j, k, m, w).

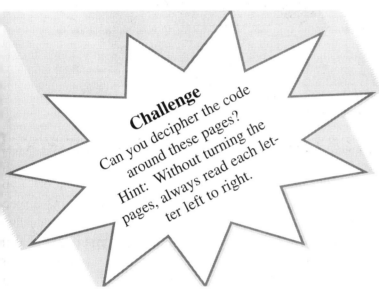

Challenge
Can you decipher the code around these pages? Hint: Without turning the pages, always read each letter left to right.

Comparing Words: Ask the children to write two three-letter words using the code. You may wish to brainstorm possible three-letter words on the chalkboard for the children to refer to. Challenge the children to write an addition equation for each word showing the number of dots and dashes. Invite them to share the equations with the class. Together, identify the equations with: the greatest sum, the smallest sum, an odd sum, an even sum, the most popular sum. Challenge each child to find the difference between the sums of their two equations. Together, compare the differences. Identify the equations with the smallest difference and the greatest difference.

What's in a Name?: Your class will be eager to find out the number of dots and dashes in their names. You may wish to have the class write both their first and last names at the same time, or prefer to begin by working with just their first names. When the writing is complete, display a large piece of chart paper for the children to share their results on. Ask each child to step up to the chart and write the number of letters in their name, as well as the number of dashes and dots needed to write it. (Example: An entry for the name Nancy would read: NANCY—5 letters, 10 dots, 3 dashes.) While the children nibble on a few dots and dashes, ask them to make true statements about the data displayed on the chart. Their statements may range from "Nancy's name used fewer dashes than dots" or "Mark's name used an odd number of dashes" to "Kathy's name and Cindy's name used a sum of 22 dots" or "Richard's name used sixteen more dots than dashes."

Cracking the Code: Is your class becoming Morse masters? Challenge them to create a four-letter word that uses: less than four dots (tall, meat, late, time); more than 10 dots (ripe, push, buzz, very, pony); five dashes (glad, game, jump, know); an odd number of dots (nest, room, took, four). Invite the children to create their own challenges for their classmates to solve.

by Nancy Silva

Clapping the Code

Creating Patterns: Samuel Morse needed the telegraph to send his messages; your class will just need their hands. Ask them to quickly clap their hands together for each dot and to slowly clap their hands against their laps for each dash. Explain that a dash is twice as long as a dot. Since a long dash is twice as long as a short dash, you may wish to demonstrate the difference between clapping the letter *t* and the letter *l*. Ask the children to touch their shoulders once to indicate a space within a letter, as with *c, o, r* and *y,* and twice to show a space between two letters.

Begin by clapping simple patterns such as S T D T D T D T (three dots/one dash) or M H M H M H M H (two dashes/four dots) and progress to more complicated patterns such as P T I T L P T I T L (five dots/one dash/two dots/one dash/one long dash) or I G B M I G B M I G B M (two dots/two dashes/one dot/one dash—three dots/two dashes). Increase or decrease the difficulty depending on the age and ability of your class. Invite a child to clap a simple code while classmates try to decode it.

Clapping Sums and Differences

Review sums and differences using Morse code numerals! Present your class with addition and/or subtraction flash cards having a sum or difference of zero to nine. Invite them to answer by clapping the code. Your class will eagerly respond to the equation 10 - 6 = by clapping dot-dot-dot-dot-dash. Dash-dash-dot-dot will be how they'll reply when you display the flash card 5 + 2 =.

Morse code numerals may also be used to answer questions such as "How old are you?" "How many brothers do you have?" or "How many vowels are in your first name?" Challenge the children to create questions for their classmates that will have an answer of zero to nine. Invite the class to take turns asking and responding.

Alphabet		Numbers	
A	• —	0	—
B	— • • •	1	• — — •
C	• • •	2	• • — • •
D	— • •	3	• • • — •
E	•	4	• • • • —
F	• — •	5	— — —
G	— — •	6	• • • • • •
H	• • • •	7	— — • •
I	• •	8	— • • • •
J	— • • — •	9	• • • • •
K	— • —		
L	—		
M	— —	**Punctuation**	
N	— •	comma	
O	• •	• — • —	
P	• • • • •		
Q	• • — •	period	
R	• • •	• • — • — • •	
S	• • •		
T	—	semicolon	
U	• • —	• • • • •	
V	• • • —	interrogation	
W	• — —	— • • — •	
X	• — • •		
Y	• • • •		
Z	• • • •		

February

February

Though February may be short,
It's filled with special days.
We're always glad to have it come
To celebrate in many ways.

> *(Place February above the flannel board calendar.)*

A sleepy, little groundhog yawns,
He knows that on this day each year
He must look for his shadow and
Let us know if spring is here.

> *(Place groundhog on February 2nd square on the calendar.)*

On Lincoln's birthday we remember
A great man from our country's past,
The President who freed the slaves,
And worked to make our Union last.

> *(Put silhouette of Lincoln on February 12th square.)*

What fun to send, what fun to get,
A lovely, lacy valentine,
And lots of little candy hearts
That say, "Guess Who? Be Mine!"

> *(Put a valentine heart on February 14th square.)*

The President who served first
Was General George Washington,
And on his birthday we have
A holiday for everyone.

> *(Put Washington's silhouette on February 22nd square.)*

The shortest month of all the year
Is one that's sure to please
Because it's filled with special days,
Holidays like these!

> *(Put child's smiling face on flannel board.)*

A Flannel Board Story

Cut-Outs Needed:

1. The word *February* (top of this page)
2. Dated squares for a monthly calendar
3. A groundhog
4. A silhouette of Lincoln
5. A valentine heart
6. A silhouette of Washington
7. A child's smiling face

1	2	3	4	5	6	7
8	9	10	11	12	13	14
15	16	17	18	19	20	21
22	23	24	25	26	27	28
29						

by Phyllis J. Perry

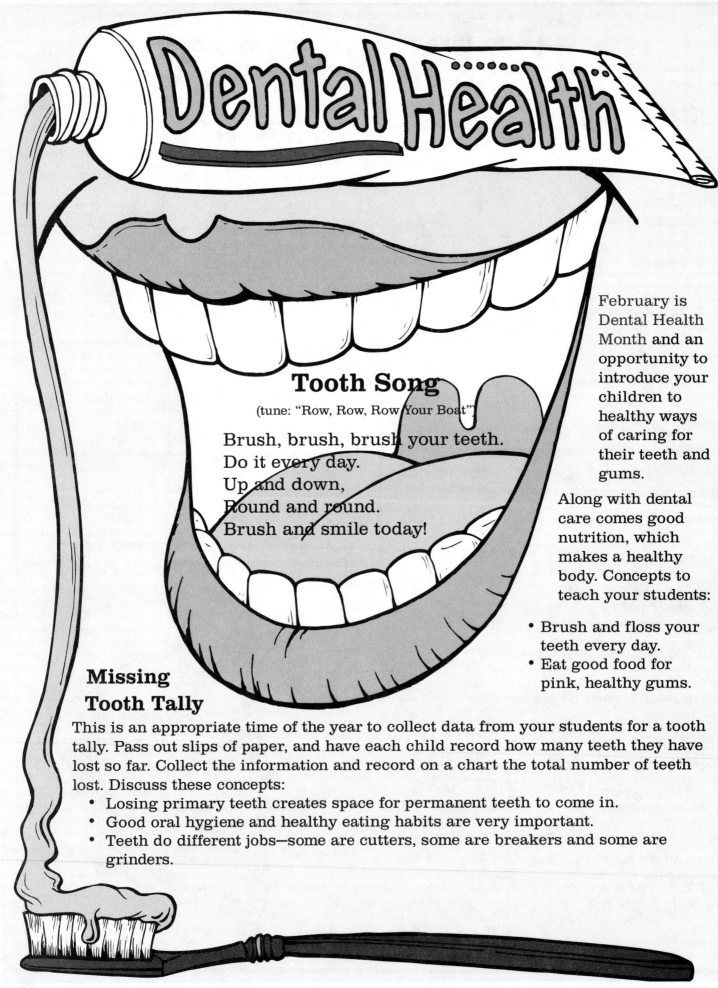

Dental Health

Tooth Song

(tune: "Row, Row, Row Your Boat")

Brush, brush, brush your teeth.
Do it every day.
Up and down,
Round and round.
Brush and smile today!

February is Dental Health Month and an opportunity to introduce your children to healthy ways of caring for their teeth and gums.

Along with dental care comes good nutrition, which makes a healthy body. Concepts to teach your students:

- Brush and floss your teeth every day.
- Eat good food for pink, healthy gums.

Missing Tooth Tally

This is an appropriate time of the year to collect data from your students for a tooth tally. Pass out slips of paper, and have each child record how many teeth they have lost so far. Collect the information and record on a chart the total number of teeth lost. Discuss these concepts:

- Losing primary teeth creates space for permanent teeth to come in.
- Good oral hygiene and healthy eating habits are very important.
- Teeth do different jobs—some are cutters, some are breakers and some are grinders.

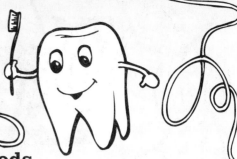

Healthy Bingo

Make cards like Bingo. Instead of using numbers on the cards, glue magazine pictures of healthy foods and snacks. As the caller names a food, the students mark their cards with a piece of popcorn. After the game is over, students can eat their playing pieces.

Sorting Foods

Spend time cutting out pictures of foods from magazines. Ask students to find healthy foods like fruits, vegetables and milk and unhealthy snacks such as candy and soda. Put all these pictures into a large pile. Take two small brown bags and draw a "happy tooth" on one and a "sad tooth" on the other. Together, sort out the pictures and place them in the correct bag according to whether the foods are healthy or not.

Smiles

Draw a mouth shape on red construction paper. Across the middle of each shape, draw a horizontal line. Spread glue across the line and press on white navy beans to represent teeth. Create a "white shiny smile!"

Toothbrush Painting

Cut a large tooth shape from white construction paper. Using old toothbrushes, let students dip them into tempera paint and "brush" the paper tooth. Have students use up and down, back and forth and circular motion strokes as they paint. This art activity is fun and stresses the concepts of proper brushing. Remind the children that these old toothbrushes are not intended to be put into their mouths.

Tooth Card (individual)

Let each child make a round tooth card with their name on it. When the child loses a baby tooth, they can blacken the corresponding tooth on the card Hang all the cards on your classroom wall.

NOTE: The card is more symbolic of the oral cavity than accurate. Its design is conceptual rather than factual.

by Tania Kourempis-Cowling

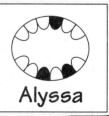

Alyssa

Black *Americans*

Who Had a Dream

Dr. Charles Dre[w]

Benjamin Davis, Sr.

Benjamin Banneker

Marian Anderson

Black Americans have contributed to every field of achievement in our country. Black men fought against the British in the Revolution. As explorers, they traveled with Lewis and Clark. As miners, they dug for gold in California. In Texas, these cowboys rode cattle trails and rounded up stray longhorns. As inventors, they discovered products for a better life for everyone. They have been scientists, entertainers, educators, doctors and ministers. These men and women, often working under great handicaps, have made tremendous contributions to the United States' growth.

During Black History Month, involve your students in various activities to remember these great Americans. Use the following list for several activities as you focus on these famous people.

1 What's My Line?

Ask students to select one name from the list and bring an item from home that provides a clue to the person's contribution to history. For example, a student could bring a baseball for Jackie Robinson, a peanut for George Washington Carver. If the item isn't available, suggest they bring a picture of the object. Display on a table for observation.

2 Hats on Parade

Write a note to parents requesting their child bring a hat that is associated with a famous Black American. For example: baseball cap, cowboy, sailor, soldier, explorer, trader. Plan a parade around your school wearing the hats.

3 T-Shirt Art

Ask each child to bring an inexpensive white T-shirt. Using fabric paint, print the name of a famous Black American on the front. Allow children to experiment with different colors of paint for an original design. Plan a special day for all students to wear their T-shirts.

by Carolyn Ross Tomlin

TLC10047 Copyright © Teaching & Learning Company, Carthage, IL 623[?]

Teacher/Student Activities

Bulletin Board

Caption: "Honoring Black Americans from A to Z "

Display pictures of famous Black Americans and the field in which they are known. If unable to locate pictures, print the name in large letters. Cut out a "cloud" shape and position it above each portrait.

Lewis Latimer

- a. Marian Anderson—music
- b. Crispus Attucks—first American killed in the fight for independence in the Boston Massacre
- c. Benjamin Banneker—compiler of almanacs
- d. James A. Bland—songwriter
- e. George Washington Carver—agriculturist who discovered many uses for the peanut
- f. Alvin A. Coffey—gold miner
- g. Benjamin O. Davis—first Black American general in American history
- h. Dean C. Dixon—musical conductor for major orchestras
- i. Dr. Charles Richard Drew—pioneer in blood research
- j. Jean Baptist Point DuSable—frontier trader
- k. Catherine Ferguson—started the first Sunday School for poor children in New York City
- l. Mary Fields—freight hauler, mail coach driver, laundress
- m. Althea Gibson—tennis star
- n. Matthew Alexander Henson—co-discoverer of the North Pole
- o. Bose Ikard—American cowboy
- p. Percy L. Julian—chemist
- q. Martin Luther King, Jr.—leader of the Civil Rights Movement
- r. Lewis H. Latimer—pioneer in the field of electricity
- s. Thurgood Marshall—first Black American justice of the U.S. Supreme Court
- t. Issac "Ike" Murphy—racing jockey
- u. Jesse Owens—Olympic gold medal winner for track
- v. Rosa Parks—arrested for refusing to give her bus seat to a white man
- w. Bill Pickett—rodeo star
- x. Sidney Poitier—actor
- y. Jackie Robinson—baseball player
- z. Booker T. Washington—educator

Martin Luther King, Jr.

Footprints of History

Invite students to select a famous Black American and print their name on a footprint. In a reading center, collect a group of books on African Americans. Tape all the footprints in a line leading to the center.

Jesse Owens

Storytelling Festival

Invite parents and community helpers to your school to read stories about Black Americans. Ask each reader to dress in the character of the story, using a piece of clothing appropriate to the period of history or the person's contribution. Display books on African American culture in a book center.

Booker T. Washington

Martin Luther King, Jr. Day

*D*r. Martin Luther King, Jr. was born on January 15, 1929. He grew up with his family in Atlanta, Georgia. He was a very intelligent man who furthered his education with a doctorate degree and became the minister of a Baptist Church in Montgomery, Alabama. He was a man who was moved by Gandhi's belief in "equal rights for all people" and was also influenced by Thoreau's essay, "On Civil Disobedience."

*T*his holiday is a good time to help your students understand and appreciate the differences among all people. It's a time to help the children comprehend distinctions between races and cultures. Encourage them to notice all the ways in which they are alike and different—hair color, skin color, eyes, height, shape and so on.

*D*r. King believed in nonviolence. He organized many marches so that people could gather and make their point in a nonviolent way. In 1963, he led the famous "March on Washington." This march ended at the Lincoln Memorial where he gave his famous "I Have a Dream" speech to thousands of people who marched along with him. He was awarded the Nobel Peace Prize in 1964. Under his leadership, progress in African American civil rights led to equal education and equal opportunity for jobs.

*M*artin Luther King, Jr. was assassinated on April 4, 1968, in Memphis, Tennessee. The United States celebrates a holiday in his honor on the third Monday in January. On the following page are a few activities to use in your classroom. These exercises increase a child's self-esteem and awareness of others.

REDEEM THE AMERICAN PROMISE LIFE LIBERTY HAPPINESS FOR ALL

REDEEM THE AMERICAN PROMISE LIFE, LIBERTY, HAPPINESS FOR ALL

EMERGENCY WELFARE SERVICE

ALL Rights For ALL People

Friendship Booklet

Staple five small sheets of paper together in booklet form (one booklet for each student). Cut out each child's silhouette from orange, yellow, white, brown and red paper. Paste one cut-out on each page. Discuss with the children the skin colors and what cultures they represent. On each silhouette, print one word: *friendship, joy, trust, love*. Place the orange cut-out on the cover and title the book *Hand in Hand*.

Hand and Footprints

Using two different colors of tempera paints, spread a thin layer on the child's hand and on a bare foot. Press the prints onto white paper. Label the page with the child's name. Hang these around the classroom and have the children notice differences between sizes and shapes.

Pictures Are Perfect

A photograph of each child hung on a bulletin board makes them feel special. Pictures of children from other countries help the class become culturally aware.

Languages

Many classrooms have children from other countries. It is a great listening activity to hear another language spoken. Ask students and parents to come into class and teach a few simple words or an easy song. Always make copies of these words or songs for the child to take home to share with their family.

March

Obtain a copy of Dr. King's "I Have a Dream" speech. It is slightly overpowering for the young child; however, a few simple phrases could be discussed with the children. Organize the children in a line and march across the room chanting the phrase "We shall overcome," used during the historic marches many years ago.

I Have a Dream . . .

So I say to you, my friends, that even though we must face the difficulties of today and tomorrow, I still have a dream. It is a dream deeply rooted in the American dream that one day this nation will rise up and live out the true meaning of its creed—we hold these truths to be self-evident, that all men are created equal.

by Tania Kourempis-Cowling

Groundhog Day

When February rolls around
    With winter winds and snow,
When an icy chill is in the air
    And I'm cold from head to toe,

It's nice to think of Groundhog Day
    When people tell us tales
Of a furry little animal
    Who never, ever fails

To pop out of his cozy den
    On February Two.
(I'm quite surprised. I'd stay indoors
    With better things to do

Than watch to see if the morning sun
    Was rising in the east,
And if I saw the shadow of
    A rather sleepy beast!)

I also wonder what they'd say
    If on this special date,
That groundhog turned off his alarm
    And chose to hibernate.

Then how would we know if spring was near
    Or if wild winds would blow
To bring us six more weeks of chill
    With storms of ice and snow?

I surely hope that furry beast
    Will keep his weather date.
We've had enough of winter now—
    It's time to celebrate!

by Jean Conder Soule

Groundhog & Friends

Spark your students' enthusiasm for Groundhog Day on February 2nd with these motivating holiday activities. According to legend, if the groundhog comes out on this day and sees his shadow, winter will last six weeks longer.

Set the stage for this holiday by reading *It's Groundhog Day* by Steven Kroll (New York: Holiday House, 1987). This entertaining story tells about Roland Raccoon's attempts to prevent Godfrey Groundhog from looking for his shadow on Groundhog Day. It seems that the sly raccoon is afraid that an early spring might ruin his ski lodge business.

Groundhog & Friends Weather Kit

Celebrate Groundhog Day with your class by giving each student their "official" weather kit for February 2nd. First, ask your students to decorate their Groundhog Day Weather Forecaster's Badge. Next, have them color and cut out the groundhog puppets and glue them to craft sticks. After that, discuss the weather report for February 2nd from your local newspaper. You may want to write the main facts on the board. Have the students decide whether or not the groundhog will see his shadow based on the newspaper report. Finally, ask your students to fill in their own "Groundhog Day Weather Station" reports.

Now it's time for your students to write a television weather news script and Greta Groundhog's Animal Report about an animal that hibernates in winter.

Hooray for groundhogs! Treat your class to a party to celebrate Groundhog Day. Have your students feast on animal cookies and punch while sharing their groundhog activities with the class!

by Mary Ellen Switzer

Groundhog & Friends Weather Kit

Gary G. Groundhog   Greta Groundho[g]

_____
(name)

Groundhog Day
Weather Forecaster's Badge

Color and cut out puppets. Glue them on craft sticks.
Write or tell a story about Gary and Greta.

Groundhog Day
Weather Station

Date: _____

By: _____
   Weather Forecaster's Name

Groundhog Day Weather Report

_____
_____
_____
_____
_____
_____
_____

Groundhog & Friends Weather Kit

Be a TV News Star!

Draw your picture.

Today's weather is brought to you by: _____

Write a television weather news report telling about your Groundhog Day weather report.

Weather News Flash!

_____

_____

_____

_____

_____

_____

_____

_____

_____

_____

_____

_____

Greta Groundhog's Animal Report

Brrr . . . When winter comes, Gary and Greta and their other animal friends hibernate for the seaso Choose another animal that hibernates and find out all about it. Use an encyclopedia and other re erence books to help. Write your facts below.

Greta Groundhog's Animal Report

Name of animal: _____

Where this animal lives: _____

What it eats: _____

Write two facts about this animal.

1. _____

   _____

   _____

2. _____

   _____

   _____

Draw a picture of this animal.

Be My Valentine

Try something different this year for Valentine's Day. Instead of having children exchange valentines with each other, let them make valentines for all the people who help to make their school days enjoyable. These might include bus drivers, cafeteria workers, classroom aides, crossing guards, playground aides, secretaries, special teachers, volunteers and your principal.

Cut a large circle (at least 15" in diameter) from white butcher paper. Fold it into quarters, then fold again into eighths. Cut half a heart by rounding off the corners.

Open up your circle. Draw lines to delineate four hearts.

Let four children take turns decorating the valentine (each doing one heart). Have them sign their art. Other children will decorate other valentines.

When all the valentines are finished, turn them over and print the recipient's name on each one. Then have everyone, including you, sign each valentine on the undecorated side.

Before delivering, refold each one into a heart.

Valentine

I know it isn't fancy,
And it's really rather small.
It doesn't have bright flowers—
Or any kind at all.
It doesn't have a border
Of silver, gold or lace.
But I can make it pretty
With a happy, smiley face.
Then I'll write a message
And add a heart or two.
I hope that you will like it.
My valentine to you.

by Mabel Duch

Hearts Are Falling

"Hearts are falling from above—
Hearts so red and full of love—
Some are big and some are small—
But there is lots of love in all!"

Seven-year-old Audrey cheerfully sang her specially made-up Valentine's Day song as she smoothed out her bed. Valentine's Day was just three days away, and Audrey didn't feel ready at all.

"Valentine's Day is supposed to be about love," thought Audrey. Her teacher had shared the story of St. Valentine, who had died on February the 14th, many hundreds of years earlier. St. Valentine believed that people should be kind and loving, and so did Audrey. The only problem was that she did not have a valentine's gift to give her Granny Annie, the most special person in Audrey's life.

"Ever since I came to live with Granny Annie, she has made me feel special. Now what can I do for her?" Audrey asked this important question to Raggamuff, her favorite handmade rag doll. But Raggamuff just smiled. Audrey placed Raggamuff on the neatly made bed and began another round of her song.

> *"Hearts are falling from above—*
> *Hearts so red and full of love—*
> *Some are big and some are small—*
> *But there is lots of love in all!"*

Finishing the song, Audrey skipped into the kitchen and hugged Granny Annie, who was taking a pan of biscuits out of the oven.

"Morning, Granny Annie!" said Audrey.

"Morning to you, precious girl," and Granny Annie returned the hug. "What's that I heard you singing?"

"Just a little song I made up," said Audrey, as she reached for a hot biscuit.

"Sounds like a pretty little tune," Granny Annie replied.

After breakfast, Audrey walked to school with her neighbor, Laura Lee. "What will you give your granny for Valentine's Day?" Laura Lee asked Audrey.

"Don't know yet," answered Audrey.

"My daddy is going to take me to Shopping City this evening, and let me pick out silver pierced earrings for Mama. She got her ears pierced when she was 12, you know, and I'm gonna do my ears when I'm 12, too!"

Laura Lee finished her speech with a big nod, and Audrey nodded in agreement. Pierced earrings seemed like a wonderful gift, but they would cost lots of money. Laura Lee's daddy worked at the paper mill, and he made a good wage. That's what everybody said.

"Audrey! Watch out for that tree root. You're not paying attention," Laura Lee warned.

"You're right," replied Audrey. "But I'm worried about Valentine's Day. I want to do something special for Granny Annie. She's like a mama and a daddy to me. She deserves two presents if I could get them."

"Don't worry so much" Laura Lee patted her friend's arm. "My mama says you're smart as a whip. You'll think of something."

In school that day, Mr. Washington, their teacher, gave a lesson on ways to say "I love you" in other languages. Since Valentine's Day was just three days away, it seemed like a good idea.

"Je t'aime," said Mr. Washington. "That means 'I love you' in the French language." The class chanted: "Je t'aime!"

"Lo ti amo," said Mr. Washington. "That means 'I love you' in the Italian language." "Lo ti amo," everybody shouted.

"This is my favorite," added Mr. Washington. "*Yo te amo* means 'I love you' in the Spanish language."

"Yo te amo, Mr. Washington," said the second graders, and Mr. Washington smiled.

That afternoon, after school, Audrey walked home and opened the door with her key. Granny Annie would be home in an hour, after she finished her shift at the nursing home. Granny Annie was a licensed practical nurse, and the old folks at the Golden Pines Resort Home loved Granny Annie. Last year at Valentine's Day, sev-eral of the folks had given Granny Annie boxes of chocolate-covered cherries and a gift certificate from Shopping City. Of course, Granny Annie used the gift certificate to buy Audrey a pair of new school shoes. "You should buy something for yourself," Audrey had told her.

"Oh, I will," said Granny Annie, and she picked up a pair of white stockings for work.

Audrey sat down to do her homework. She reached for a leftover breakfast biscuit and drizzled some honey on it. "If only I could give Granny Annie something as sweet as this honey," thought Audrey. "Then she would know for sure how much I love her."

Licking the honey from her fingers, Audrey got a wonderful idea. She washed her hands and pulled out her tin of crayons. Then she looked in the desk drawer, where Granny Annie kept wrapping paper and writing things. There it was . . . the lacy white doily that had been nestled under the box of chocolate-covered cherries. Granny Annie saved everything.

With the lacy white doily as a background, Audrey created a special Valentine's card for Granny. She drew plump, smiling honeybees, buzzing around a picture of her and her granny that had been hanging on the refrigerator. Mr. Washington had taken the picture of Audrey and her granny when they attended the Christmas play. He took pictures of all the children and their families, and then sent them in the mail inside a Christmas card.

"Now for the writing," Audrey mused. "What should I say about Granny Annie?" This is what she wrote:

> *"Hearts are falling from above—*
> *Hearts so red and full of love—*
> *Some are big and some are small—*
> *But there is lots of love in all!"*

She signed her name: Love, Audrey.

On Valentine's Day, Audrey skipped into the kitchen with the card hidden behind her back. Granny Annie was carefully placing heart-shaped cookies into a white box lined with paper.

The cookies were a treat for Audrey's clas[s] Granny Annie wrapped a big, special cookie f[or] Mr. Washington.

"Happy Valentine's Day, Granny Annie!" shoute[d] Audrey. Granny Annie sat down at the table an[d] pulled on her reading glasses. She careful[ly] inspected the card. "The honeybees are swarmin[g] because you're as sweet as honey," Audr[ey] explained.

"It's too beautiful for words," sighed Grann[y] Annie. "Listen to this verse. My precious girl is [a] poet!" And Granny Annie read the poem aloud:

> *"Hearts are falling from above—*
> *Hearts so red and full of love—*
> *Some are big and some are small—*
> *But there is lots of love in all!"*

"If I had a dozen hearts, I couldn't love you a[ny] better, Granny Annie," said Audrey.

"That's my precious girl," replied Granny Anni[e] and they looked at the card for a long time.

by Dr. Linda Karges-Bone

Activities for "Hearts Are Falling"

Language Enrichment

1. After reading the story aloud, ask children to list all the free, creative ways that Audrey could make a gift for Granny Annie. Use chart paper and red, scented markers for the children to write their responses.

2. Create an acrostic poem as a class using the letters in the word LOVE to describe characteristics of loving relationships with friends and family.

3. Use sentence strips to complete this sentence: "I can show love and kindness by . . . ." Place the sentence strips in a display that forms a large heart shape.

4. Read aloud from Jack Prelutsky's humorous collection of Valentine's Day poetry, *It's Valentine's Day*. (Greenwillow Books, 1983). Create humorous valentine verses of your own and compile the verses in a big book.

5. Use words from the story "Hearts Are Falling" in the weekly spelling lesson. Words to choose for grades 2-3: *valentines, biscuit, heart, love, special, cookie, honey, handmade*.

Math and Logic Enrichment

1. Use red and white Unifix™ cubes to make a graph of whether children prefer honey or butter on their biscuits. Compare the results.

2. Fill a jelly jar with confection hearts or red cinnamon candies. Have children estimate the number of candies in the jar. Ask them to write their estimates and their names on a red heart and pin the hearts to a bulletin board. On Valentine's Day, count the candies together, and discuss the results of the estimating activity.

3. Empty the hearts into paper cups. Give a full cup of hearts to each group of four children. Have the cooperative groups figure out ways to divide the hearts in their cup into equal portions. Ask them to write number sentences about their solutions.
(For example: 26 hearts divided into 4 parts gives us 6 hearts each and 2 hearts left over.)

4. Hearty Math Game: Pull all of the "hearts" out of a deck of cards. Use the hearts to practice number facts. Place the four of hearts and the five of hearts on the table, then quickly turn them facedown. Have the children write the sum on a mini chalkboard. (Small group activity: 4-6 students at a time.)

5. Use the heart cards to add groups of numbers: 4 plus 6 plus 3 equals _____. Children can do this game with a partner and check their results with a calculator.

Creative Arts Enrichment

1. Set up a card-making center with lace doilies, glue, glitter, paper, markers and stickers. Encourage children to create their own Valentine's Day cards or invitations to the Valentine's Day Tea (see #4 below).

2. Use heart-shaped sponges and red and pink paint to decorate small flowerpots for gifts. Ask a local hardware store or business partner to donate the flowerpots.

3. Fold tissue paper flowers to place into the sponge-painted flowerpots.

4. Roll out tubes of sugar cookie dough and give the children heart-shaped cookie cutters and assorted decorations to make valentine cookies. Make enough to invite a loved one to Valentine's Day Tea. You can make the tea an opportunity to invite a parent or grandparent to school or a time to bring a favorite stuffed doll or stuffed bear to school for sharing time!

A Party with *Heart*

Valentine's Day, February 14th, is not a legal nor a religious holiday, yet it is widely celebrated in the United States.

Its origin is very old, dating back to ancient Rome where sweethearts were chosen during a festival called *Lupercalia*. Young people drew names from a box and exchanged gifts. This old custom has emerged into traditional Valentine's Day when people tell others how much they care about them. Love and friendship can be expressed in many ways other than gifts. Examples are sharing, helping, talking and playing with each other in kind ways. On this page and the following are a few ideas to include in your next classroom party.

Halved Hearts

As your students arrive in the classroom, give them a "half" cut from a commercial valentine card. When all the children are present, have them mingle to find the matching half of their card. These two children will become partners in a project or activity assigned by the teacher. This is a good way to make new friends!

Valentine Centerpiece

A great table centerpiece or decoration for the teacher's desk can be made by inverting a colander and sticking red lollipops into each hole. Tie pink and white ribbons or yarn around the sticks.

Lacy Ice Cream Dessert

Place a scoop of vanilla ice cream into a plastic dish. Drape a lacy doily over the mound and sprinkle dry cocoa on top. Remove the doily and you will have a fancy lace treat with a chocolate flavor.

by Tania Kourempis-Cowling

Pizza Hearts

Order a pizza, but ask the baker not to cut it into slices. Instead, use a heart-shaped cookie cutter to make as many mini heart pizzas as possible. Serve with fruity heart punch.

Heartthrob Rock

Do this dance using the music for the "Bunny Hop." Find an instrumental recording or sing to this tune.

Step out to the left,
Step out to the right,
Then jump, jump, jump,
To the "Heartthrob" rock.

"By Hand" Decorations

Lay your hand down on red construction paper and trace around it. Using one end of an opened paper clip, poke holes along the outline. Years ago people used pins and needles to prick holes, making cards and decorations that had the appearance of lace.

NOTE: You could draw a heart shape instead of the hand!

Carnation Science

Purchase white carnations from a local florist. Slice off a piece from the bottom of the stems. Place the flowers in a jar or vase filled with water and a dark shade of red food coloring. In time, the flowers will absorb the color through the stem, and the carnations will turn a beautiful shade of pink. These flowers are lovely to decorate with and to teach a science lesson, also!

Which Friend Is Missing?

Have students hide their eyes as the teacher taps one child on the shoulder. That child quietly tiptoes out of the room. The teacher then asks the class, "Which friend is missing?" as the students guess who is gone. Repeat the game, sending out two or three children at a time to make the game slightly difficult.

Fruity Heart Punch

Mix one large can of unsweetened pineapple juice, six cups of water and one package of tropical fruit punch soft drink mix. Stir well. Prior to the party, freeze maraschino cherries into each section of several ice cube trays. Place a "cherried" ice cube into a clear cup and add this delicious punch.

Valentine Activities
for Kids

Here are some activities and gifts your children will enjoy doing and making that utilize items you probably have around the house. The gifts will be appreciated as they will have a personal touch, and they will help children develop creativity, awareness and practice recycling. Just pick some projects and enjoy the fun. If you are a leader of a children's group, they may be just what you need.

by Carol Smallwood

An empty box suitable for a wastebasket can result in an attractive gift. Have your child cover it with cut-out pictures, messages and drawings of their own. Covering it with clear plastic paper will make it useful for many years.

Old valentines can be spread out and children can play I Spy. Have one child look at the valentines and choose one object to focus on. He or she can name that object by saying, "I spy an angel." The other students try to find the picture in the question.

Have children arrange old valentines in alphabetical order by the name of the company that made them. Then challenge them to arrange the valentines by price if indicated on the back or by UPC symbol numbers. Exercises in math can develop by using numbers in different ways children can think of.

Valentine's Day is a perfect time for personalized cards. Give your children some garden and flower catalogs and magazines, pink or red construction paper, scissors, glue, scraps of ribbon or yarn and a pencil. Use envelopes from any type of greeting card previously received in good condition—names can be covered with decorations.

Ask children to look at some old valentines or use new ones to list and categorize words or objects they see according to letters of the alphabet: under H—heart, happy, have or under L—lace, love, lasting.

See how many words children can make by using the letters found in valentine. For example: ant, tale, nine. This is a good timed activity (try 3 minutes) to do with friends. It can also be done with words associated with Valentine's Day such as: flowers, February, heart, friend.

Have children try writing messages using extra words, and have their friends figure them out such as: Happy apple number Valentine's with dry Day France to order Arizona coupon you care. After crossing out the extra words the message would read: Happy Valentine's Day to you. Or make fill-ins such as: __e m__ f__ie__d (be my friend)

Children can do story fill-ins such as: Mary was very _____, because _____ didn't have a good _____ to send _____ to. valentine _____ to. (Possible answer could be: Mary was very sad, because she didn't have a good friend to send a valentine card to.) This is fun when other children also do it and then make comparisons. They could make fill-ins to give to people in hospitals or nursing homes in decorated old cards.

Have children cut out a side of a box to make a "movie screen." Then tape a series of valentines side by side to pull through the cut-out space. A mini screen could be an envelope with the center part cut out. Or a stand-up, accordion-style multipanel card could be made by taping valentines or pictures together.

Try a cryptogram like:

OJLS YGJJEQJ, DLVVB CLWJFEQFJ'Y OLB EP BPA! ULB QE TJ EDJ TJYE PFJ. WPCJ, RAVQO

Answer Key: *Dear Sweetie, Happy Valentine's Day to you! May it be the best one. Love, Cupid*

A B C D E F G H I J L M N O P R S T U V W X Y

L T R O J K M D Q X W U F P V S Y E A C G Z B

Kids will love making up different keys and messages. Numbers can be used instead of letters.

Use old valentines (or use those not sent out yet) to have children develop organizational skills by giving them a collection and having them make a chart showing such things as: name of manufacturer, UPC number, number of words used, size, how many times certain words like *love* appear, colors used. Provide a ruler, paper and pencil. If they are doing this with some other children, they can see who can think of the most comparisons.

Make heart-shaped seed collages from kidney beans, colored popcorn and other seeds that look like valentine colors. Cardboard or scraps of wood may be used as background and covered or painted before seeds are glued on.

Have children think of gifts they can make from small seashells, pinecones and pebbles. Covering a can with these after applying red or pink paper will make a great pencil and pen holder for a desk. Lining it with adhesive plastic paper will add to its usefulness and appearance.

Old valentines can be used to make puzzles. Have children glue them to stiff paper and cut into pieces. To give as gifts, decorate a box or envelope to put the puzzle in with bits of paper arranged in the shape of a heart like a mosaic. Gum wrappers that have foil can be cut or punched with a paper punch to make various designs or letters. Rebus-type messages can be made by cutting out pictures or words from the valentines—for example, the picture of an eye would mean "I."

Gift booklets may be made from folded sheets held together with shoelaces, string or ribbon. They may hold whatever the child wants, such as pictures or poems. Encourage children to look in reference books and write down interesting facts about how Valentine's Day started, when cards were first sent, why it is called Valentine's Day, who Cupid is and why he has arrows. They can use short quotations or poems about love and friendship.

A Valentine Book Nook

Treat your students to our exciting array of valentine book surprises. Set the stage with some zany holiday poems from *It's Valentine's Day* by Jack Prelutsky (New York: Greenwillow Books, 1983). Your students will love this collection of entertaining poetry, including such hits as "Jelly Loves Weasel Will" and "I Made My Dog a Valentine." *Good Morning to You, Valentine* is a variety of holiday poems selected by Lee Bennett Hopkins (New York: Harcourt, Brace, Jovanovich, 1976). "If I Were a Mailman" and "Snowman's Valentine" are two of the selections in the book. Have your students create their own Valentine's Day poems and make a class poetry book.

Lights, Cameras, Action! Put your budding young actresses and actors to work performing in seasonal plays. *The Valentine Box* by Marjorie Mayer (Chicago: Childrens Press, 1977) is a book in drama form that is sure to be a big hit with your class. Have your students make props and design a set for this production. "Good Day Giant," a short Valentine's Day play for two actors, can be found in *Small Plays for Special Days* by Sue Alexander (New York: Clarion Books 1977).

A Valentine Fantasy

Haywood, Caroline. *A Valentine Fantasy.* New York: William Morrow & Company, 1976.

Your class will love this whimsical holiday fable about how Valentine's Day originated. Travel back to medieval times, as a young boy named Valentine is faced with a terrible dilemma. He has been directed to bring in the bluebird's golden heart to the king, in order for the king to marry a princess. When Valentine refuses the king's command, the tiny bluebird comes to his rescue.

❤ Here's how it all started! Write your own fable about how Valentine's Day began.

❤ How do you think Valentine's Day will be celebrated in the future? Draw a picture of a Valentine's Day party in the year 2050.

❤ Puppets, please! Make stick puppets of the main characters in this book, and write the dialogue of the story. Invite another class to see your puppet performance.

A Great Big Valentine

Hoban, Lillian. *A Great Big Valentine.* New York: HarperTrophy, 1989.

Arthur just can't seem to get into the Valentine's Day spirit! He and his good friend Norman are mad at each other. Will they be able to patch things up in time to celebrate Valentine's Day?

❤ In the story, Arthur made a special valentine in the snow. Draw a picture of a snowy valentine for your best friend.

❤ Valentine's Day is a time for friendship and sharing. Create a picture booklet called "My Special Friend." On each page, draw a picture of something you enjoy doing with your friend.

❤ Design a trophy in honor of your best friend.

❤ If you could have a Valentine's Day party for your special friends, who would you invite? Draw a picture of the food you would serve and write a list of the games you would play.

by Mary Ellen Switzer

Will You Be My Valentine?

Kroll, Steven, *Will You Be My Valentine?* New York: Holiday House, 1993.

Uh oh! Thomas picked Gretchen's name in the class Valentine's Day drawing. There's one big problem—she doesn't seem to like Thomas and won't play with him at school. Thomas' mom invites Gretchen to their house to see if she and Thomas can become better friends. Will his mom's plan work?

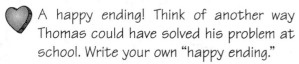 A happy ending! Think of another way Thomas could have solved his problem at school. Write your own "happy ending."

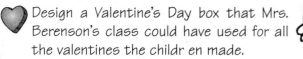 Design a Valentine's Day box that Mrs. Berenson's class could have used for all the valentines the children made.

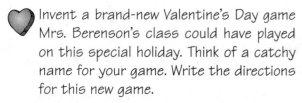 Invent a brand-new Valentine's Day game Mrs. Berenson's class could have played on this special holiday. Think of a catchy name for your game. Write the directions for this new game.

A Valentine for Cousin Archie

Williams, Barbara, *A Valentine for Cousin Archie.* New York: E.P. Dutton, 1981.

When Cousin Archie receives a strange anonymous valentine, he decides that it must be from the Widow Cottontail. He, in turn, sends her an unsigned valentine and begins one of the funniest valentine exchanges ever!

 Retell the story from Chester's point of view.

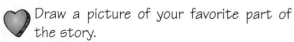 Draw a picture of your favorite part of the story.

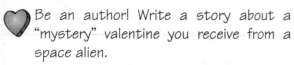 Be an author! Write a story about a "mystery" valentine you receive from a space alien.

Secret Valentine

Stock, Catherine. *Secret Valentine.* New Yo[rk]: Bradbury Press, 1991.

A child is busy making valentines to send, a[nd] decides to make a special one for the lonely [old] lady who lives next door. When Valentine's D[ay] arrives, the child is surprised by a beauti[ful] "secret" valentine.

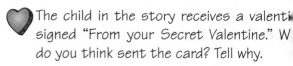 The child in the story receives a valenti[ne] signed "From your Secret Valentine." W[ho] do you think sent the card? Tell why.

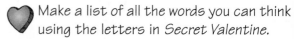 Make a list of all the words you can think [of] using the letters in *Secret Valentine.*

Design a bookmark to "advertise" th[is] valentine book.

A Valentine for Ms. Vanilla

Ehrlich, Fred. *A Valentine for Ms. Vanilla.* N[ew] York: Puffin Books, 1991.

Join Ms. Vanilla's class as they get ready f[or] their Valentine's Day party. Your class will chuc[k]le as Ms. Vanilla's students share their humo[r]ous valentines at the party. Surprise! There['s] even a valentine for Ms. Vanilla.

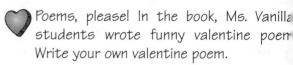 Poems, please! In the book, Ms. Vanilla['s] students wrote funny valentine poem[s]. Write your own valentine poem.

Think of a new Valentine's Day treat—wi[th] a vanilla flavor, of course! Draw a picture [of] your new concoction and tell how it [is] made.

Move over, Ms. Vanilla! There's a ne[w] teacher at school called Ms. Chocolat[e]. Design a valentine for her with a chocola[te] theme.

After sharing this valentine book with yo[ur] class, plan to serve vanilla refreshments a[s] a special treat. You could serve a variety [of] vanilla cookies or maybe even whip up [a] batch of vanilla pudding. Here's think[ing] vanilla!

Valentine Heartgram

Calling all book lovers! Choose a book that you enjoyed and would recommend to others. Write a heartgram message telling about your book.

Name of Book: _____

Author: _____

Message: (Write what you liked best about this book.)

_____

_____

_____

_____

_____

Heartgram sent by: _____

Be Mine, Dear Valentine!

Create a valentine for your favorite book character in this heart!

HOORAY FOR
PRESIDENTS' DAY

Strike up the band . . . it's Presidents' Day! The United States celebrates Presidents' Day on the third Monday in February to honor two of America's greatest Presidents—George Washington and Abraham Lincoln. Celebrate this holiday with your class by using the following array of activities.

Let's Plan a Party!

Plan a special Presidents' Day celebration party for your class. Ask your students to design a place mat for the party with a patriotic theme using red, white and blue crayons. Delight your youngsters with Teddy's (Roosevelt) bear treats (bear-shaped cookies or crackers) and George Washington's "cheery cherry" pie and punch.

Read All About It!

*Set the stage by reading to your class **A Picture Book of George Washington** and **A Picture Book of Abraham Lincoln** by David A. Adler (New York: Holiday House). Your students will get a firsthand look at the interesting lives of those two famous Presidents. The appealing, colorful illustrations add to the enjoyment of these books.*

*Delight your students with another read-aloud favorite—**Arthur Meets the President** by Marc Brown (Boston: Little, Brown and Company). When Arthur wins the "How I Can Make America Great" essay contest, he is invited to a special ceremony at the White House. Join Arthur on his trip to meet the President!*

Presidents on Parade Fan Club

- *Design a Celebrate Presidents' Day badge.*

- *Imagine that you are President of the United States. What would you do to help endangered animals in the United States?*

- *What do you think would be the best thing about being President of the United States?*

- *What would you like least about being the President?*

- *Ask three classmates or relatives this question: Who is your favorite United States President and why?*

- *Congratulations! You plan to run for President of the United States. Design a campaign poster that you would use to tell about yourself.*

- *Write two sentences telling why people should vote for you!*

- *Draw a picture of the special jet airplane that you would use as President.*

- *Make a list of all the words you can think of using the letters in **Presidents***

- *Voters put their choices for the candidates on ballots and drop them in a ballot box. Design a ballot box that would encourage everyone to vote.*

Presidents' Day Book Nook

Here is a list of books to enhance your Presidents' Day celebration.

by Mary Ellen Switzer

Abe Lincoln's Hat
by Martha Brenner
New York: Random House, 1994

True Stories About Abraham Lincoln
by Ruth Belov Gross
New York: Lothrop, Lee & Shepard
    Books, 1973

Abraham Lincoln for the People
by Anne Colver
New York: Chelsea Juniors, 1992

George Washington:
First President of the United States
by Carol Greene
Chicago: Childrens Press, 1991

George Washington:
A Picture Book Biography
by James Cross Giblin
New York: Scholastic, Inc., 1992

George Washington's
Breakfast
by Jean Fritz
New York: Coward-McCann, Inc., 1969

Martha Washington:
First Lady of the Land
by Lavere Anderson
New York: Chelsea Juniors, 1991

Marvelous Monument Dot-to-Dot

Connect the dots in the picture below and create the famous monument built to honor George Washington. Did you know that more than one million people visit the Washington Monument every year? This popular landmark is located in Washington, D.C., near the Potomac River. It measures 555 feet, 5$\frac{1}{8}$" high. If you ride the elevator to the top, you can get a wonderful view of the city.

Lincoln Memorial Puzzle

Tourists flock to another popular landmark when visiting Washington, D.C.—the Lincoln Memorial, also located near the banks of the Potomac River. This beautiful memorial was built in honor of Abraham Lincoln, the 16th President of the United States. One of the highlights of this memorial is the huge statue of a seated Abraham Lincoln.

Cut out the puzzle pieces below and glue them in place on a piece of construction paper. You will have a picture of this famous landmark. Have fun coloring your picture.

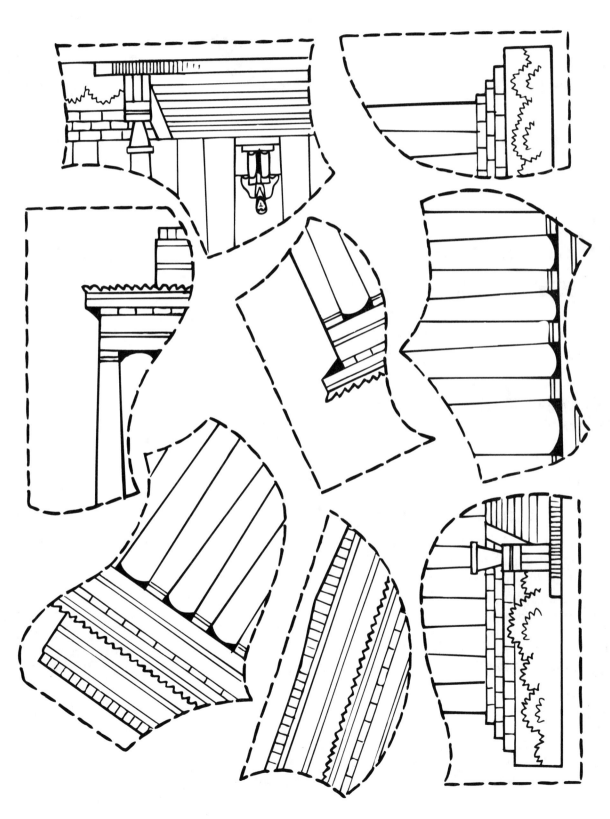

100
Day Celebration

On the hundredth day of school, sing and celebrate. Introduce Kid One Hundred to kick off your Hundredth Holiday with number concepts stories and measuring.

Kid One Hundred

Kid One Hundred can count to 100 in a single day, lift two 50s with ease and leap higher than 99. Kid One Hundred is the hero of the celebration.

To find your Kid One Hundred, locate an old stuffed doll or figure. Add a 100 sticker, belt, paper hat and fabric cape to the figure. Prepare for Kid One Hundred's coming by giving hints to the class. On the hundredth day, decorate your room with 100s from the entrance into the room. Kid One Hundred has struck again!

Home Participation

Ask each student to bring 100 of any small objects from home. These might be 100 pieces of dry cereal, raisins or rubber washers. Have additional bags of objects on hand for those who forget or are not able to bring anything. These objects are the basis for the following activities:

Using a balance scale, let students compare which bag of 100 objects weighs more and which one weighs the least.

At another center, let students lay 10 of the objects end to end. See which objects are the longest.

Select a bag of 100 objects. Have students close their eyes and from a list of describing words, see if they can figure out which one of three bags was described.

One Hundred Day Songs

One Hundred Days Have Passed
(Tune: "Farmer in the Dell")

ne hundred days have passed,
ne hundred days have passed.
ho the school's half done
ne hundred days have passed.

n, twenty we go.
irty, forty and so
n to one hundred we count
 we go.

ty, sixty, seventy then,
ghty, ninety by tens
e're counting to 100
nd start over again.

My Friends and I
(Tune: "My Bonnie Lies over the Ocean")

y friends and I are all counting
ne days from one to one hundred,
y friends and I are all counting
 celebrate one hundred days of school.

ok back, look back
om day one to now, day 100.
ok back, look back
om day one to now, day 100.

100 Seed Science

aterials

100 marigold seeds
potting soil
cardboard milk cartons
spoons
newspaper
water

1. Count out and divide seeds into groups of five. Practice counting by fives to 100.
2. Fill 20 cleaned 1/2 pint or pint milk cartons with soil to 1" of the top.
3. Space out and plant five marigold seeds per milk carton. Cover with 1/2" of soil.
4. Water and place in a sunny window.

by Terry Healy

Internet Connection

Imagine receiving 100 greetings from across the world. Many educational list servers are available on the "net" through which classroom teachers may request E-mail messages. As the messages come in, the class can count them and locate their origin on a large map.

Have You Counted?

(Tune: "Frere Jacques")

Have you counted? Have you counted?
Ten sets of fingers?
Or ten sets of toes?
We count to 100,
We counted to 100,
As we go, as we go.

One Hundred Day Punch

Punch bowl
200 centiliters (2 liters) lemon lime soda
200 centiliters (2 liters) grape soda
100 liters of crushed ice
100 liter plastic measuring container

Let students help measure and mix punch. Serve with any edible 100 snacks brought by the students.

Celebrating

Every four years, we have an extra day in the month of February. It will be February 29, and it is called Leap Year Day. It takes the Earth 365¼ days to go around the sun. This accounts for the extra day on our calendar to catch up every four years, and we call this Leap Year. The next leap year will be in the year 2000.

Leap Year Day does not really affect most people, except those that were born on February 29. They have to deal with celebrating their special day either on February 28 or March 1.

Since this is an extra day at school, ask your students for ideas to make this day stand out among the others. On this page and the following page are a few activities to try.

Calendars

Have each child draw a calendar grid for the month of February. Fill in numerals for each day, drawing a red circle around the 29th to denote its "specialness." This would be a good time to review the month and draw specific pictures in the boxes of the holidays of February: Groundhog Day (February 2); Lincoln's Birthday (February 12); Valentine's Day (February 14); Presidents' Day (February 19); Washington's Birthday (February 22). On the remaining days, let the children draw in pictures of favorite tasks they like to do.

Topsy-Turvy Party

Because Leap Year is associated with a mix-up in the calendar and traditional roles, having a witty party could be a lot of fun. During the day, let the students switch seats, call each other their friends' names, wear unmatched or backwards clothes and even role-play becoming the teacher and administrators.

Silly Games

Tune: "Hokey Pokey"
(Do the complete opposite of the commands called. Make up other actions and continue the game.)

You put your right foot in,
You put your left foot in,
You put your right foot in
And you turn yourself around.
You do the "Topsy-turvy" and do the opposite.
That's what it's all about!

by Tania Kourempis-Cowling

LEAP YEAR

Daffy Drawing Day

Give everyone paper and crayons to draw a scene putting objects out of place, such as a lady walking a fish on a leash or a child riding a bicycle with square wheels. Allow time for children to create this picture; then spend time with a picture "show and tell" to see all the clever ideas.

Student Activities

1. Explain the meaning of Leap Year to students, identifying February 29th on the calendar. Tell them that this will be a *leap day*. What special events can they suggest to celebrate? You might call it the Big L Day, and have them create a design for a special February calendar.

2. Ask if anyone was born on February 29th. How might a birthday be celebrated for someone born in a Leap Year? Would they celebrate a birthday every four years? Explain that the person would be one when others were four, two when they were eight, etc. How could this problem be overcome? Divide students into small groups and ask them to figure out a way to solve the problem.

3. Create some limericks with students, using the letter L. A starter might be "Let's look lovely on leap day and lick lollipops."

4. Play leapfrog outside of the classroom. Place several large objects in a row with 2-3 feet between them. Tell students they are frogs and must leap over each object without touching it.

5. Students can create a "Leap Day" booklet. Each page can be titled as follows: "L Animal, L Vegetable, L Fruit, L Clothing." They can think of an object that fits into each category and draw a picture of it. More able students might brainstorm as many things as they can for each category and write these down.

FEBRUARY						
Sun	Mon.	Tues	Wed	Thurs	Fri	Sat
						1
2	3	4	5	6	7	8
9	10	11	12	13	14	15
16	17	18	1	20	21	22
23	24	25	26	27	28	29

by Teddy Meister

Cooking with Kids

by Marie E. Cecchi

Cottage Cheese Snowman

- cottage cheese
- block of cheddar cheese
- carrot
- raisins

Use an ice cream scoop to put two or three cottage cheese "snowballs" on a plate, in the shape of a snowman. Set a carrot stick across the top of his head for a brim. Cube the cheese and set one cube above the carrot stick for the top of his hat. Set raisins into his head for eyes and a mouth, and three into his belly for buttons. Use a small slice of carrot for his nose.

Hands-on snacks are a fun way to teach children about proper nutrition. It also introduces new vocabulary, reinforces counting and promotes growth in following directions and sequential order. Creating a personal snack will also give children a wonderful feeling of accomplishment and success. They will truly be able to say, "I did it all by myself!"

Snowballs

- cream cheese
- cheddar cheese
- crushed cereal of choice

Soften the cream cheese and grate the cheddar. Mix equal amounts of both together and form into balls. Roll each ball in crushed cereal.

214

Sun Sandwich

- bread
- peanut butter
- raisins
- carrot
- celery

Cut a slice of bread into a circle shape. Spread peanut butter over the top. Use two slices of celery to make "happy" eyes. Use one slice of celery to make a smiling mouth. Use a raisin for the nose. Use carrot sticks to surround the bread as rays.

Banana Sled

- cottage cheese
- banana
- raisins
- carrot
- peanut butter

Spread some cottage cheese out on a plate for "snow." Set two carrot sticks into the "snow" for sled runners. Cut the banana in half, then slice one half lengthwise. Spread peanut butter on the flat surface. Place this banana piece on the carrot sticks to form the sled. Stick raisins into the peanut butter on the sled as passengers.

Birdseed Pops

- banana
- vanilla yogurt
- sunflower seeds
- craft stick

Slice the banana in half. Insert the craft stick into the flat end. Dip the banana into the yogurt, then roll it in the sunflower seeds.

Snowballs in

Winter—a great time for making snowballs! Bu[t] what if you live in a place where it doesn't snow much, or what if you would like to toss a few snowballs right inside the classroom? There is a solution. Yes, you CAN have an old-fashioned (and harmless) snowball fight right in school, and the snowballs won't even melt. In fact, they will be soft and puffy and children will be able to use their math computation skills while tossing them.

All you need for your in-class snow-ball throw are cotton balls, self-sticking round labels and a bucket or pail of some kind.

First, place the numbers 1- 25 on the round labels. Write one number per label using a dark marker of some kind. Then stick the round labels onto the cotton balls (one number per cotton ball). Place a plastic bucket in the center of the room. Have students sit in a circle around the bucket and toss their "snowballs" at the bucket.

Now you're ready to have that math snowball fight. Let one child at a time pick up as many cotton balls as possible in a given amount of time. The teacher sets the time limit from 30 to 40 seconds and tells the students when to begin picking up and tossing the cotton balls and when to stop.

the Classroom?

When the designated time for "throwing snowballs" is up, the child retrieves them from the pail and must compute their total by adding the numbers on the balls together. Another child or the teacher could be writing all of the numbers on the board so the whole class can check the "thrower's" computation. If the computation is correct, the student receives that number of points as his score. For instance, if a child got the numbers 8, 9, 10 and 12 in the bucket, the total score would be 8 + 9 + 10 + 12 or 39! Of course, the student with the highest score at the end of the allotted playing time is the math "snow king" or "snow queen" of the day.

Snowball games like these are especially fun at winter holiday parties or on snowy days when children may be too excited to do

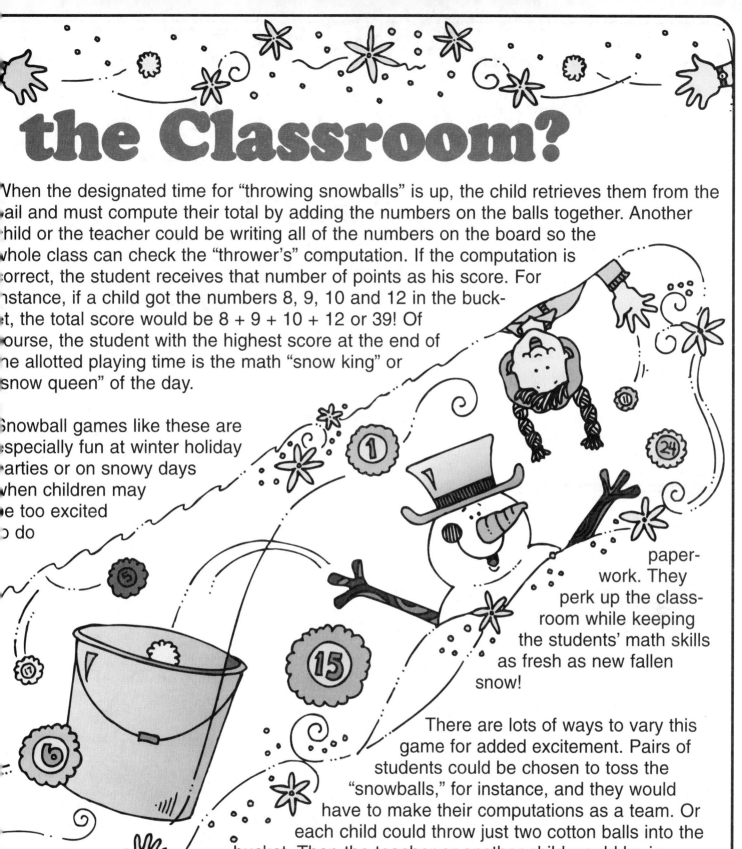

paperwork. They perk up the classroom while keeping the students' math skills as fresh as new fallen snow!

There are lots of ways to vary this game for added excitement. Pairs of students could be chosen to toss the "snowballs," for instance, and they would have to make their computations as a team. Or each child could throw just two cotton balls into the bucket. Then the teacher or another child would be in charge of calling out, "add," "multiply," "subtract" or "divide." The student would then have to perform the operation called out. If the computation is correct, the child gets to keep the balls. The person with the most "snowballs" at the end of the playing time is the new "snowmaster" of the day.

by Joanne Coughlin

Kid Space
School Yard Learning Adventures

Winter and Early Spring

Kid Space is a place of school yard (and backyard) beginnings. It is an ever-changing, fascinating place where children can connect with the natural world and enjoy opportunities not readily available inside. Kid Space is a stage for school yard (or backyard) adventures. It is a safe place where kids can explore freely and make first-hand discoveries. Make the most of the smells, the colors, the textures, the sounds, the excitement, the freedom and the peace.

Timed Sketches

Enjoy the excitement of seasonal changes with this close-up look at nature. Children will develop skills of observation and sketching in this exercise designed to bring kids close to the Earth and open the door to questions about the natural environment.

You Need (for each child):
sketch pads with hard back or clipboard
pencils
eraser

What to Do:
1. Take children out to your Kid Space at the same time each week, regardless of the weather.
2. Each child can choose their own sketch spot.
3. Once each child is settled in their sketch spot, a timed observation will begin. (One to three minutes of observation time is appropriate, depending upon the ages of the children.) Encourage children to look very closely at small details and the larger vista that they see. Allow time for silent observation and then a discussion of details.
4. Prepare for the timed sketching. Once children are comfortable, with pencil in hand and sketch pad in place, begin a silent timed sketching of 2-20 minutes, depending upon the attention span of the group of children. Children will sketch the details that they see around them until time is called. At this point, children date the work and put away their pencils.
5. Each week children will notice differences in their "sketch spot" and its surroundings. Encourage discussion of their observations of the seasonal changes.

Try This:
Instead of sketching, substitute a timed writing exercise about the particular spot.

by Robynne Eagan

218

Winter Olympics

Just when winter is starting to lose its appeal, turn your Kid Space into the site of the Winter Olympics. The Winter Olympics is just the thing for fitness, fun and cool excitement. This event can be designed to include a few children or an entire school.

1. Decide whether you want to make your games competitive or non-competitive.

2. Divide participants into teams representing real or imaginary countries with accompanying uniforms and opening ceremonies. Take this opportunity to teach children the history of the Olympics, skills needed for various winter sports, the customs of represented countries and the value of good sportsmanship.

3. Each team invents, or is assigned, its own Winter Olympic event. These activities can be new and zany, trendy and popular, or traditional sports. You may point children in a particular direction or let them use their imaginations. Students plan how the event will be run, what materials will be needed, design and make a sign, and set up on the big day. Consider the following events:

The Great Snow Race

Runners clad in boots and proper outerwear must run from point A to point B through the white stuff. The slipping, sliding, tripping fun adds to the excitement.

Winter Tracking

Squeeze some tempera paint onto the bottom of your boots and take a walk through the snow, leaving an easy-to-spot footprint track. (You may have to carry the squeeze bottle around with you and reapply it as needed.) Young Olympians must follow the track from start to finish. Players can be timed or various tracks of equal distance can be laid out so players can race against one another.

The Snow Hare Hop

Provide a good supply of snow for Olympians to jump into in this wintry version of the broad jump.

A"maze"ing Winter Hike

A fresh snowfall is needed to make this snowy maze. Pre-plan the maze or create it as you go. Tramp down or shovel a tricky maze through the snow. Include a start, a finish and lots of tricky deadends! Olympians can be timed as they find their way.

Snowshoe Shuffle

Try to round up enough pairs of snowshoes to allow the entire group to hike from one spot to another, to race across a great white expanse, or to just try a new means of winter travel. Parents, outdoor education centers, winter resorts and community centers are good sources of equipment.

Snowball Toss

Using colored water in a spray bottle, make a starting line in the snow, a 3' (1 m) line, a 6' (2 m) line and 9' (3 m) line. Young Olympians make and toss their snowballs in turn to determine the distance of their throws.

1. Plan an opening ceremony that includes music; a brief pep talk about efforts, personal achievements and fun; a parade of competitors; and the distribution or display of maps showing the location and time of various events. Provide an indoor "warming station" for chilly participants.

2. Teachers, students and/or volunteers can be assigned to run the various events as team captains direct their teams to the events at the appropriate times. A bell will be rung at 5 to 20-minute intervals to signal participants to move onto the next event.

3. Close the games with brief words highlighting the successes of the event and distribute awards for athletic competence, spirit, effort or humorous contributions. Host a "Hang Our Mitts to Dry" Hot Chocolate Social.

Try This:
- Enlist the help of volunteers to run or assist with events.
- Request a change of clothing and mittens for participants. Invite parents to prepare a hot lunch for frosty participants or order pizza.

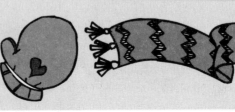

Fox and Geese

Enjoy a freshly fallen snow with an old game.

You Need:
- three or more players
- freshly fallen snow
- winter wear, especially good footwear for tramping out the paths

How to Play:

1. Stamp a large circle in the snow. Make a smaller circle in the center of this circle.

2. Stamp six straight paths from one side of the outer circle to the other, crossing in the center circle. (Like cutting up a pie—discuss how many pieces the circle is broken into and what fraction of the circle one or several pieces are.)

3. Designate one player to be the fox and the remaining players to be the geese.

4. You may not need to explain that the fox chases the geese around! The fox and geese may not step off the paths at anytime during the game. A goose who steps off the path is "cooked" and must become the new fox.

5. The geese can take refuge in the center safe zone for a short time (about 30 seconds).

6. A tagged goose becomes the new fox and the game continues.

Snowsnakes

The Iroquois natives took advantage of the ice and snow for their unique game of Snowsnakes. This traditional race involves long smooth wooden sticks better known as Snowsnakes. Snowsnakes race in specially prepared ice tracks. Snowsnake tournaments are held in late January in Ontario, Canada. For an interesting lesson in design and technology, traction, art and physical education, make and race your own snowsnakes.

You Need:
- patch of snow 18" (6 cm) by about 25' (8 m)
- plastic container with lid (e.g. soda bottle)
- hose or spray bottles
- doweling, broom handles or hand-carved and shaped sticks 3' to 5' (1 to 2 m) in length
- paraffin wax

How to Play:
1. Mark out the flat playing area. Include a starting line made by spraying water colored with food coloring from a spray bottle.

2. Form two parallel snowsnake tracks about 6" (15 cm) apart. Tie a rope to the handle of a clean plastic container. Fill the container with hot water, put a lid on it and drag it behind you to form a track.

3. Prepare the tracks by spraying them with water from mist spray bottles or a hose turned onto a fine mist. When one layer freezes, additional layers can be sprayed on for a slicker surface.

4. Players can fashion their snakes from simple broom handles; doweling with ends that have been shaped and sanded; or from chosen sticks that have been carved, shaped and sanded in a more traditional manner.

5. Snowsnakes can be prepared with a polish of wax, a coating of water, ice or other means to reduce the friction. This exercise can incorporate a science lesson on friction and heat.

6. Players position themselves behind the starting line and await the pre-determined signal to begin.

7. Each player tosses his snowsnake along the tracks and urges it on with calls, hoots and chants.

8. Children can use their measurement skills to determine the distance traveled by each snowsnake. Results can be recorded for later graphing, averaging and problem-solving activities.

9. The player whose snowsnake travels the farthest goes on to throw against the next opponent. The final winner is the Snowsnake Champion.

Clip Art for Winter

223

Clip Art for Winter

Be Mine

Happy New Year

Presidents' Day

We're Having a
Valentine Party!

Dear Parents,

Our Valentine Party will be held on

_____ (day), at _____ (time). If you

would be willing to help with the party, please fill out the

following form and return it to class by _____ (date).

I will then send a note home telling how you can help.

Our plan for exchanging valentines is as follows:

_____

_____

_____

_____

Thank you!

_____

(Teacher/Room Mother)

Valentine Party Volunteer List

I can help with the following:

____ refreshments ____ games ____ cleanup

____ drinks ____ cups/napkins ____ extra hand at party

____ before-party preparations Name _____

Spring Romp

We're swinging,
and sliding,
we're *jumping* in place.
We're pulling,
and tugging,
we're running a race.
We're whirling
and twirling,
we're spinning outside.
We're leaping
and laughing,
we're racing to hide.
We're wiggling
and giggling,
we're playing together,
in kite-flying,
sun-singing,
wind-waving weather!

by Rebecca Kai Dotlich

PURIM IS SPECIAL

Every year on Purim, Jewish children will hear the story of Queen Esther. With the help of her cousin, Mordecai, Esther saved the Jews from the plan of Haman, a wicked man who tried to have all the Jews killed.

The story is read by the rabbi from a special scroll called a Megillah. Every time Haman's name is read, the children whirl noisemakers, stamp their feet and make a lot of noise so Haman's name can't be heard. It is the only time that noise can be made in the synagogue or temple.

Purim is a happy holiday. Children dress up in costumes and have parades and parties. They eat Hamantaschen, a special three-cornered cookie filled with jelly. It reminds the children of Haman's three-cornered hat.

Purim is also a time to share. Gifts of Hamantaschen, cookies, fruit and candy are given to family and friends. Special baskets of food and toys are given to people who are poor, sick or lonely. Money is collected or raised at the Purim carnival and given to charities.

Jews all over the world look forward to this happy holiday!

Hamantaschen Recipe

Try this special Purim treat! Makes about 4 dozen Hamantaschen.

1 cup sugar
1/3 cup oil
1/3 cup shortening
3 eggs
1/2 cup orange juice

4 cups flour
3 tsp. baking powder
1 tsp. salt
1 egg, beaten
jelly for filling

PROCESS:
1. Cream the sugar, oil and shortening.
2. Add the 3 eggs and juice. Mix well.
3. Blend with the dry ingredients. Roll into a ball.
4. Divide into 4 parts. Roll out each piece very thin (about 1/8") on a floured board.
5. With the rim of a cup or glass, cut into the dough to make circles.
6. Place 1/2 to 2/3 teaspoon of filling in the middle of each circle.
7. Shape into a triangle—lift up right and left sides of circle, leaving the bottom side down. Bring both sides to meet at the center, above the filling. Lift the bottom side up to meet the other two sides.
8. Preheat oven to 350°F. Brush the dough with beaten egg before baking.
9. Place on a greased cookie sheet. Bake approximately 20 minutes.

Purim Projects

Purim is a festival of joy, noise and creative costumes.

1. Have students draw a picture of a costume they could wear for a Purim celebration. They might want to be a "Queen Esther" or a mean old "Haman." Provide scraps of construction paper, cloth and any other materials that can be pasted on paper to make the costume.

2. Baskets of food are given as gifts to friends and family. Provide students with an outline shape of a basket drawn on art paper. Ask them to draw food items they think others would like to receive as a Purim gift. Have them consider such items as fruits, nuts, candies, cakes and cookies.

3. Gifts are also given to the poor, homeless and sick at this time of year. Ask children to create a Purim get- well card for someone sick. Are there any children in class who are ill? This would be a good opportunity to start a class get-well card to help cheer up classmates who are absent from school.

4. Lots of happy noises are made during a Purim service at temple, where the holiday is observed. Have students save empty milk cartons. Rinse thoroughly, cover with decorations or art paper, place 8 to 10 lima beans inside, and students will have a Purim "groger" or noisemaker!

5. Thinking happy thoughts is another part of a Purim celebration. Ask students to think about what makes them happy. Have them draw several happy faces on art paper and create a drawing showing things that make them happy.

228   **by Teddy Meister**

Focusing on Women's History

Ella Fitzgerald

Throughout the history of our nation, women have made important contributions. These achievements have affected the lives of all our citizens. Teach young children more about these people as you focus on women's history.

Teacher/Student Activities

Women and Their Work

Teach nonreaders to identify the word-picture with the correct response in a matching game. Glue the pictures on the next page on index cards. Laminate for durability. Use in a center or duplicate a set for each student in the group. Read these directions before you begin:

1. Place the cards faceup on your desk.
2. Listen as your teacher reads a name.
3. Choose a card that shows something about this woman. For example, if the name called is Amelia Earhart, you will hold up a plane. She was the first woman to pilot an aircraft across the Atlantic Ocean.
4. Hold the card up when you know the correct answer.

* Adapt to early readers by having students take turns calling out a name.

Annie Oakley

1. Jane Addams—worked to improve living conditions for poor people
2. Louisa May Alcott—wrote *Little Women*
3. Susan B. Anthony—fought for the rights of women
4. Clara Barton—started the American Red Cross
5. Catherine E. Beecher—founded schools for girls
6. Mary Cassatt—artist
7. Amelia Earhart—first woman to pilot an aircraft across the Atlantic Ocean
8. Fannie Farmer—cookbook author and food expert
9. Ella Fitzgerald—singer
10. Mahalia Jackson—African American singer of gospel songs
11. Helen Keller—blind, deaf and mute author
12. Juliette G. Low—founder of Girl Scouts
13. Margaret Mead—anthropologist
14. Annie Oakley—known for being a trick-shot rifle expert
15. Annie Peck—mountain climber, women's suffrage fighter
16. Pocahontas—Native American princess who aided settlers of Virginia
17. Marjorie K. Rawlings—wrote *The Yearling*, a Pulitzer Prize winner
18. Eleanor Roosevelt—social reformer and President's wife
19. Margaret Chase Smith—member of the U.S. Senate for 24 years
20. Louise Suggs—professional golfer
21. Marie Tallchief—ballerina
22. Shirley Temple—child movie star, delegate to the U.N.
23. Harriet Tubman—aided escaped slaves
24. Eudora Welty—Southern writer

by Carolyn Ross Tomlin

Eleanor Roosevelt

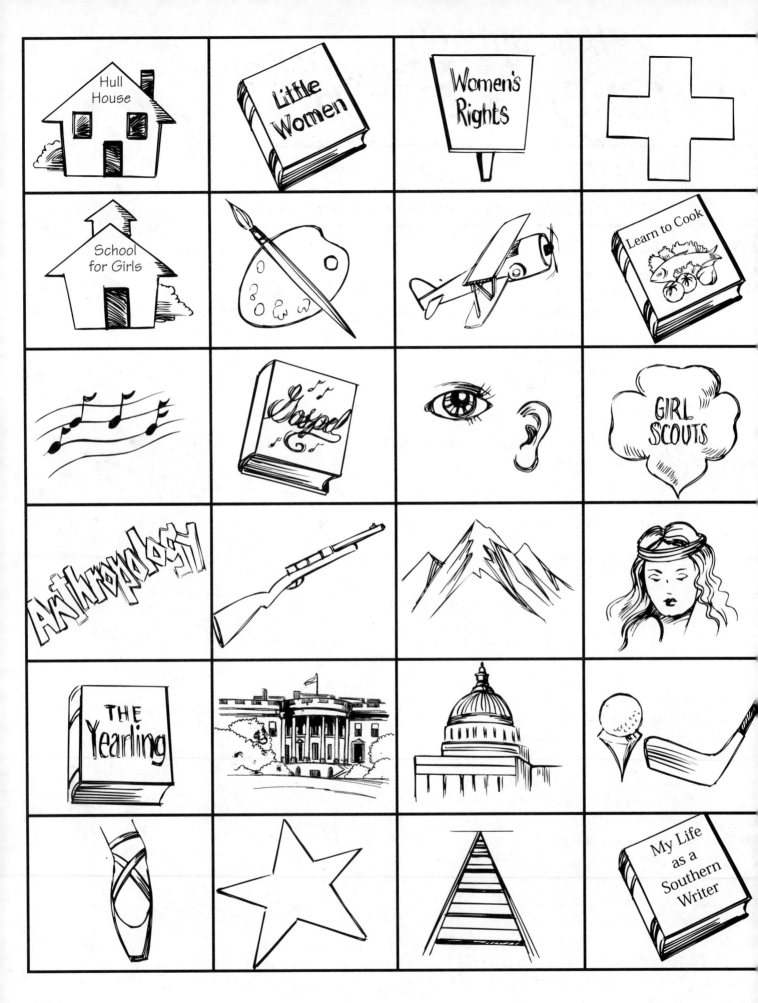

The Magic Wish

I caught myself a leprechaun —
Caught him by the toe.
He promised me a magic wish
If I would let him go.

Wanting to be like him,
For just a little while,
I used my wish for wishing
To play in fairy style!

We plucked some
four-leaf clovers,
Danced a highland jig,
Drank cool apple cider
And rode a fairy pig.

We swung the gate as we ran by.
We pranced the fairy ring.
I got to meet her majesty,
The lovely Fairy Queen.

I caught myself a leprechaun
And had a lot of fun.
If you can catch
a leprechaun . . .
You'll be the
lucky one!

by Jeanene Engelhardt

St. Patrick's Day

Celebrate St. Patrick's Day on March 17 by making it a Green Day. The color green symbolizes Ireland and the Irish. Here are a few Green Day activities:

1. Wear green clothes.
2. Go on a hunt for green things around the classroom and school.
3. Serve green eggs for snack by adding a little spinach or green food coloring to scramble eggs before cooking.
4. Make an all-green salad.
5. Walk and play on green grass.

The Irish are also famous for their folklore about leprechauns: these tiny old fairies bring good luck, if you can find their pot of gold. Leprechauns love to hide near rainbows. Encourage the children to use their imaginations to answer these questions. All answers are individual thoughts and correct.

1. If you caught a leprechaun, what would you wish for? What does he look like?
2. What do you think you would find at the end of a rainbow?

Hearty Shamrock

Cut three hearts out of green construction paper. Form a shamrock by gluing the points of the hearts together on a separate piece of paper. Now, draw a stem or make one from construction paper. To decorate these shamrocks, make paper confetti (holes punched with a hole punch) out of all colors of construction paper. Glue these colorful dots randomly over the shamrock.

Shamrock Crown

Cut a band of heavy-duty paper or tagboard to fit around the child's head. Glue or staple the ends. Attach green pipe cleaners around the top edge of the crown. To the pipe cleaners, glue or staple construction paper shamrocks. Personalize these crowns by writing the child's name and *Happy St. Patrick's Day!*

Over the Rainbow

On a piece of black construction paper, draw six arches with chalk or a white crayon. Fill each arch by tearing small pieces of construction paper and gluing them down within the arch. Fill in the entire area of each arch as you follow this order of the rainbow: red, orange, yellow, green, blue and purple.

by Tania Kourempis-Cowling

A Good Day to Be Green!

Shamrock Mask

From green construction paper, cut a shamrock large enough to cover the child's face. Mark the eyes and cut out two eyeholes. Attach a tongue depressor to the base for a holder. Cut out a nose and mouth from colorful paper and glue these into place. Glue on two shiny pennies for bright cheeks. With mask in place, act out this traditional rhyme with a twist!

Shamrock, shamrock, turn
   around.
Shamrock, shamrock, touch
   the ground.
Shamrock, shamrock, reach
   up high,
Shamrock, shamrock, touch
   the sky.
Shamrock, shamrock, don't
   make a sound,
Fall to the ground and roll
   around!

Who's Sitting on Gold?

First, make a gold coin by covering a real coin with gold foil or drawing one and coloring it with a gold crayon.

One player is IT and leaves the room. The other players are seated, with one sitting on the coin. The person who is IT returns and tries to guess who is sitting on the coin by listening to singing clues—any tune will do. The closer he comes to the hidden coin, the louder the children sing; the farther away he moves, the softer they sing. When the coin is found, the player who was sitting on it leaves the room next.

Shamrock Shake

Blend one banana, two cups of lime sherbet and two cups of milk. This makes a yummy drink!

St. Patrick's Favorites

Favors are made by placing a handful of green candies in the center of a square of plastic food wrap and tying this package with a green ribbon or yarn. Gold foil-wrapped Hershey's Kisses™ can become "the leprechaun's gold."

Shamrock Bounce

Paint an old tennis ball green. Set five aluminum pie or cake pans on the floor, fairly close together. Number the pans from one to five. Give each child five bounces of the ball. Each time it lands in a pan, add up the score. See who gets the highest score in the class.

Green Spin Art

Place a white paper plate in a cardboard box. Drop small drips of watery poster paints from a paintbrush onto the plate. Use blue and yellow paints to make green. Give the box a quick spin. With each spin, the design will change a bit.

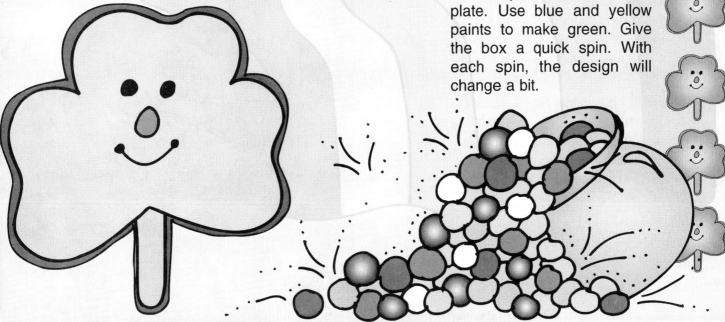

233

Listen Up for St. Patrick's Day

Dancing Letters

Skills: Beginning sounds, vowels and consonants
Materials: Lined paper, pencil

In this short lesson, we will find the name of a lively dance people might do on St. Patrick's Day. Number your paper from 1 to 5. On each line you will write a different three-letter word.

1. On line 1, write the word *hat*.

2. On line 2, write a new word that uses the same consonants. Change the *a* in *hat* to the vowel you hear at the beginning of *igloo* and *in*.

3. On line 3, write a new word keeping the last two letters of the word in line 2. Change the first consonant to the letter you hear at the beginning of *pie* and *pet*.

4. On line 4, change the second consonant to the letter you hear at the beginning of *gum* and *gorilla*. Keep the other letters the same as in line 3, and write the new word.

5. On line 5, change the first consonant to the letter that you hear at the beginning of *jelly* and *jump*. Keep the other letters the same as in line 4, and write the new word. Now you have the name of a lively dance.

6. Write your name under the last word on your page.

Green Rhymes

Skill: Rhyming words
Materials: Lined paper, green and brown crayons

On St. Patrick's Day, people like to wear green. In this lesson we will work on words that rhyme with *green*. Number your paper from 1 to 15. For each number I will say a word. If the word rhymes with *green*, make a small green circle by the number. If the word does not rhyme with *green*, make a brown *X* by the number.

1. bean
2. teen
3. same
4. hen
5. screen
6. clean
7. greet
8. mean
9. sheet
10. learn
11. seen
12. men
13. spleen
14. keep
15. Write your name with a green crayon.

by Ann Richmond Fisher

Shamrock Search

Skills: Following directions,
top/bottom, right/left

Materials: Reproducible on page
236, pencil

A not-so-lucky leprechaun lost his pot of gold,
and he searched under the shamrocks on your
paper until he found it. Listen carefully to find out
where the leprechaun looked. Follow the directions
to mark your page.

1. The leprechaun started at the shamrock
   that is on the top left of your page. Put a
   number 1 on that shamrock.

2. The second one he went to was just below
   the first one. Put a number 2 on the second
   shamrock.

3. The third shamrock the leprechaun examined
   was just to the right of the second one. Put
   a number 3 on this shamrock.

4. The fourth shamrock he checked was in the
   bottom left corner. Put a 4 on this shamrock.

5. The fifth shamrock the leprechaun visited
   was the one to the right of the fourth one.
   Write a number 5 on this shamrock.

6. Then the leprechaun looked under his sixth
   shamrock. It was the one in the top right
   corner. Put a number 6 on the sixth shamrock.

7. Finally, the leprechaun looked under one more
   shamrock. It was right below his sixth shamrock. Put a number 7 on this shamrock. Circle
   it.

8. Now go back and draw lines with your pencil,
   connecting the shamrocks in order.

9. Write your name under the bottom right
   shamrock.

Shamrock Search

Take your students for an outdoor walk in search of the finest blarney stones. Discuss ahead of time what kind of stone you are looking for. You may find them in a bed of clover or on a dirt path. The best blarney stones are oval and smooth. Riverbed stone is ideal for making blarney stones. (If these are not available in your school yard, you may have to "plant" them there.)

Spray your stones gold or green or leave them the natural color. Decorate them with small bits of moss, pressed flowers, ribbon, green yarn or clover from your walk.

Give the stones as gifts or use them to make wishes on and write stories about your wishes. Keep them around for good luck.

Attach the following poem when giving the stone as a gift. Write the poem on your classroom chalkboard and discuss its meaning.

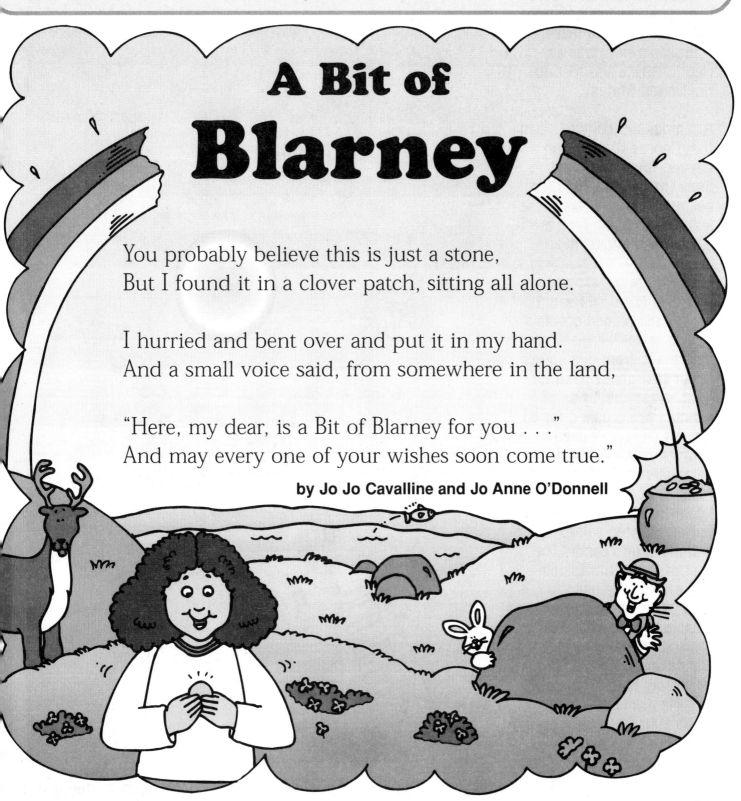

A Bit of Blarney

You probably believe this is just a stone,
But I found it in a clover patch, sitting all alone.

I hurried and bent over and put it in my hand.
And a small voice said, from somewhere in the land,

"Here, my dear, is a Bit of Blarney for you . . ."
And may every one of your wishes soon come true."

by Jo Jo Cavalline and Jo Anne O'Donnell

A Parade of Peanut Projects

The peanut is native to South America. They have been growing for more than 1000 years. From there, the plant apparently was carried to Africa and then to the United States.

A famous agricultural scientist, George Washington Carver, found the most uses (more than 300) for peanuts. Carver used these legumes to make fuel, medicines, cosmetics, ink and dyes.

March is National Peanut Month and a good opportunity to study the many products made from this source. Other than those used for food, great quantities of peanuts are crushed for oil. Peanut oil is now used in shortenings, margarines, salad oils and soaps. Millions of pounds of peanuts are used for peanut butter, roasted salted nuts and made into candy. The rest of the plants (skins and stems) are used to feed cattle and to make cleaning products.

Hands-on exploration is a great tool to learn about this plant, taste this delicious substance and create interesting art with the product itself.

Peanut Puppet

Draw and cut a peanut shape out of brown paper. Next, cut rubber bands to make four equal pieces. Draw facial features on your peanut with crayons or markers. Wiggly eyes glued on would be quite humorous. On the back side, tape the rubber bands as arms and legs. Use another rubber band at the top as your manipulator. Pick up your peanut puppet by the top band and make him dance.

Peanut Printing

Use a whole peanut in its shell, a broken half shell and the peanut itself. Set out containers of tempera paint in various colors. Dip these products into the paint and make prints on white paper by pressing down on the peanut. Make random designs and use many colors for effect.

by Tania K. Cowling

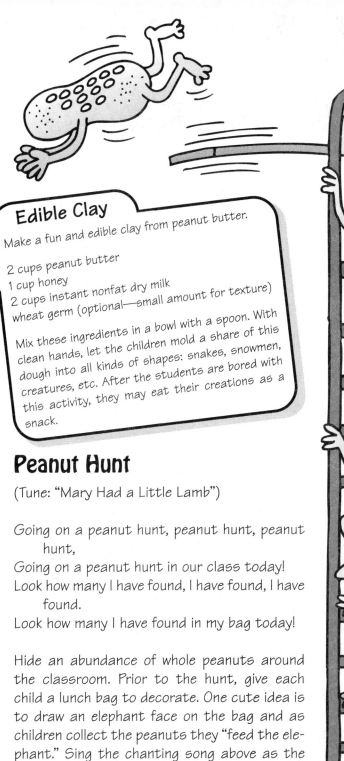

Edible Clay

Make a fun and edible clay from peanut butter.

2 cups peanut butter
1 cup honey
2 cups instant nonfat dry milk
wheat germ (optional—small amount for texture)

Mix these ingredients in a bowl with a spoon. With clean hands, let the children mold a share of this dough into all kinds of shapes: snakes, snowmen, creatures, etc. After the students are bored with this activity, they may eat their creations as a snack.

Peanut Hunt

(Tune: "Mary Had a Little Lamb")

Going on a peanut hunt, peanut hunt, peanut hunt,
Going on a peanut hunt in our class today!
Look how many I have found, I have found, I have found.
Look how many I have found in my bag today!

Hide an abundance of whole peanuts around the classroom. Prior to the hunt, give each child a lunch bag to decorate. One cute idea is to draw an elephant face on the bag and as children collect the peanuts they "feed the elephant." Sing the chanting song above as the students search the room high and low for peanuts.

Peanut Photo Frame

Paste a favorite photo inside a jar lid. Glue this lid onto a larger circle of heavy cardboard. Decorate the larger circle with peanut shells. Paint and decorate as desired. Tape a large paper clip to the cardboard base as a hanger.

Peanut Butter & Jelly Art

Cut out two bread shapes from white construction paper. Sponge-paint one using red paint for strawberry jelly or purple paint for grape jam. Paint the other slice light brown for the peanut butter. You can even mix a small amount of cornmeal into the paint for texture. Punch holes at the top and tie with a piece of yarn or secure the two shapes with a brad fastener.

Peanut Wreaths

Cut a circular wreath shape from heavy cardboard. Glue on an arrangement of peanuts (in shells) all around the wreath. There are many options for decorating: painting the shells, gluing on trims, glitter or a decorative bow. Tape a large paper clip to the back for a hanger.

Peanut Snack Tray

Glue an inverted foam cup between the bottom of a large plastic-coated plate and the top of a small plate or bowl. Decorate as desired. Use as a snack tray by placing peanuts on top and sliced fruit pieces on the bottom.

Spring and Summer in the Great Outdoors

What Is Kid Space?

Kid Space is a place of school yard (and backyard) beginnings. It is an ever-changing, fascinating place where children can connect with the natural world and enjoy opportunities not readily available inside.

Kid Space is a stage for back-yard adventures. It is a safe place where kids can explore freely and make firsthand dis-coveries on their own turf. It offers artistic mediums like mud, sand, water and color; a world of smells and textures and sounds; a world of critters and edible wilds. It offers excitement, freedom and peace.

Kid Space will help children develop the sense of adven-ture, control and self-confi-dence needed to explore on their own. Children can help create their space to make it interesting, enriching and unique.

Kids have an instinctual sense of wonder that draws them to the wonderful world of nature. Why not make the most of your outdoor space, be it a balcony, a backyard or a school yard, to create Kid Space in the great outdoors.

Mud Puddles and Raindrops

Rain, Rain, Come and Play! Who says you can't go out in the rain to play? A rainy day, especially a warm rainy day, is an exhilarating adventure wait-ing to be explored. Go ahead; make a splash, unless there's lightning!

(Request that students have com-plete rain wear for those days when you can enjoy the rain. Suggest a rain-suit with hood and high boots, a rain-coat with hood, nylon splash plants and rubber boots, minimal under-clothes on hot days, warm underwear on cold days and large cozy towels for after!

by Robynne Eagan

Puddle Fun

Waterscope

Take a closer look—beneath the surface of a puddle!

Materials:
large plastic ice cream container   a knife
clear plastic wrap   strong rubber band

1. Cut the bottom out of a plastic container.
2. Let students stretch cellophane over the bottom.
3. Secure the cellophane with a rubber band.
4. Lower the cellophane viewing end of the scope into the puddle.
5. Talk about what you see beneath the surface.

Puddle Boats: Make a Boat Center

Make some boats and float them on a puddle. Boats can be made out of recycled containers, Styrofoam™ trays, reeds, bark, feathers, leaves, straws, walnut shells, sheets of wax and so on. Set them afloat for a flotilla, regatta or boat races. Talk about what makes a boat float.

Puddle Bug Search

Take a closer look at a puddle. What do you see? Investigate a mud puddle—there is so much to see!
- mud puddles
- small glass jar
- magnifying glass

After a rain, find a large puddle, get close and take a look. Do you see small animals, stones, dirt, rocks, grasses? Take a water sample by dipping a small container in the puddle. What do you see with your magnifying glass? Examine the puddle in half an hour, after the dirt has settled. Do you notice any changes?

Puddle Jumping

Kids won't need any instructions for this activity. Let them experiment with the physical properties of water and mud as they splash, slosh, slip, skip and wade in.

Trace a Puddle

Trace a puddle with some chalk. What happens as the weather changes and the day goes on?

Mud Glorious Mud

Mud Craft

Put on some old clothes and rubber boots to explore mud!

Materials:
mud   water   old spoon
thick cardboard   old paintbrush

Process:
1. Stir up some mud in the bucket.
2. Spread the mud on the ground until you have a path about six feet long and one inch wide.
3. Put on shoes and take a walk down the path.
4. Take big steps, little steps, hop, use your hands, wear two different shoes and try various combinations.

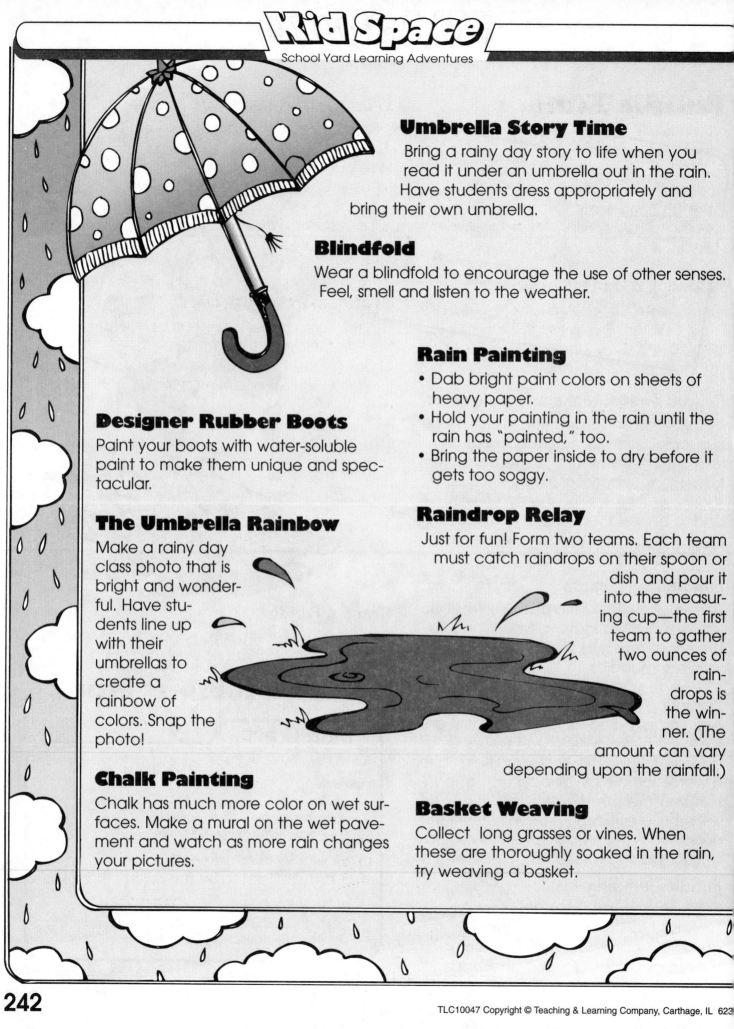

Umbrella Story Time

Bring a rainy day story to life when you read it under an umbrella out in the rain. Have students dress appropriately and bring their own umbrella.

Blindfold

Wear a blindfold to encourage the use of other senses. Feel, smell and listen to the weather.

Rain Painting

- Dab bright paint colors on sheets of heavy paper.
- Hold your painting in the rain until the rain has "painted," too.
- Bring the paper inside to dry before it gets too soggy.

Designer Rubber Boots

Paint your boots with water-soluble paint to make them unique and spectacular.

The Umbrella Rainbow

Make a rainy day class photo that is bright and wonderful. Have students line up with their umbrellas to create a rainbow of colors. Snap the photo!

Raindrop Relay

Just for fun! Form two teams. Each team must catch raindrops on their spoon or dish and pour it into the measuring cup—the first team to gather two ounces of raindrops is the winner. (The amount can vary depending upon the rainfall.)

Chalk Painting

Chalk has much more color on wet surfaces. Make a mural on the wet pavement and watch as more rain changes your pictures.

Basket Weaving

Collect long grasses or vines. When these are thoroughly soaked in the rain, try weaving a basket.

Center in the Rain

A real water center at last! Take students out in the rain and offer them an outdoor water center that includes basins, buckets, cups, tubs, soap, sponges, ice, snow, sieves, funnels, straws, tubes, shaving cream, spray bottles, food coloring and so on.

Take a Closer Look

Encourage students to look to the distance. What do they see? Look at a tiny patch. What do they see? Supply magnifying glasses and look again.

Sound Catchers

Use your ears! What do you hear? Introduce new vocabulary such as rustling, swishing, splashing, crashing, dripping, dropping, blowing, singing, thumping, buzzing, tapping, etc.

How Does It Feel?

Sharpen the sense of touch. If it is warm enough, wear bathing suits and feel the rain all over. Lie on the ground and feel the Earth, the wind, the sun, the water, warmth, dampness, rough bark, plants, flowers, etc.

Where Is the Sun's Heat Stored?

Find a warm surface, lay down on it to soak up the heat. A large rock or pavement surface will give off heat. Can you see steam coming off of any surfaces? Feel with your hands.

Sketch a Raindrop

When you look at a raindrop what do you see? Use a sketch pad and pencil to sketch raindrops in the air, as they hit a surface and settle on a surface.

Let a raindrop fall on your paper. Trace it with a marker and watch the colors change.

Sharpen the Senses

Help children experience nature: feel the wind, feel the temperature changes, touch the rain, smell the air, listen for thunder and watch for lightning.

Observe changes: smell the earth and damp air, look for creatures, check the plants, check the sky, listen to the sounds.

Observe a Spiderweb

A web catches raindrops as well as unwary insects who are later eaten by the spider.

Creative Movements for Spring

Ferris Wheel

My father and I took a wonderful ride
On a carnival ferris wheel
   (*make big circles with arm*)
You get in a seat with a place for your
   feet
   (*sit down slightly*)
And go up and come down with a
   squeeeeeal!
   (*stand up on tippy toes then back to
   "sitting"*)
And when you go up and stop at the top
   (*back to tippy toes*)
You can see all the people below
   (*point down*)
It's funny, but true: they look smaller than
   you
   (*show small with index finger and
   thumb*)
Until suddenly back down you go
   (*back up "sitting"*)

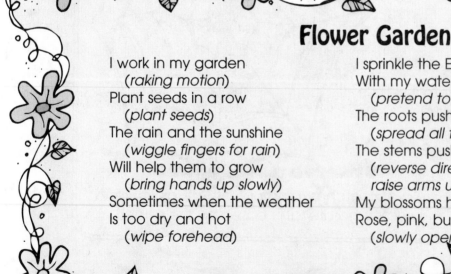

Flower Garden

I work in my garden
   (*raking motion*)
Plant seeds in a row
   (*plant seeds*)
The rain and the sunshine
   (*wiggle fingers for rain*)
Will help them to grow
   (*bring hands up slowly*)
Sometimes when the weather
Is too dry and hot
   (*wipe forehead*)
I sprinkle the Earth
With my watering pot
   (*pretend to water plants*)
The roots pushing downward
   (*spread all ten fingers, pointing down*)
The stems pushing up
   (*reverse direction, close hand and slowly
   raise arms up*)
My blossoms have opened
Rose, pink, buttercup
   (*slowly open hands as a flower*)

by Judy Wolfman

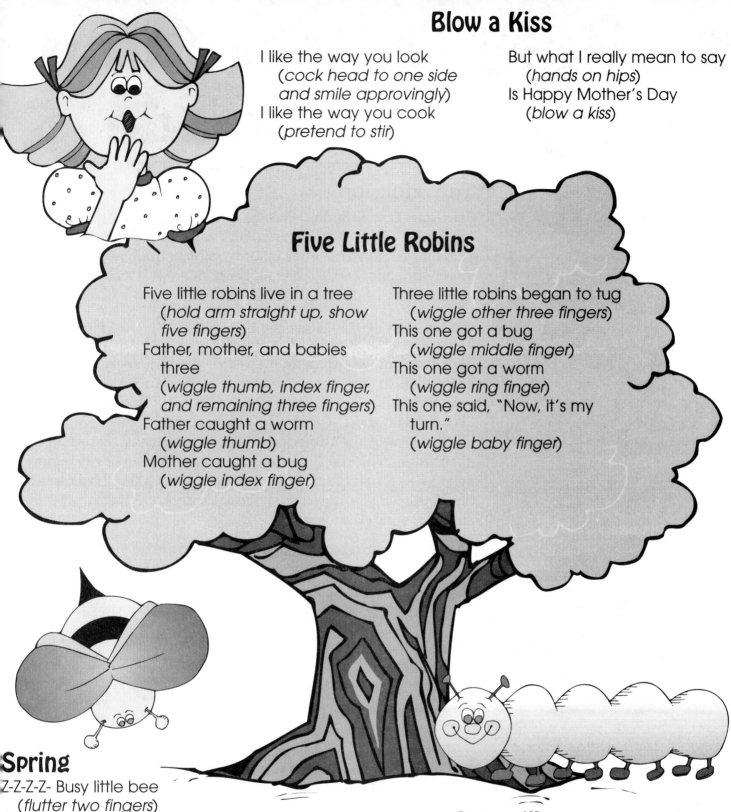

Blow a Kiss

I like the way you look
(*cock head to one side
and smile approvingly*)
I like the way you cook
(*pretend to stir*)

But what I really mean to say
(*hands on hips*)
Is Happy Mother's Day
(*blow a kiss*)

Five Little Robins

Five little robins live in a tree
(*hold arm straight up, show
five fingers*)
Father, mother, and babies
three
(*wiggle thumb, index finger,
and remaining three fingers*)
Father caught a worm
(*wiggle thumb*)
Mother caught a bug
(*wiggle index finger*)

Three little robins began to tug
(*wiggle other three fingers*)
This one got a bug
(*wiggle middle finger*)
This one got a worm
(*wiggle ring finger*)
This one said, "Now, it's my
turn."
(*wiggle baby finger*)

Spring

Z-Z-Z-Z- Busy little bee
(*flutter two fingers*)
Fly away from me
(*flutter fingers away from
body*)
I am not a flower and there's
No honey in me!
(*shake head back and forth*)
Z-Z-Z-Z- Busy little bee
(*flutter fingers all around,
ending behind your back*)

Caterpillars

"Let's go to sleep."
The little caterpillars said
(*yawn, rub eyes*)
As they tucked themselves
(*tuck fingers of right hand
into fist of left hand*)
Into their beds
They will awaken by and by

(*bring out fingers and
lock thumbs*)
And each one will be
A lovely butterfly
(*fingers together, flap
hands and "fly" as a
butterfly*)

Easter Bunny Parade

Introduction

Join our Easter Bunny Parade for an "eggs"citing array of springtime activities. Your students will enjoy every minute of this unit as they create scripts for Cottontail Playhouse; start a Bunny Brigade Story Center; and clip, color and create their very own Easter Bunny and friends.

Set the stage by starting a Bunny Brigade Story Center in your classroom. Ask students who have stuffed animals or puppets (rabbits or other spring animals such as chickens or lambs) to bring them in to be story characters for this center. Use our name tags for the stuffed animals if you wish. Ask your students to write and illustrate stories using a bunny theme. Tell them to use at least two of the stuffed animals or puppets as characters in their stories. For example, they could write about a lonely bunny who looks for and finds other animals to be his friends. Display the stories and pictures on a "Bunny Brigade Stories" bulletin board in your classroom.

Plan to have a Create-a-Cookie party at the end of your unit, and have your students decorate rabbit and spring animal-shaped cookies. Ask volunteers to bring in unfrosted animal-shaped cookies, icing and decorations for the party.

Bunny Brigade Name Tag

Introducing: _____
(Animal's Name)

Belongs to: _____
(Student's Name)

Description: _____

_____

Bunny Brigade Name Tag

Introducing: _____
(Animal's Name)

Belongs to: _____
(Student's Name)

Description: _____

_____

by Mary Ellen Switzer

Easter Bunny Parade Activities

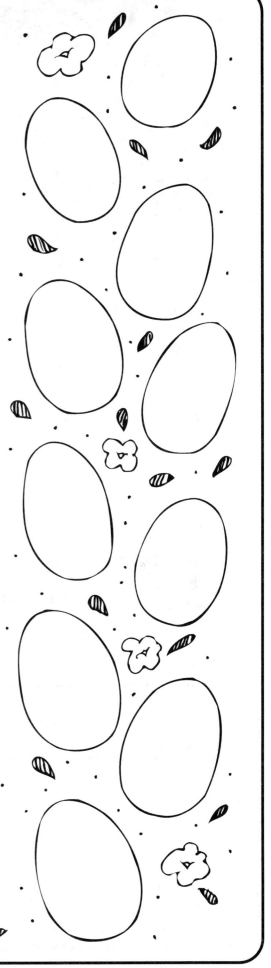

Decorate and color an egg for every activity completed from the springtime activities below.

1. Be a rabbit "eggs"pert. Find out more about that favorite spring animal, the rabbit! Using an encyclopedia or reference book, write four interesting facts about rabbits.

2. Be an inventor! Put wheels on an egg and create an Egg Mobile. Draw a picture of your design.

3. Create a billboard advertisement to tell the world about the new Egg Mobile.

4. *B* is for *bunny.* How many other animals can you think of that start with the letter *B*? Make a list.

5. Make a list of all of the words you can think of using the letters in *Easter Bunny Parade.*

6. Let's pretend! Imagine that you were on an egg hunt and found a magic egg. Tell what happens next.

7. Marvelous map! Pretend you were asked to design the perfect egg hunt in your backyard (or your school's playground). Draw a map showing where you would hide the eggs.

8. Write a diary entry about the adventures of the first rabbit on the moon.

9. Give a four-carrot salute! Plan a special holiday to honor that cuddly, lovable animal—the rabbit! What would you call the holiday? What special activities would you plan? Write a paragraph telling about your holiday and illustrate.

10. Design a board game with a rabbit theme. Draw a picture of how your game will look, and write directions for how to play the game.

by Becky Radtke

Cottontail Playhouse

Turn your young writers into Cottontail Playhouse performers with these motivating script-writing activities. Divide your class into small groups of playwrights and give each "team" one of the script starters below. Ask each group to write a script, practice it and then share it with the class.

Friends to the Rescue!

Setting: Easter Bunny's house

Characters: Narrator, Easter Bunny and any number of animal friends

Plot: Uh, oh! It's the night before Easter, and that forgetful Easter Bunny has forgotten to dye the eggs. Tell how his animal friends think of the perfect plan and come to his rescue.

Ron Rabbit's Magic Trick

Setting: Ron Rabbit's backyard

Characters: Narrator, Ron Rabbit, Randa Rabbit (Ron's sister), Mother Rabbit and any number of animal neighbors

Plot: Ron Rabbit was playing with his new magic set, when POOF—his sister Randa disappears! Tell how he gets his sister back.

The Disappearing Egg

Setting: The Johnson mansion

Characters: Detective Dan and Lisa from A-1 Detective Agency, Mr. and Mrs. Johnson, butler, gardener, maid and any number of suspects

Plot: Help! A valuable gold egg has disappeared from the Johnson mansion. Detectives Dan and Lisa arrive at the mansion to solve the mystery. First, they will look for clues and then interview everyone at the mansion. Tell how they solve the crime.

Those Amazing Rabbits

Setting: Television studio

Characters: Announcer and any number of reporters

Plot: Announcer—Welcome to our TV special *Those Amazing Rabbits*. Today, our reporters will be giving you some interesting information about rabbits. (Each reporter will give facts about rabbits. Use encyclopedias or other books to gather information.)

Clip, Color and Create

Theme: Easter Bunny and Friends

Spark up your creative writing program with these motivating story and script-writing activities pertaining to the Easter Bunny and his animal friends. Your students will be delighted as they make character stick puppets. Children can work independently or in small groups on these kid-pleasing writing activities.

Create-a-Play Starters

The Easter Bunny's Eggs

Setting: The Easter Bunny's house

Characters: Easter Bunny, Dee Dee Duck, Lucy Lamb, Sam E. Sparrow, Tommy Turtle and C.H. Chick

Plot: Help! The Easter Bunny has a big problem! It's a week before Easter, and his new Deluxe Egg-Coloring Machine is broken. How will he be able to finish coloring all the eggs in time for Easter? Will his friends be able to help him?

Where's the Easter Bunny?

Setting: The Easter Bunny's house

Characters: Easter Bunny, Dee Dee Duck, Lucy Lamb, Sam E. Sparrow, Tommy Turtle and C.H. Chick

Plot: Tomorrow is Easter, and all the Easter Bunny's friends are worried. They can't find him anywhere. Lucy Lamb suggests that they start a search party and begin looking for him. Where could he be?

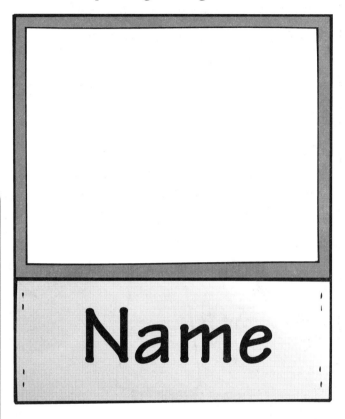

Name

Cottontail Tote Stage

Your students will enjoy creating a mini stage which can also double as a handy tote for their puppets. Follow these easy directions.

First, take a large sheet of white construction paper. Fold the paper to make a 4" pocket at the bottom. Staple the pocket on both sides. Write a child's name on the front of the pocket.

Next, have the students draw and color a picture which will be the stage backdrop. Have the children cut out and color the helpful props on the "Create a Stage" sheet on page 250 to glue to their pictures. After the puppet plays have been performed, store the puppets in the stage pockets.

Create a Stage

Be a stage designer! Cut out the props below and glue to your stage.
Add your own artwork to finish the stage!

Create-a-Character Puppet Page

Attention, young authors! Create your own mini puppet plays featuring the Easter Bunny and his friends, using these handy puppet characters. First, cut out the puppets, color them and glue to craft sticks. Next, use a Create-a-Play Starter to begin writing your play. Use as many of the puppet characters in your script, and add more if you wish.

Easter Bunny

Dee Dee Duck

Lucy Lamb

Tommy Turtle

Sam E. Sparrow

C.H. Chick

Easter Bunny Book Nook

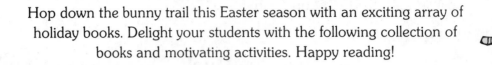

Hop down the bunny trail this Easter season with an exciting array of holiday books. Delight your students with the following collection of books and motivating activities. Happy reading!

The Chocolate Rabbit

Claret, Maria. *The Chocolate Rabbit.* New York: Barron's Educational Series, Inc., 1985.

Oops! When Bertie Rabbit accidentally knocks a pan of chocolate all over himself, he becomes the first chocolate Easter bunny! His father gets the bright idea of making wooden rabbit molds for more chocolate bunnies, and you know what happens next!

Activities
- Bertie Rabbit's father was an artist who painted colorful eggs. Design an Easter basket for his eggs.
- Yummy chocolate bunnies! Use a reference book to find out all about chocolate and how it is made. Write four facts that you have found.
- Draw a picture of your favorite chocolate treat and tell why you like it.
- Congratulations! You have just made the biggest chocolate rabbit in the world! Create a picture of a billboard to advertise your giant rabbit.

by Mary Ellen Switzer

Cranberry Easter

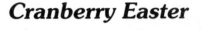

Devlin, Wende and Harry. *Cranberry Easter.* New York: Macmillan Publishing Co., 1990.

Spring has come, and it's time for Cranberryport's annual egg hunt. Seth, the owner of the general store, usually hosts the town's egg hunt, but he wants to retire and move away. A girl named Maggie comes to the rescue and devises a plan to convince him to stay. And Cranberryport gets the best Easter egg hunt ever!

Activities
- Extra . . . Extra . . . Read all about it! Write a news story about the Cranberryport egg hunt. Tell about Mr. Whiskers dressing up as a fat Easter Bunny. Include where the event took place and other details about the egg hunt.
- Pictures, please! Draw a picture that would go with your news article about the Easter egg hunt.
- As an extra surprise in this book, there is a recipe for cranberry cobbler. Create a new cranberry dessert of your very own. Draw a picture of your dessert and tell how it is made.
- Plan an Easter egg hunt that all your friends would rave about! Draw a map of your yard, a park or school playground and show where your eggs would be hidden! Happy hunting!

62

Hopper's Easter Surprise

egenthaler, Kathrin, and Marcus Pfister. *Hopper's Easter Surprise.* New York: North-South Books, 1993.

Activities

Think you'd like to be an Easter Bunny? A young Arctic hare named Hopper decides he would like the job but soon finds out it's harder than he thinks!

Be an ad writer! Create a "help wanted" ad for an Easter Bunny. Include the qualifications you think a bunny would need for the job.

Hopper meets a brown hare in the story, and soon they become friends. Draw a picture of a special friend you have and write three sentences telling about that person.

Draw a picture to show how Hopper decorated his special Easter egg that the Easter Bunny left for him.

Silly Tilly and the Easter Bunny

oban, Lillian. *Silly Tilly and the Easter Bunny.* New York: Harper & Row, 1987.

ll Silly Tilly Mole ever be ready for the Easter unny? It's Easter morning and the forgetful ole can't remember where she put anything! in in the fun, as Silly Tilly rushes around the use trying to get ready.

Activities

Calling all Silly Tilly Fans! Find out more about moles. Look in a reference or animal book and read all about moles. Create a *Marvelous Moles* picture book with pictures and information about this animal on each page.

Silly Tilly used a flowerpot for a hat. Draw a picture of what her "hat" looked like.

Be an author! Write a story about Silly Tilly getting ready for another holiday.

Happy Easter

Wiese, Kurt. *Happy Easter.* New York: Puffin Books, 1980.

A mother rabbit sends her two children out to collect some eggs for Easter. After the eggs have been colored, everyone gets a real surprise—a bright bunch of Easter chicks.

Activities

- The rabbit family got a big surprise in the story. Write about a time that you received a surprise. Draw a picture of the event.
- Write the story from the mother hen's point of view.
- Be an artist! Draw a picture of the colorful little chicks. Give each chick a new name.

The Easter Bunny That Overslept

Friedrich, Priscilla and Otto. *The Easter Bunny That Overslept.* New York: Mulberry Books, 1957.

One spring, the Easter Bunny had a big problem—seems he slept right through Easter! He still tried to give his eggs out on Mother's Day, the Fourth of July and Halloween, but no one wanted them! On Christmas Eve, he helps Santa deliver presents, and Santa gives him the *perfect* gift—a gold alarm clock.

Activities

- Be an inventor! Invent a new alarm clock that would remind the Easter Bunny to deliver his eggs. Draw a picture of your invention, and label the parts.
- Cottontail Playhouse! Make stick puppets of some of the characters in this book. Write a script of the story, and use your puppets to present your skit.
- What is your favorite part in this book? Draw a picture of the scene.

Name _____

Bunny Trivia Trackdown

Are you a bunny "eggs"pert? Grab your pencils and let the fun begin! See how many rabbit trivia questions you can answer.

_____ 1. What rabbit got in trouble for going into Mr. McGregor's garden?

_____ 2. The March Hare is a character from what book?

_____ 3. A baby rabbit is called a _____.

_____ 4. Who did the Hare race in the popular Aesop's fable?

_____ 5. What is a rabbit cage called?

_____ 6. This rabbit book character got stuck to a tar-baby.

_____ 7. Are wild rabbits nocturnal (active at night)?

_____ 8. How do rabbits communicate with each other?

_____ 9. Bugs Bunny was a pest to who?

_____ 10. This old, shabby toy rabbit wanted to be real.

_____ 11. True or false? Rabbits do not have very good hearing.

• Write two trivia questions and answers about rabbits. Trade with a classmate.
• Rabbit Whiz-Kid Bonus! Make a list of all the rabbit book characters you can.

Answer Key: 1. Peter Rabbit, 2. *Alice in Wonderland*, 3. kit or kitten, 4. the Tortoise, 5. hutch, 6. Brer Rabbit, 7. yes, 8. They thump the ground with their back feet. 9. Elmer Fudd, 10. the Velveteen Rabbit, 11. false

Easter Egg Mix-Up

The Easter Bunny is delivering eggs to quintuplets. Can you find and circle the five eggs below that are exactly the same? Color the picture.

Cooking with Kids

Pastel Fruit Salad

Ingredients:
1 large can pineapple chunks, drained
1 can mandarin oranges, drained
1 small jar Maraschino cherries, drained
1 cup flaked coconut
1 cup pastel-colored marshmallows
1 to 2 cups sour cream (enough to coat)

Mix all the ingredients together and refrigerate. Serve in clear plastic cups for all the pretty colors to show through.

Note: The recipe may need to be doubled or tripled according to class size.

Bunny Salad

Rabbits are famous for eating carrots. Make and serve a favorite carrot-raisin salad with your students.

Ingredients:
4 cups grated carrots
1 cup raisins
1/2 cup mayonnaise or Miracle Whip™

Grate the carrots. Put all the ingredients into a bowl. Mix well and refrigerate till serving time. Put a scoop onto a lettuce leaf and serve with crackers.

Marshmallow Milk

Serve a cup of warm milk with a floating chocolate-covered marshmallow egg. Use a small straw to stir and sip.

by Tania Kourempis-Cowlin

Colorful Scrambled Eggs

Ingredients:
1 dozen or more eggs
   (according to class size)
food coloring
margarine to coat frying pans

Crack the eggs into a mixing bowl. Whip the eggs thoroughly. Divide the mixture into several bowls. Add a drop or two of food coloring; use green, blue and red. You will need several frying pans to cook the colored eggs separately. Serve a small scoop of scrambled eggs in each color along with buttered toast strips.

Bunny Bird Gorp

A handful of this irresistible mix means crunchy-coated popcorn and a menagerie of gummy bunnies and jelly bird eggs.

Ingredients:
6 cups popped popcorn
1 cup dry roasted peanuts
1/2 cup brown sugar
1/4 cup margarine
2 tablespoons honey
1/2 teaspoon ground cinnamon
Gummy bunnies and jelly bird eggs

Place the popcorn and peanuts in a greased 15" x 10" x 1" baking pan. In saucepan, combine brown sugar, margarine, honey and cinnamon. Cook and stir over low heat until boiling. Continue boiling for about 4 minutes. Pour over the popcorn mixture and stir to coat.

Now, bake the mixture in a 300° oven for about 20 minutes (stirring frequently). Transfer the cooled mixture into a large bowl, adding the bunnies and jelly beans. Serve or make treat bags!

Easter Cupcake Cones

Ingredients:
1 box yellow cake mix
30-36 flat bottom ice-cream cones
1 can vanilla frosting
food coloring
cake sprinkles and small jelly beans

Prepare the cake mix according to package directions. Fill each ice-cream cone with cake batter to within 3/4" of the top. Place the cones in a baking pan and carefully bake them in a 350°F oven for 20-25 minutes or until a toothpick inserted comes out clean. Cool completely.

Decide which color you would like to frost your cupcake cones. Use a drop or two of food coloring to change the vanilla frosting into pink, yellow or lilac.
   red with frosting = pink
   yellow with frosting = pastel yellow
   red and blue with frosting = lilac
Decorate with sprinkles or jelly beans!

Dear Earth of Mine

I'd like to scrub you fresh
and clean,
with soap and sponges
'till you gleam
again,
just like you first began,
free of tar
and old tin cans.
I'd like to see you strong
and mended,
perfect like
you were intended.
Cobbled new,
I'd rescue you,
and rinse you clean,
and make you *green*
again.

by Rebecca Kai Dotlich

259

Earth-Friendly Ways to Help Our Planet

Objective: Recognize differences between actions that are Earth friendly and those that are not.

Earth-Friendly Games

Make a set of of interlocking cards. Draw a frown face on one half and paste or draw an unfriendly act (for example: litter on the ground) next to the frown face. On the other half, draw a smile face and a friendly act (for example: a garbage can). Mix up pieces and have children match them by fitting them together correctly. (**Note:** 5" x 7" file cards work well for this.)

Make a set of cards similar to the ones mentioned above but, instead of pictures, write words. (For example: *Instead of using a paper lunch bag . . .* on one side and *I will use a reusable lunch box,* on the other side.) (**Note:** 3" x 5" cards work well for this.)

Help students design a board game that uses a path that leads to a healthy Earth. In some spaces write good things to do, with an instruction to move ahead. On other spaces write harmful things, with an instruction to go back. (For example: "Put a can in recycle bin. Move ahead 1 space." "Let the water faucet drip all day. Move back 2 spaces.") Number of spaces ahead or back can depend on the degree of action. For example: "Accidentally started a forest fire" could say "Move back 5 spaces," while "Started a recycle paper drive at school" could say "Move ahead 3 spaces." Use dice to determine number of moves. First person to reach healthy Earth wins.

by Elaine Cleary

Earth-Friendly Role Playing

Objective: Reinforce "do's" of Earth-friendly actions through role playing of age-appropriate situations.

Note: In all of these situations, the action to complete the play is left undirected, but students should be able to figure out the best course of action in each. If they can't, hints from the teacher and other students may be given, or another set of characters may take their places. After some practice, the teacher should be able to just put out props and let the students create characters and situations.

Characters: two students
Props: candy wrapper, trash can
Situation: One child sees another throw a candy wrapper on the ground.

Characters: two students
Props: bowl, plastic spoon, trash can
Situation: One child finishes eating pudding and starts to throw a plastic spoon in the trash can.

Characters: two students
Props: pencil, loose-leaf paper, wastebasket
Situation: Student is writing on paper, makes a mistake, starts to crush paper and throw it away, even though the back of the paper is clean.

Characters: parent, child
Props: shelf for a pretend store, paper towels, cotton dish towels
Situation: Mother starts to take paper towels off shelf, but the child points to cloth ones instead.

Characters: two children
Props: gift box, fancy wrapping paper, gift card, colored comic pages from newspaper, old greeting cards, tape, scissors, string
Situation: Children have a package to wrap for a birthday party.

Characters: teacher, two students
Props: two paperback books (or magazines), wastebasket
Situation: Teacher gives books to both students, and they pretend to read until finished; one starts to throw away his book.

Earth-Friendly Art

Objective: Create a visual reminder to be Earth friendly. Show how "junk" can be reused to make something new.

Make a "Junk-a-Saurus"

Materials: Have children bring in empty cans, toilet paper/paper towel rolls, shoe/tissue boxes, empty soda pop/milk/detergent plastic bottles, empty thread spools, old yarn, buttons, any other "junk" found around the house.

Talk about dinosaurs, especially their shapes. Discuss how models could be made using the junk. Let each child design and "build" her own Junk-a-saurus, fastening it together with paste, tape or brackets. When finished, she should give it a name and make up a story. Put all finished creatures together in a display.

I-Love-Nature Mobile

Materials: magazines from which to cut pictures and/or drawing paper on which to draw pictures of sun, rain, grass, tree, flower, bird, ocean, lake, fish, wild animal, soil; crayons/markers; paper straws; thread or thin string; scissors; glue; cardboard

In class, discuss the gifts nature gives us. List them on the board. The list should include those mentioned above but children may have other suggestions, too. Let each student make his own mobile, including as many things from the list as he wishes. Hang mobiles in the classroom before taking them home.

Wear-a-Message T-Shirts

Materials: old, solid-color T-shirts; permanent color markers/crayons; big pieces of cardboard

Together in class make a list of Earth-friendly sayings. Have each student choose a saying and (on scrap paper) design a simple picture using words and/or designs. Stretch T-shirt over cardboard and, using markers or crayons (or a combination), draw the same picture on the front of the T-Shirt. Some may want to do the back, too. If marker is used, let it dry on the cardboard. If crayon is used, put a piece of brown craft paper on top and apply hot iron to set color. Have a Wear-Your-T-shirt Day, perhaps having a parade through other classes. The recycled T-shirt can be washed and worn again and again!

Earth-Friendly Music

Objective: Use simple songs to help children remember Earth-friendly rules.

Tune: "Mary Had a Little Lamb"

Teacher: What is something that can be recycled? (object) What should we do with it? (action)

Resulting Song:
Soup cans can be recycled, recycled, recycled;
Soup cans can be recycled,
So put them in the blue bin.

Teacher: What is something we can't reuse? (object) What could we use instead? (action)

Resulting Song:
We can't reuse paper towels, paper towels,
    paper towels;
We can't reuse paper towels,
So use cloth ones instead.

Tune: "On Top of Old Smokey"

Teacher: Suggests first line; children supply rest.
Resulting Song:
My family recycles, _____

_____

_____

_____

(Blank lines should list items to recycle.)

Another introductory line might be:
When I take a long shower, _____
(Go on to tell why that's wrong and what should be done instead.)

After doing several songs this way, students may want to suggest their own first lines or possibly other tunes to put words to.

Tune: "Twinkle, Twinkle, Little Star"

Teacher: Suggests first and last lines; children fill in the rest.

Resulting Song:
We use paper every day; this is what we have to say:

_____

_____

By saving paper, we save trees.
(Blank lines should suggest ways to save paper.)

Earth-Friendly Language

Objective: Use written language skills to communicate with parents, sharing with them the importance of ecology.

Teacher will lead a group discussion on:

- Which Earth-friendly practices take place mainly in the home?
- Why parents need to be aware of these practices
- How parents can help children be Earth friends

Together (children talk/teacher write) put these ideas into a letter explaining the need to be Earth friendly and asking parents to help. Teacher makes copies of this letter. Children sign their names and decorate the paper; then deliver it to parents.

Follow same discussion process as above, but teacher writes letter on the board. Children copy letter themselves, sign it, decorate paper and deliver to parents.

Briefly discuss the importance of communication between home and school, together with ways parents can help the Earth-friendly cause. Review rules for writing a letter. Then have each student write his own letter asking parents to help.

Option: Decorate paper. Then address envelopes and send letters home through the mail.

Follow-up for all levels will be a discussion of parents' reaction to the letter and how they will help.

Earth-Friendly Vocabulary

Objective: Children should already be acquainted with the basic ecology-associated vocabulary. The following activities are intended for reinforcement and retention.

Words: The 3 Rs— reduce, reuse, recycle

Reduce: Discuss how many paper napkins they use at lunch if each child uses one for face, one for hands, one to clean off eating space. Have each child take three napkins and make a stack. Next, discuss how each child could manage with only one napkin. Pass out one napkin to each child; then make a second stack. Note the difference in the two stacks.

Reduce: Put bucket under faucet in sink. Turn on water and pretend to brush teeth, leaving the water on for the entire time. Note the amount of water collected in the bucket. Repeat procedure leaving water on only to wet and rinse brush and mouth. Note how much less water is used.

Reuse: Put an empty soda pop bottle, an empty peanut butter jar and a shoe box on the table. See how many ways children can think of to use each in a different way. Ask: What other things can be reused?

Recycle: Show the recycle sign stamped on selected plastic and paper products. Explain the significance of the arrows. Tell how each one was made into another new item. Add glass and aluminum to the display. Have a lesson to identify which materials your community recycles. Put a collection of these materials in a box. Have children take turns taking out one object and telling which material it is. Together, sort all items into proper categories. Find out if your cafeteria has recycle containers. If not, write a letter to the school suggesting they begin recycling.

264

Save That Junk

When Earth Day arrives on April 22nd, it's a time to teach concepts on the preservation of our planet. Children need to learn how important it is to conserve natural resources, reduce the amount of garbage and to recycle. In our classrooms, we can encourage students to save and collect supplies rather than buying new products. The idea is to "save that junk" and turn throwaways into creative and fun art media.

Set up a recycle bin for the collection of items the children bring in. Save papers, plastics, Styrofoam™ and other materials to use in everyday art activities. Items from the Earth also make great projects: leaves, rocks, shells, feathers, etc.

Below is a complied list of saveable junk media. Don't forget the popular forms of creative art—the collage and mosaic. Included are several fun activities to try in your classroom.

What to Collect

boxes—all sizes
egg and milk cartons
berry boxes—paper and plastic
twine and string
cardboard tubes
salt and oatmeal boxes
straws
old magazines and catalogs
cotton
Styrofoam™ pieces and trays
wire and hangers
fabric and trims
glass jars
plastic containers and bottles
clothespins
lumber scraps
aluminum foil and cans
nature items
nylon stockings
nuts and bolts
clock parts
cancelled stamps

The list is endless!

Nifty Newspaper Art

Glue a piece of newspaper (a classified page looks great) onto an 8" x 10" piece of cardboard. Plan a picture, a garden of flowers, a clown with balloons or maybe a train with a trail of boxcars, just to name a few. Cut out pieces from colorful felt, fabric, trims, wallpaper and magazine pages. Glue these onto the cardboard. You have now created a design that stands out from its newsprint background.

by Tania Kourempis-Cowling

3-D Foil Art

Collect items from the junk box to use for this project. Examples are nails, screws, yarn or twine, paper clips, coins, beads, clock parts, nuts and bolts. Glue these objects to a piece of cardboard or scrap of lumber. Let the objects dry.

Paint a thick coat of white glue over the entire top surface. Lay a sheet of aluminum foil over the top. Press gently to adhere the foil over the objects. Use enough foil to crumple and mold it to all the lumps of this sculptured art.

Movable Mobiles

Attach strings to a clothes hanger to make the mobile. *Mobile* means "movement." Add items to the strings to blow in the breeze. Look in the junk bin for art media to be used as mobile pieces. Example:

- Cut animal shapes from margarine lids, Styrofoam™ trays, cardboard boxes, etc.
- Make a holiday theme mobile.
- Use blown-out eggs, colored and decorated for an Easter theme mobile.
- Make a nature mobile from leaves, flowers, feathers, acorns.

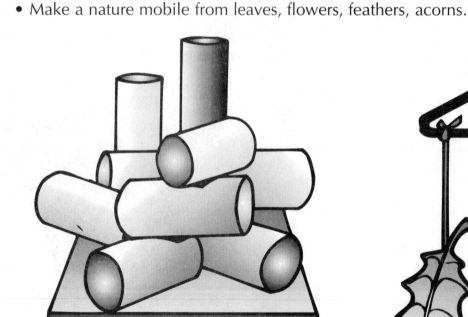

Tube Art

Collect cardboard tubes (toilet, paper towel, gift wrap). Cut these tubes into different lengths. Spread a layer of glue onto a cardboard base. Stand some cylinders in the glue, and lay some on their sides. Let this sculpture dry completely. Paint the tubes with colorful tempera.

Puppets

There are endless possibilities to make puppets from the recycle bin. Bases could be old socks, tin cans, margarine tubs, dish detergent bottles, oatmeal/salt boxes and the standard lunch bag.

Boxy Puzzles

Take the front panel from a favorite cereal or cookie box. Cut this into zigzag puzzle pieces. The amount of pieces and difficulty vary according to the age of the students. Code the back of each piece with a number or symbol and store these in a locking plastic bag.

Can Shakers

Make rhythm shakers or noisemakers with empty aluminum soda cans. Put dried beans or small pebbles inside; tape the opening shut. Cover the entire can with aluminum foil. Press the foil securely around the can. Decorate with colorful stickers and stars.

Stencil Fun

Plastic lids from margarine tubs and coffee cans make great stencils. Cut out geometric shapes, animals, stars or any favorite design. The kids can use these stencils to trace shapes and color pictures.

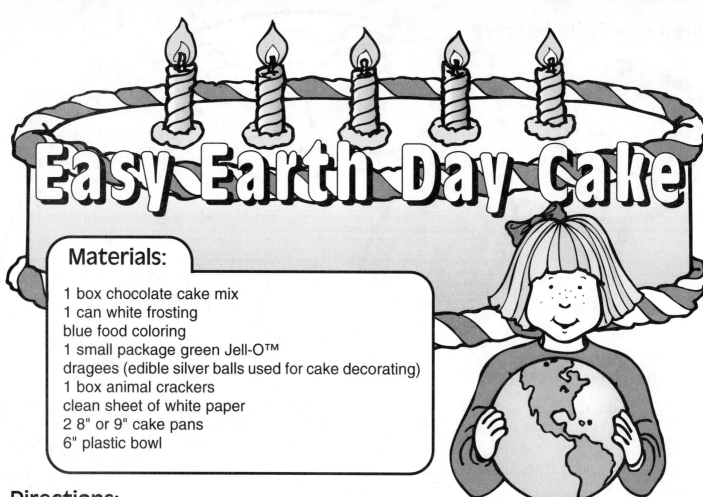

Easy Earth Day Cake

Materials:

1 box chocolate cake mix
1 can white frosting
blue food coloring
1 small package green Jell-O™
dragees (edible silver balls used for cake decorating)
1 box animal crackers
clean sheet of white paper
2 8" or 9" cake pans
6" plastic bowl

Directions:

Bake chocolate cake according to package directions. Let cake cool! If you don't, you will have crumbs littering your Earth! Frost with white icing. (Save about 1 cup of the icing in a separate bowl to use with blue food coloring for the oceans.)

Next, place a plastic bowl (approximately 6") upside down, lightly stenciling a circle in the middle of the cake. Mix blue food coloring into the remaining white icing and frost the round Earth blue.

Cut out the stencil of continents (found on the next page), being careful not to cut into the "oceans." Tape any places together that you might cut. Next, lay your "stencil" on

top of the blue Earth frosted on the cake. Sprinkle a light coating of green Jell-O™ over the open stencil. Lift carefully. (Have someone help if possible.) If you do not have any Jell-O™, you could also use white icing mixed with green food coloring and spread over stencil with your finger.

Place animal crackers along edges of cake to represent our endangered species! Use your imagination! Add other decorations to your Earth cake.

Optional: Place a few edible dragees, which are round silver cake-decorating balls, around the universe as stars. Or use silver star decals. Just remember to remove before serving. For a different look, a 13" x 9" pan may be used for the cake.

by Rebecca Kai Dotlich

268

Earth Day Cake Pattern

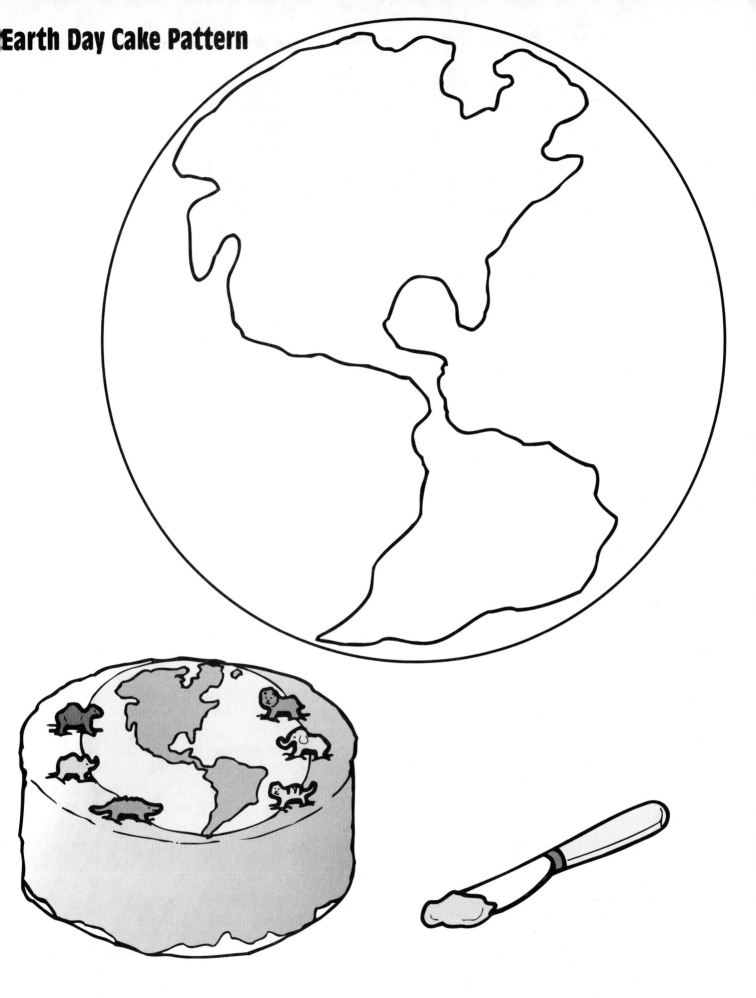

arden Magic

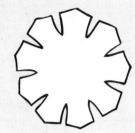

Five little seeds sleeping in the ground;
Up comes a flower and looks all around;
Says "I'm lonesome. I wish I had a brother."
He gets his wish. Up comes another.
Two little flowers, pretty as can be;
Here comes a third one; now there are three.
Three little flowers. Do you want any more?
Say that you do, and we'll have four.
Four little flowers in my flower bed;
A fifth one lifts her pretty little head.
Five little flowers grow and
grow and grow.
From where did they come?
Do you know? Do you know?

To Make Finger Puppets

- The pointed flowers should be cut from lightweight cardboard.
- You can use construction paper for the other flowers and the leaves. For strength, cut them double and glue together.
- Use a dime as a pattern for the center of the smallest flower. Use a nickel for center pattern of the other flowers.
- Use markers or pens to draw faces on the centers, and glue them to the flowers.
- On the largest flowers, cut slashes from the edges to the faces. Glue the leaves in back of their heads.
- Using small loops of strapping tape, fasten flowers to the back of a green glove, near the tips of fingers and thumb. (This can be done easily if you put the glove on your hand and press down on the flowers.)

To Perform

Work with the back of your hand to the audience. Fold your thumb and fingers down and raise them one at a time at the appropriate places in the poem.

by Mabel Duch

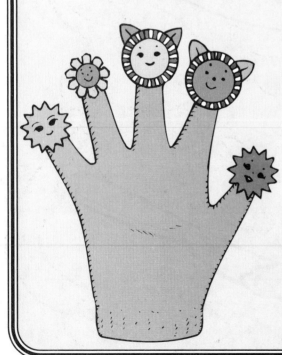

Gertie's Garden

Here's Gertie O'Hare,
Giving her garden good care.
She plants, then she waters the tiny new seeds,
And soon she has all the "veggies" she needs!

Materials

- patterns
- straw
- scissors
- crayons
- glue
- 8 oz. whipped topping container

Directions

1. Color and cut out pieces A through D.

2. Flatten top of straw. Glue A and B together carefully, with straw placed securely in between. Trim edges and straw as needed.

3. Invert an 8 oz. whipped topping container and glue pieces C and D to side, matching seams appropriately.

4. If desired, cut one E using brown construction paper. Glue to top.

5. In top center, poke a hole large enough for the straw to fit though loosely.

6. Place straw with Gertie attached in center hole and rotate.

by Barb Casper

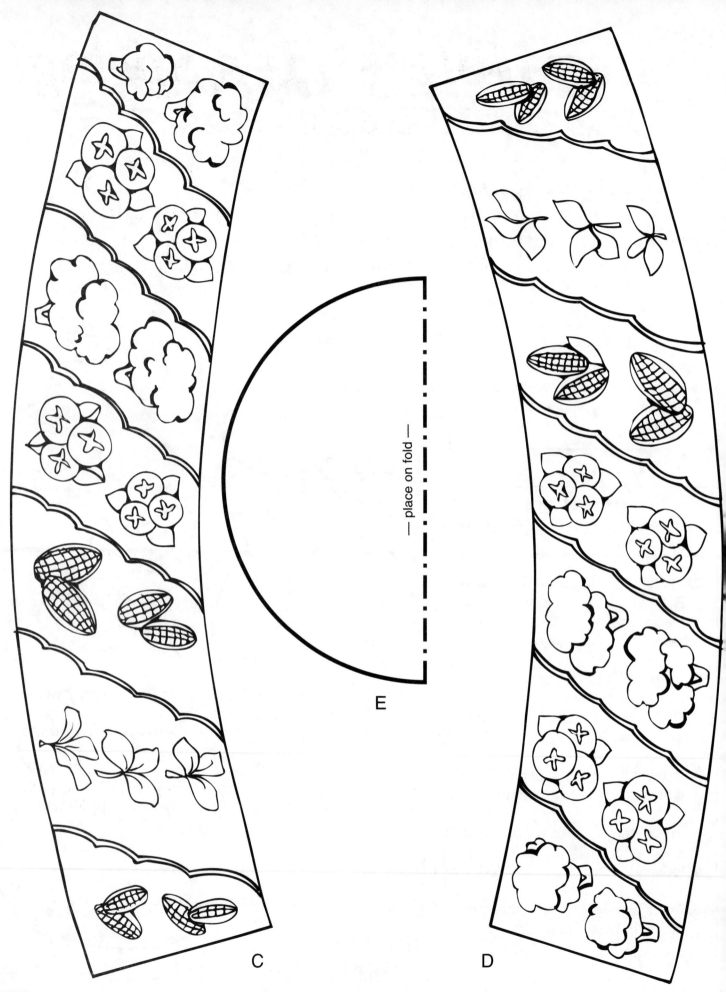

— place on fold —

E

C

D

Listen Up! It's Spring!

 ## Flower Phonics

Materials: Blank paper, pencil

Skills: Beginning sounds

First number your paper from 1 to 10. For each number, I will read you a pair of flower names. If the two names begin with the *same* sound, write *S* by the number. If the two names begin with *different* sounds, write *D* by the number.

1. tulip, sweet pea
2. marigold, mum
3. poppy, pussywillow
4. heather, hollyhock
5. pansy, bluebell
6. zinnia, aster
7. daisy, rose
8. daffodil, dandelion
9. lilac, lily
10. orchid, buttercup

11. Write your name under the number 10.

 ## May Day Flowers

Materials: Reproducible on page 275
Crayons: red, yellow, blue and brown

Skills: Color recognition, counting 1-10

In Row A

1. Write your name at the top of your paper.
2. Find the flower with 6 petals. Color it yellow.
3. Find the flower with 5 petals. Color it red.
4. Find the flower with 7 petals. Color it blue.

In Row B

1. Find the May Day basket with 8 flowers. Color just the basket brown.
2. Find the May Day basket with 10 flowers. Color just the basket blue.
3. In the last basket, draw 3 red flowers.

In Row C

1. Find the Maypole with 4 streamers. Draw 4 yellow flowers under it.
2. Find the Maypole with 5 streamers. Circle it with your brown crayon.
3. On the back of your paper, draw a tall Maypole with 2 streamers, one on each side. Draw 2 children around the Maypole.

by Ann Richmond Fisher

May Day Deliveries

Materials: Blank paper, pencil

Skills: Addition and subtraction with addends up to 8

Divide your paper into quarters by folding it once horizontally and once vertically. (Demonstrate this if necessary.) Crease the folds and then open your paper and lay it flat. In the top left portion of your paper, write your name.

I am going to read you a story about a boy who delivered flowers on May Day. At the end of the story, I will ask you how many baskets he had left. Use the top right corner of your page as work space. Write down the numbers you need to solve the problems as I read.

Story: Austin Helps His Mom

Austin liked to help his mother at the flower shop. His favorite times to work there were at Christmas because l loved the smell of holly and evergreens and May Day because his mom always planned surprises. This year she w giving free surprise May Day baskets to some special people, and Austin was going to have the fun job of helpi deliver them!

Bright and early on May first (which of course is May Day), Aust helped his mom load 12 baskets of flowers into the van. Their fir stop was Bayview Nursing Home where Austin carried in 6 ba kets for the great-grandparents of some of his friends. Next th stopped at the mayor's office where they left 1 basket for th mayor and 1 for his secretary. Their third stop was the childrer wing of the hospital. But since visiting hours had not begun, th weren't able to leave any flowers. They'd have to stop in a litt later.

About noon, Austin and his mother drove back to the flower sh where they ate lunch and loaded 8 more baskets into the va Then they drove to the library and delivered 3 baskets to the libra ians. Next they drove by their own house, wrote a note on one the baskets and left it on the front porch for their mailman. The last stop for the afternoon was their church where they left 3 ba kets for the Sunday services.

1. How many baskets were left in the van for Austin and h mom to take back to the hospital? (Repeat story if desire
2. In the bottom left corner of your paper, write your fir answer.
3. In the bottom right corner, list three of the places whe Austin delivered baskets.

274

May Day Flowers

Row A

Row B

Row C

 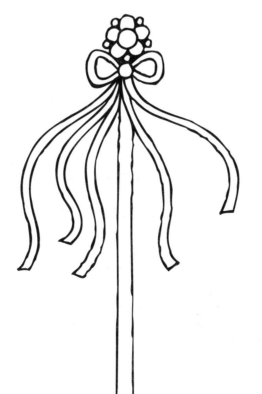 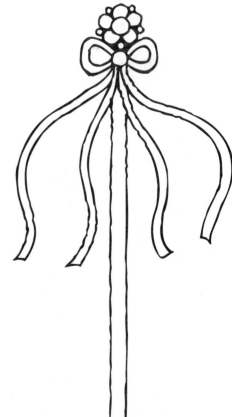

Spring into Action
Multicultural Games for the Classroom

Korean Children's Day

This holiday is celebrated May 5 as a time to make children feel special. School in Korea is out for the day, and kids have parties and get small gifts from their parents. Yoot is a game Korean children often play on Children's Day.

Make a Yoot gameboard (shown as a border around this activity) and three craft sticks colored with markers on only one side. The object is for a player to move his marker around the board and be the first to get back to Start.

To play, toss the three craft sticks. Movement of the markers depends on how the sticks land.
- Move one space if the sticks land with two blank sides up.
- Move two spaces if the sticks land with two decorated sides up.
- Move three spaces for three blank sticks.
- Move four spaces for three decorated sticks.

Start ➡

Pinata Game

Instead of filling a pinata with "goodies," try filling it with slips of paper, each containing a letter of the alphabet. Choose a couple of letters beforehand, say B and Q, and when the papers fall from the broken pinata, the children who find the most Bs and Qs are the winners. This can be done with numbers, colors and shapes and is a great game for teaching recognition skills.

Variations:
Another fun color recognition game is to fill a pinata with colored "pony" beads (can be purchased at a local crafts store). Assign each child a color and the child who collects the most of their color wins.

Do the same as above, only write each child's name on a slip of folded paper and put inside the pinata. When the papers fall, the child who finds his name first is the winner.

Firecracker Hunt

Cut out numerous construction paper firecrackers and hide them around the room while the children are not there. Put some in obvious places and some in more difficult places. Hold a treasure hunt and see who can find the most.

Variations:
Cut one firecracker from gold paper. The finder receives a treat.

Attach clues to each firecracker that tell where the next one can be found. The class works as a group figuring out where each firecracker is as they get closer and closer to finding the gold firecracker. Have a special treat for the class when the treasure hunt is over.

by Donna Stringfellow

Spring Games for the Classroom

Egg Hop

Divide players into two teams. Have children choose partners within their team. The first pair on each team is given the cardboard eggs. One player starts off as the rabbit, the other as the helper. To begin playing, the helper places one egg in front of the rabbit who hops on it with both feet. The helper puts down the next egg, and they continue moving eggs and hopping. When they reach a set goal, the players switch places and come back. The winner is the team that finishes the relay first.

Preparation: Make large cardboard cutout Easter eggs for each team.

Bunny Nose

Divide the children into two teams. At the other end of the room place two piles of cotton balls. Put a rather large dab of petroleum jelly on each child's nose. The first child on each team crawls to the cotton balls, picks one up on his nose (without using hands), then crawls back and the next child in line follows suit. The winner is the team who finishes first.

Preparation: Have a pile of cotton balls and a jar of petroleum jelly ready.

Popcorn Lamb

Divide players into teams and give each team the necessary materials. Each player glues a set number of popcorn onto the lamb and passes it on to the next player. The winner is the team that finishes their lamb first.

Materials: A large copy of a lamb, a bowl of popcorn and a bottle of glue for each team.

Jelly Bean Count

Divide children into two teams. On a table at the opposite end of the room, spread out 20 cut-out Easter eggs, 10 for each team, each set numbered 1-10.

Place a bowl of jelly beans in front of each team. The object is for the first child on each team to take one jelly bean, run to the table and place it on the egg marked "1." The next child in line picks up two jelly beans, finds the number "2" egg and places his candy there and so forth. The winner is the team who fills up their eggs first and correctly.

Me, Me

Have children stand in a circle with one child blindfolded in the center. Give the blindfolded child an egg and spin her around several times. Designate one child in the group to call "Me, me, toss it to me." If the blindfolded child successfully tosses the egg to the right caller, the caller then becomes the tosser. You can use plastic eggs for this game, but if you're really brave, you can try hard-boiled eggs or blown eggs.

62

Lei Day

Place: Hawaii
Date: May 1st

Lei Day is celebrated on May 1st in Hawaii. On this festive occasion, people wear leis—beautiful wreaths made of flowers strung together. Events held on this holiday include lei competitions, dancing and musical concerts.

Leis have always been an important part of the Hawaiian culture and are worn during celebrations, such as weddings, birthdays and holidays. Tourists arriving in Hawaii often receive leis as they leave their airplanes. Some of the flowers used for leis are orchids, carnations, jasmine and ginger.

Hawaii, the 50th state in the U.S., is nicknamed the Aloha State. This beautiful state is a group of islands located in the middle of the Pacific Ocean. The state flower is the hibiscus, and the state bird is the nene (Hawaiian goose). Sugarcane and pineapples are two important products of Hawaii.

Pineapples are a popular food in Hawaii. Think of a new dessert using pineapples that your friends will rave about. On the pineapple, draw a picture of your dessert and tell how it is made.

by Mary Ellen Switzer

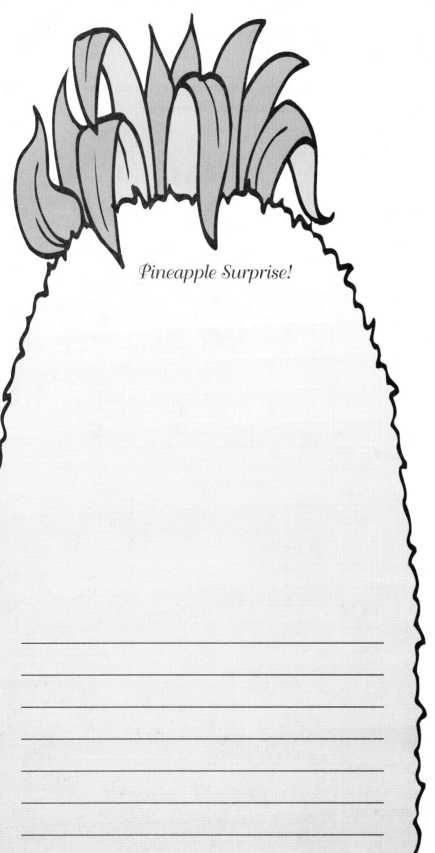

Pineapple Surprise!

Celebrate Cinco de Mayo

After providing your students with background information about Cinco de Mayo, use these activities to increase their knowledge about the importance of this national Mexican holiday.

Let's Visit Mexico

Place books about Mexico and its people on your reading table. We have provided a few suggestions, but there are many good selections available.

Place bright colored paper flowers, baskets, Mexican flags and other Mexican decorations nearby to carry out the Cinco de Mayo theme.

Gilberto and the Wind

Ets, Marie Hall. *Gilberto and the Wind.* New York: Viking, 1963.

A little Mexican boy finds the wind to be a changeable playmate. Sometimes the wind can fly kites, capture balloons, scatter leaves and run races. Other times the wind is a quiet companion. Pencil sketches add to the charm.

Nine Days to Christmas

Ets, Marie Hall, and Aurora Labstida. *Nine Days to Christmas.* New York: Viking, 1959.

A five-year-old girl named Ceci selects a pinata for Christmas. Modern-day Mexico is pictured in illustrations and text. Good for reading to small groups.

by Carolyn Ross Tomlin

Food in Mexico

Gomez, Paul. *Food in Mexico.* Vero Beach, Florida: Rourke Publications, Inc., 1989.

This book offers a summary of food products, customs and preparation in Mexico. Describes regional dishes, cooking techniques and recipes for a variety of meals.

My Dog Is Lost!

Keats, Ezra Jack, and Pat Cherr. *My Dog Is Lost!* New York: Crowell, 1960.

Juanita, a Spanish-speaking boy has just arrived in New York. He is sad because his dog is lost. Friends, who speak other languages, help him find his dog. Simple Spanish phrases introduced.

A Family in Mexico

Moran, Tom. *A Family in Mexico.* Minneapolis: Lerner Publications, 1987.

Describes the life of a Mexican family, residents of a suburb of Oaxaca, following especially the activities of nine-year-old Paula Maria.

Simple Mexican Recipes

Young children learn in a variety of methods—one of which is combining and preparing food for tasting. Here are some Mexican foods your children will enjoy. Invite parents or guardians to celebrate Cinco de Mayo with you.

Helpful Hints for Food Preparation

- Wash hands before handling food or equipment.
- Keep all utensils clean. Use hot, soapy water.
- Teachers and children with colds or open cuts on hands should avoid helping with food preparation.

Tortillas

Tortillas are a staple food of Mexico. Purchase these in the dairy case of your supermarket. Cook on a hot griddle or electric skillet in a small amount of oil. Turn frequently. Spread with cheese and roll up.

Cinco de Mayo Salad

1 head lettuce, shredded
1 pound cheddar cheese, grated
3 tomatoes, cubed
1 onion, chopped
1 large package corn chips
1 pound ground chuck, browned
1¼ package taco seasoning mix
2 cups red kidney beans, drained

Using a plastic knife, allow the children to shred, grate, cube and chop the ingredients. (Always watch children closely when using knives.) Toss vegetables and corn chips. Have ground chuck already prepared or do this yourself. Stir in taco seasoning and beans. Parents, children and other guests can make individual servings. Serves 25 to 30.

South of the Border Lemonade

6 lemons
1½ cups sugar
2½ quarts water

Allow children to squeeze lemons, making sure each child has a turn. Combine water, sugar and juice in a gallon container. Stir until well blended. Serve over ice. Makes 3 quarts.

J.Armbrust

Note: You may want to ask room parents to contribute enchiladas, refried beans and tacos for guests and children to sample during your Cinco de Mayo celebration.

Musical Instruments

Music is an important part of Mexico's celebrations and festivals. Encourage young children to participate in Mexican music by making their own instruments.

Shakers

Use empty egg-shaped hosiery packages. (Ask mothers to save these in advance of your celebrations.) Place several dried beans or small pebbles inside. Tape edges together. Decorate.

Bell Wristbands

Sew small bells onto a piece of elastic. Sew ends of the elastic together. Wear on wrists and shake to music.

Music Sticks

Cut wooden dowels into 12" pieces. Paint bright colors. Two sticks are needed for each child.

Use these simple musical instruments as children sing and dance to Mexican songs in celebration of Cinco de Mayo.

Sawdust Modeling Clay

Pottery has many uses in the Mexican family. It is used to hold food for cooking and serving. Young children will enjoy making a vessel from these inexpensive ingredients.

To make sawdust modeling clay, beat 2 cups dry wallpaper paste and 4 cups water until you have a smooth paste. Add 8 cups dry sawdust. Work together with hands. Place in airtight bags overnight for sawdust to absorb moisture.

Pinch off one ball-shaped clump for each child. Keep hands wet while modeling. Form into a vessel for holding food. Allow to dry for several days. Painting with tempera paint is optional.

282

Spanish Words

Print these Spanish words on index cards, with the English spellings on the back. Make a small star in the lower right-hand corner to indicate which is the Spanish term. Check a Spanish dictionary for pronunciation. Have fun teaching this language to your students.

Spanish	English
adios	good-bye
hola	hello
uno	one
dos	two
tres	three
cuatro	four
cinco	five
seis	six
siete	seven
ocho	eight
nueve	nine
diez	ten
rojo,-a	red
azul	blue
amarillo,-a	yellow
verde	green
negro,-a	black
blanco,-a	white

Name _____

Cut out the numbers at the bottom and paste them by the correct Spanish words.

☐ tres ☐ uno

☐ seis ☐ ocho

☐ dos ☐ cuatro

☐ siete ☐ nueve

☐ cinco ☐ diez

1	2	3	4	5
6	7	8	9	10

A Mexican Fiesta

Activities to Bring Mexican Customs to Your Classroom

Mexican Table Toppers

by Tania Kourempis-Cowling

Tie-Dyed Flowers

You will need about three or four paper coffee filters per flower. Using several containers, place several drops of food coloring into a tablespoon of water. Fold the filter into quarters. Dip one end into the mixture, letting it absorb color. Continue dipping the other filters in different colors. Lay these filters flat to dry. Later, place all filters on top of one another. Gather them together at the bottom and wrap a pipe cleaner tightly around the end for the stem. Place these around the room in vases or attach to walls.

Place Mats
(Mantelitos)

Make a place mat out of construction paper to set a Mexican table for either snack or lunch. Use the Mexican flag colors of red, white and green. Fold an 8½" x 11" piece of construction paper lengthwise. Cut slits up from the fold. Stop cutting about ½" from the edge of the paper. Make the slits an inch or so apart. Open. Now, weave construction paper strips over and under the slits of the place mat. Tape all the ends down to secure. Decorate the border any way you choose.

Yarn Napkin Rings

Using yarn to make colorful pictures, a famous art form in Mexico. Instead of pictures, this project will correlate with the above place mat to set a Mexican table. The napkin ring consists of a piece of toilet tube about 3" long. Spread glue on the outside of the tube, and wrap colorful yarn around the cylinder. Pass a napkin through the holder when it's dry.

Mexican Party Favors

Bag Pinata

A pinata is a decorated container usually filled with candy and small toys. The children play a traditional game, blindfolded, to break the pinata and let out all the "goodies." The first pinatas were made of clay but now papier-mâché ones have been substituted. A simple pinata for the classroom can be made from a paper grocery bag. Have the children decorate the bag as they wish with art materials. Open the bag and fold down the top a few times. Punch a hole on opposite sides of the top of the bag and thread ribbon or yarn through for a hanger. It's fun to add crepe paper streamers or ribbons to the bottom edge. These can be taped, glued or stapled on. Fill the bag with "goodies." Hang it from the ceiling or a doorway and proceed to play the pinata game with your students.

Mosaic

A mosaic is defined as a surface decoration made by inlaying small pieces of variously colored materials to form pictures or patterns. Try to obtain pictures of Mexican mosaics from books in the library or a local museum. Famous Mexican artists specializing in mosaic are Alfaro Sequeiros, Diego Rivera and Rufino Tamayo.

Make a classroom or individual mosaic using lasagna pasta. Paint the lasagna strips with tempera paint. Paint different strips various colors. When dry, break the strips into pieces. On a square of cardboard, draw a simple picture or design. Glue the pieces onto the square fitting them close together.

286

May Day Flowers

May Day Bouquet

Materials:

fresh spring flowers (violets, daffodils, lilacs, daisies)	paper doily (purchased or hand-made)
aluminum foil	paper tissue or cotton wool
ribbon	rubber bands

Directions:

The first day of May is the day to give flowers to a special friend. It is easy to make a small bouquet, or nosegay, of fresh flowers. First pick a few fresh flowers like those mentioned above. Leave the stems long and include some leaves.

Arrange the flowers into a small pleasing bouquet. Put a rubber band around the stems, close to the flowers, to hold the bouquet in place. Cut the stems so they are even at the bottom of your bouquet. Now wrap wet paper tissue or cotton wool around the cut stems to keep the flowers fresh. Cover the wet tissue with aluminum foil.

Push the aluminum foil-covered stems through the center of a paper doily. (Make a doily by cutting a lacy pattern in a circle or paper.) Finally, tie a ribbon around the bouquet just below the doily and your May Day nosegay is ready to give.

May Day Basket

Materials:

ice-cream cones	ribbon or yarn
small paper doily	fabric scraps
spray starch	pipe cleaners

Directions:

Cut several simple flower shapes from fabric scraps. Spray with spray starch to add stiffness to the petals. Make a tiny hole in the center of each flower and push a pipe cleaner through the hole for a stem.

Carefully make two holes in the upper part of an ice-cream cone. Run ribbon or yarn through these holes for a hanger. Push the pipe cleaner stems through the center of a paper doily. Arrange flowers and doily into the ice-cream cone. On May Day hang the bouquet on the doorknob of someone you love.

by D.A. Woodliff

Children's Day
in Japan

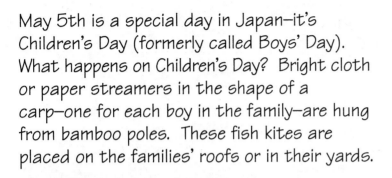

May 5th is a special day in Japan—it's Children's Day (formerly called Boys' Day). What happens on Children's Day? Bright cloth or paper streamers in the shape of a carp—one for each boy in the family—are hung from bamboo poles. These fish kites are placed on the families' roofs or in their yards.

Why was the carp chosen for this occasion? The carp is known for its strength and determination to swim upstream—worthy traits for boys to follow. Color the fish kites.

Fish Puzzle

Connect the dots of these Japanese carp streamers.

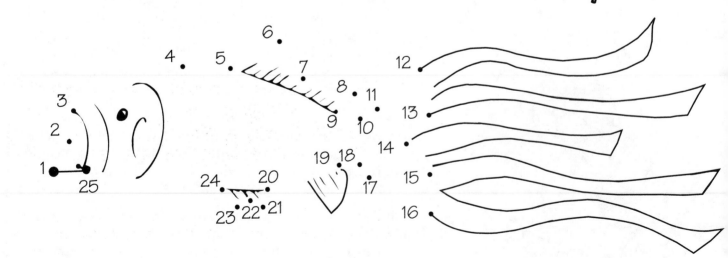

Marvelous Map

This page features Japan. Color each of the large islands of Japan a different color. Draw a circle around Tokyo, the capital of Japan. Label the major Japanese cities by the appropriate black dots.

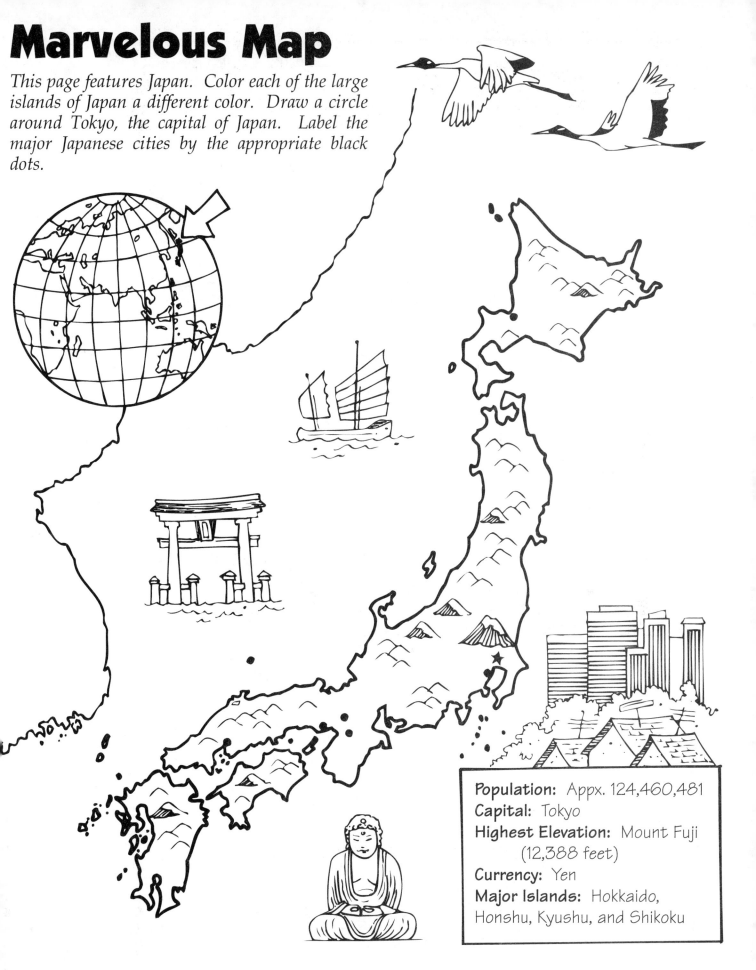

Population: Appx. 124,460,481
Capital: Tokyo
Highest Elevation: Mount Fuji
   (12,388 feet)
Currency: Yen
Major Islands: Hokkaido, Honshu, Kyushu, and Shikoku

Bonus: On the back of this page, write a fact that you have learned about Japan.

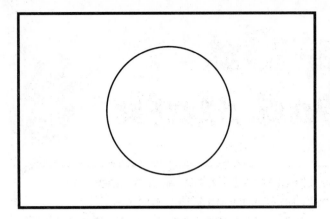

JAPANESE FLAG

Get your red and white crayons ready. It's time to color Japan's flag. This flag, which was adopted in 1854, has a red sun on a white background. Did you know that Japan is known as "The Land of the Rising Sun"?

white
shiroi

red
akai

The Magic Suitcase

Calling all tourists! Let's grab our magic suitcase and travel to Japan.

Kon-nichi wa. (This means "hello" in Japanese.) Welcome to Japan—the beautiful island country in the North Pacific Ocean. There are four large islands in Japan and thousands of smaller ones. The large islands are Honshu, Hokkaido, Shikoku and Kyushu. The capital of Japan is Tokyo, and it is also the largest city in Japan.

The Japanese manufacture many useful products, such as computers, cars, cameras, radios and television sets. These products are sold all over the world. Some of the food raised in Japan includes rice, cabbage, potatoes, strawberries and tea.

Most of Japan is covered with hills and mountains. The largest mountain in Japan is Mount Fuji.

Write or draw a picture of what you would pack in your magic suitcase for your trip to Japan.

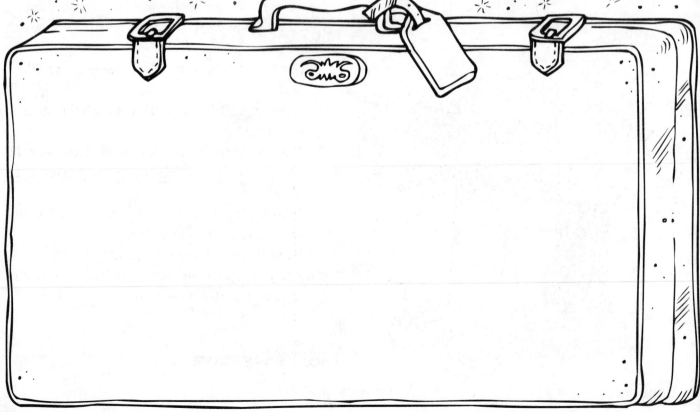

290

Hands-On
Mom and Dad Math

This year, bring the celebration of Mother's Day and Father's Day into your mathematics class with a variety of hands-on, exciting activities featuring Mom and Dad!

Pricing Mom and Dad

Provide each child with two 4" x 18" white construction paper strips. Invite the class to write their first and last names on one strip using a crayon or marker. Mom's first and last names may be written on the second strip. Using real or plastic coins, ask the children to cover each consonant with a penny and each vowel with a dime. Challenge the children to find the total value of each name. Together, identify the mom with the most expensive name and the mom with the least expensive name. Invite the class to find the difference between their names and their moms' names, the sum of their name and their mom's name. Together, identify the five smallest differences, the five greatest sums.

Father's Day

Vary this activity with Dad's name in June! Again, provide the children with two 4" x 18" strips of white construction paper. Invite the children to use a crayon or marker to write their first and last names in crayon on one strip and their dad's first and last names on the second strip. Let the letters *A-G* be worth 1¢, *H-L* be worth 5¢ and *M-Z* be worth 10¢. Invite the class to choose three bonus letters that will be worth 25¢. After the children have covered the letters with the correct real or plastic coins and identified the total of each name, challenge the children to:

- **Stand** if Dad's name has a higher value than your name.
- **Clap your hands** if your name has a higher value than Dad's name.
- **Whistle** if your dad's name has an odd value.
- **Close your eyes** if Dad's name has an even value.
- **Smile** if Dad's name has a value of $1.00 or less.
- **Turn around** if Dad's name has a value greater than $1.00.
- **Put your hands on your head** if the sum of your name and Dad's name is greater than $5.00.
- **Laugh** if the difference between your name and Dad's name is less than 25¢.
- **Hum** if this difference is greater than 50¢.
- **Put your hands behind your back** if this difference is greater than $1.00.

by Nancy Silva

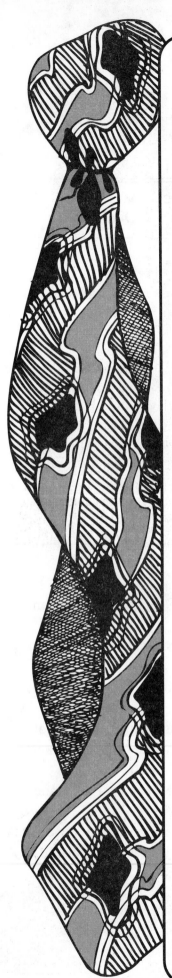

All "Tied" Up

Invite each child to bring in an old, "interesting" patterned, striped or print tie. Challenge the children to copy the tie using a variety of hands-on materials. Cusinaire™ rods, base 10 blocks and Unifix™ cubes create great stripes. Pattern blocks, tangrams and attribute blocks are ideal for forming geometric designs. Floral prints are easily represented using colorful buttons, beans and small stones. Rice, pasta and tiny beads help to add the most intricate details. You may wish to photograph the real tie, along with its clever re-creation for an unusual (and educational) Father's Day gift.

When the ties have been completed, provide the children with a list of the hands-on materials. Invite each child to tally the amount of each material that was used to create his colorful tie. Share the totals. Other classes will eagerly accept your invitation to view the ties. Display the tally charts beside each of the ties. Be sure to let each tie-maker stand beside his masterpiece to answer any questions.

Ask children to measure the tie using a yardstick or meterstick. Discuss: "Is every tie the same length, or are there several standard sizes?" Challenge the children to jump the length of the tie. Create a class equation showing the number of children who were able to accomplish this feat.

Working in small groups, ask the children to use ties to form:
- a circle
- a square
- a triangle
- a rectangle
- a pentagon
- a quadrilateral
- a parallelogram
- a hexagon

Create Venn diagrams with ties! Form a three-circle Venn diagram on your classroom floor using yarn or string. On 4" x 18" strips of white construction paper, write the three categories that you wish to use. The class will be eager to offer their suggestions. Possible categories include:

- Ties with the color _____
- Ties with _____ or more different colors
- Diagonally striped ties
- Ties with geometric shapes
- Ties with floral prints
- Ties greater than _____ inches in length
- Ties that are wider than ____ inches
- Ties made in the United States
- Ties not made in the United States
- Ties with animals on them
- Polka-dot ties
- Ties with words or people on the front

Place one of the category strips in each of the three circles. Invite children to step forward and place their ties in the correct section of the diagram. Ties that do not belong in any of the three categories may be placed along the outer edge of the circles. After the diagram has been completed, invite the children to share their observations. Begin by encouraging the class to complete sentences that begin: "Most ties ___." "More ties ___, than ___." Less ties ___, than ___." Later, work together to form equations based on the number of ties in each circle or overlapping section.

Putting Her Foot Down

Sometimes it's necessary for Mom to "put her foot down." When she does, how long is it? Invite each child to bring one of Mom's shoes to class for this activity. Some children may choose to bring in a shoe belonging to a grandmother, aunt, baby-sitter or special woman in their lives. Provide the children with a variety of materials: clips, Unifix™ cubes, keys, buttons, toothpicks, small stones, paper clips, coins, beans and so on. Challenge the children to estimate the number of each item that will be needed to measure the shoe from toe to heel. Invite the children to write the name of each material and their estimates on a large piece of construction paper. Ask the children to record the actual measurements on their charts, beside their estimates. Later, invite children to share their most accurate estimates.

Ask each child to cut a piece of yarn to match the length of the shoe. Create a class graph, ordering the yarn pieces from shortest to longest on a piece of chart paper.

Explain that you are going to create a "shoe train" using the shoes. Challenge the children to estimate where the shoe train will end if the Mother's Day shoe collection is placed toe to heel beginning right outside the classroom door and continuing down the hall. Using Post-it™ notes, allow the children to mark the spot in the hall where they predict the train will end. Test the estimates by having the chil-dren arrange the shoes. Identify the three closest estimates. Use yardsticks or metersticks to mea-sure the shoe train. Repeat this activity, this time pointing the shoe train in the opposite direc-tion. Invite several other classes to join in this activity.

Invite the children to trace the shoe on a piece of centimeter graph paper. Challenge the chil-dren to count the number of square centimeters that make up the shoe print. Ask them to fill in the shoe shape using Cuisinaire™ rods. When the shoe print has been filled in, the graph paper may be colored using crayons that match the rod colors. The colorful prints may be cut out and glued to a piece of construction paper. Ask each child to write the number of square centimeters below the print. Display the results on a bul-letin board entitled "When Mom Puts Her Foot Down."

Work together to sort the shoes. The class will be eager to create clever categories to group the shoe collection. A class tally chart list-ing these categories and the num-ber of shoes in each is the ideal way to share the results with classroom visitors. Possible cate-gories include leather, cloth, shoes that tie, shoes with buck-les, shoes with high heels and shoes with black soles. There is no limit to the creative categories that they'll think of!

Don't forget! Send shoes to school!

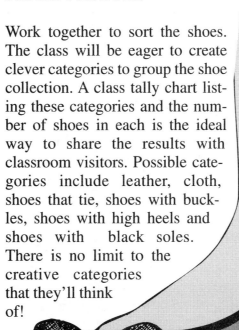

Lending a Hand

Mom is always eager to lend a hand! Invite her to do just that for this special Mother's Day activity! Provide each child with a heavy piece of oaktag or section of a cardboard box. Ask the children to trace Mom's hand at home and, with her help, neatly cut out the hand shape before bringing it to school. Some children may choose to complete this activity using the hand of an aunt, grandmother, baby-sitter or other favorite woman. Challenge each child to find the number of handprints needed to:

- cover his desktop
- make a path around his desk
- measure the width of the classroom's largest window
- measure the width of the doorway

Ask the children to use a centimeter or inch ruler to measure the length and width of the handprint. Tie in science by brainstorming the names of animal mothers with larger hand or footprints, smaller hand or footprints. Provide the children with unit cubes to find the square centimeter measure of the handprint.

The children will be delighted to cover the handprint with coins! Challenge the children to estimate the "price" of the hand if it were covered with pennies, nickels, dimes, quarters. Provide the children with real or plastic coins to test each of the four estimates by covering the hand with the coins. Ask the children to create individual charts showing their estimates, the actual price and the number of coins used. Identify the lowest priced hand when pennies were used, the highest priced hand when quarters were used. The children will welcome the opportunity to trace and cut out their own handprints. Invite each child to cover his handprint with coins, comparing the price with the price found for Mom's handprint.

Filling Dad's Shoes

No one can fill Dad's shoes, unless it's in your mathematics class! Invite each child to bring one of Dad's shoes to class. Some children may choose to bring a shoe belonging to an uncle, grandfather or special adult male. Provide a selection of materials that vary in size and shape. In addition to classroom hands-on mathematics manipulatives such as Cuisinaire™ rods, Unifix™ cubes and base 10 blocks, offer Ping-Pong™ balls, golf tees, screws, washers and small shells. The children are sure to enjoy working with elastic, cotton balls, dice, craft sticks, toothpicks and peanuts in shells! Invite the children to draw a picture of the shoe at the top of a 12" x 18" piece of white construction paper. Below the shoe illustration, ask the children to write the names of five materials that they would like to use to fill the shoe.

After having an opportunity to examine the chosen materials, challenge the children to estimate the number of each needed to completely fill the shoe. Since testing the five estimates will be quite time consuming, you may wish to allow several days for the class to complete this activity. When all of the estimates have been tested, ask the children to record the results on their individual charts. The children will be thrilled when you invite them to share their most amazing measurements with the class. There's sure to be some laughter when one of your students announces that it took 42 peanuts to fill the shoes. Display the children's posters on a bulletin board and share the humor with classroom visitors!

Father's Day Card

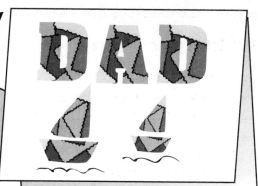

MATERIALS

construction paper
cancelled postage stamps
glue

DIRECTIONS

Soak cancelled postage stamps in water until they are released from the envelope. Allow the stamps to dry.

Fold a sheet of construction paper in half. Cut along the fold line. Now fold the cut half of paper in half to form a greeting card.

In large thick letters write the word *DAD* on the front of the card. (If you have an alphabet stencil this will help you make the letters.) Cut several of the cancelled postage stamps into various pieces, and glue these pieces inside the letters *DAD*. If desired, you can draw objects like simple boats, or baseball bats and balls, and fill these in with cancelled postage stamps as well. Outline the letters (and the pictures) with a dark crayon or felt pen. Finally, write a message or poem inside the card for your dad.

A Card for Mom

MATERIALS

construction paper   ribbon
small dried flowers   clear self-adhesive
glue   paper (optional)

DIRECTIONS

In early spring there are many tiny wildflowers. Pick a few of these tiny flowers and put them between the pages of an old catalog. Place several heavy objects (heavy books or bricks) on top of the catalog. Allow the flowers to dry and press flat between the pages for several days. Fold a sheet of construction paper in half and cut along the fold line. Fold one of these half sheets in half. These will form your greeting card. Carefully glue the tiny dried flowers onto the front of the greeting card in a pleasing arrangement. A ribbon bow, or a piece of paper shaped into a bow, is added to the stems of the flowers. Inside the Mother's Day card write a poem for your mom. (If desired, you can cut a piece of clear self-adhesive paper the same size as the card. The paper will protect the flowers from crumbling.)

by D.A. Woodliff

Messages from the Heart

Booklet Instructions

page A

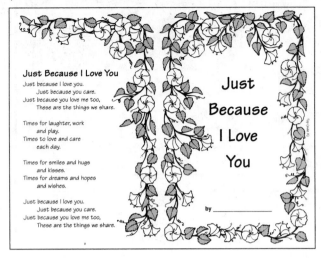

1. Duplicate page B on the back of page

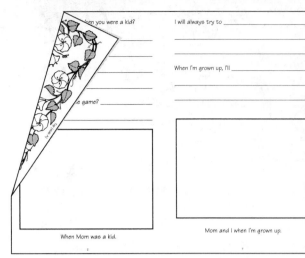

page C

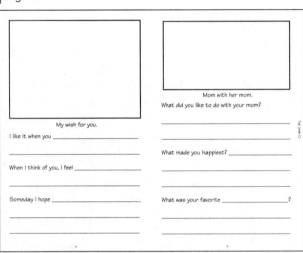

2. Duplicate page D on the back of page

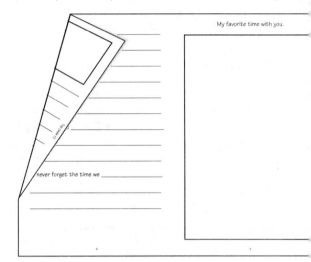

3. Lay page D on top of page B and fold.

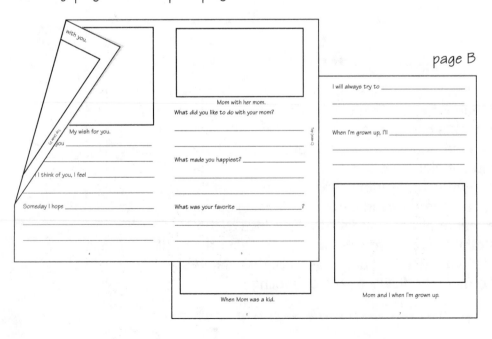

page B

Just Because I Love You

by _____

Just Because I Love You

Just because I love you.
Just because you care.
Just because you love me too,
These are the things we share.

Times for laughter, work
and play.
Times to love and care
each day.

Times for smiles and hugs
and kisses.
Times for dreams and hopes
and wishes.

Just because I love you.
Just because you care.
Just because you love me too,
These are the things we share.

8

What did you like to do when you were a kid?

_____

_____

What didn't you like to do?

_____

What was your favorite game?

_____

When Mom was a kid.

2

I will always try to _____

_____

When I'm grown up, I'll _____

_____

Mom and I when I'm grown up.

7

Mom with her mom.

What did you like to do with your mom?

_____

What made you happiest? _____

_____

What was your favorite _____

_____ ?

_____

_____

5

My wish for you.

I like it when you _____

_____

When I think of you, I feel _____

_____

Someday I hope _____

_____

_____

4

You make me happy when _____

When I'm sad, you _____

I like it when we _____

I'll never forget the time we _____

6

My favorite time with you.

3

Mother's Day Books for Children

On Mother's Lap

Scott, Ann Herbert. *On Mother's Lap*. Illustrated by Glo Coalson. Clarion, 1992. Picture book.

A warm, gentle story about an Eskimo boy's favorite place. Scott's use of repetition lends to the comforting tone of the book. The ending gives children reassurance, when the mother says, " . . . there is always room on Mother's lap."

Tell Me a Story, Mama

Johnson, Angela. *Tell Me a Story, Mama*. Illustrated by David Soman. Orchard, 1989. Picture book.

A mother and her daughter reminisce about the mother's childhood. Their dialogue charmingly portrays family sharing. Lively watercolors accompany the text.

Our Granny

Wild, Margaret. *Our Granny*. Illustrated by Julie Vivas. Ticknor and Fields, 1994. Picture book.

Bravo for a book that rids the world of stereotypical grandmothers! The vibrant, action-packed illustrations show grannies in all shapes, sizes and colors. "Some grannies have . . ." could be a nice creative writing assignment for children. Have them write their own story of a special relative, using this author's style.

Poems for Mothers

Poems for Mothers. Poems selected by Myra Cohn Livingston. Illustrated by Deborah Kogan Ray. Holiday House, 1988.

An original collection of poems. A beautiful bulletin board could be designed using these poems and children's illustations of them.

Other Mother's Day Books Worth Mentioning

Balian. Lorna. *Mother's Mother's Day*. Abingdon Press, 1982.

Bunting, Eve. *The Mother's Day Mice*. Illustrated by Jan Brett. Clarion, 1986.

Kroll, Steven. *Happy Mother's Day*. Illustrated by Marylin Hafner. Holiday House, 1985.

Wynot, Jillian. *The Mother's Day Sandwich*. Illustrated by Maxie Chambliss. Orchard, 1990.

by Liz Koehler-Pentacoff

Father's Day Books for Children

A Perfect Father's Day

Bunting, Eve. *A Perfect Father's Day.* Illustrated by Susan Meddaugh. Clarion, 1991. Picture book.

An amusing story about a little girl who makes Father's Day special by choosing *her* favorite activities to do with her dad. Lively watercolor illustrations help to create a sense of fun.

Your Dad Was Just Like You

Johnson, Dolores. *Your Dad Was Just Like You.* Macmillan, 1993.

When Peter has a disagreement with his father, he turns to his grandpa for comfort. Peter makes a discovery after Grandpa relates stories about Peter's father. The story is a touching portrayal of a father/son relationship.

Father Bear Comes Home

Minarik, Else Holmelund. *Father Bear Comes Home.* Illustrated by Maurice Sendak. HarperTrophy Easy Reader.

In this old classic, Little Bear's father comes home from a fishing trip but doesn't bring home the expected mermaid with blue and green hair. As always, Little Bear stories are warm and engaging. Great for beginning readers.

My Dad the Magnificent

Parker, Kristy. *My Dad the Magnificent.* Illustrated by Lillian Hoban. Puffin, 1987.

A child exaggerates his father's daring adventures so the father suddenly becomes a lion tamer, a cowboy and a deep sea explorer. Adorable pictures accompany the text.

End-of-the-Year Celebrations!

Celebrate summer and the end of the school year with these ideas.

Castle-Mania Celebration!

Spend the last day of school in a summery art activity. Provide "diggers" and "shapers" using your imagination and round up things like caps, cups, spoons, ladels, blunt knives, craft sticks, ice-cream cones, molds, cookie cutters, lids, empty clam shells, escargot shells, etc. Use large tools for more ambitious projects.

Pack the containers with wet sand, turn upside down and gently remove. Add finishing touches with "smoothers" and sticks, shells, pebbles, pinecones, seeds, leaves, flowers, foil, glitter and just about anything else kids can find.

Sand Sculptures

For more lasting works of castle art, try this recipe—the students will then have a take-home summer keepsake.

Materials: 1 cup sand 1 cup water
1 cup cornstarch large old pot
wooden spoon stove

Process:
1. Mix all ingredients in pot over medium heat.
2. Stir until the mixture forms a clay-like substance.
3. Pour into molds or containers sprayed with a no-stick spray, or shape freely when cool enough to handle.
4. Let harden (and remove from mold if used).

Try This:
• Add finishing touches such as flags and ornaments while the mixture is wet.
• Hardened works can be painted or coated with glue and sprinkled with glitter.

by Robynne Eagan

Lemonade

Allow students to squeeze the lemons and strain the seeds. Add cold water and sugar to taste. Add ice and serve.

"Here Comes Summer" Lunch

Enjoy a last lunch together out on the lawn. Prepare and share it together. Bring some picnic blankets or cloths and spread out for a feast!

Summer Roll-Ups

Ingredients:

luncheon meat
pickles
olives
cherry tomatoes
toothpicks

- Put all of the food items on a tray.
- Students create their own roll-up to show off, compare and eat.

Note: Remind students to remove toothpicks.

My Book

See the school year out with a "My Book" and a report card. In the two weeks leading up to the end of school, feature two or three children per day. At intervals throughout the day, feature one child. Students write a positive comment and/or draw a picture about this child on a strip of paper. The subject works on the cover page for this keepsake. Each comment is read and then added to the booklet which is stapled together. This builds self-esteem, makes a nice keepsake for summer reading, draws on students' writing skills and encourages students to look for positive attributes in one another.

Celebrate with an Art Excursion. . . Take students on an art picnic.

Materials:

sketch pads	drawing pencils
eraser	sunscreen
easels	paints
paintbrushes	palette for mixing colors
water	container for cleaning
blankets	picnic lunch
sun hats	paint boards
	(canvases, cardboard)

reading material for those who finish early

Process:

1. Take students on a short hike to a good artist's vantage point.
2. Have students sketch until they have a finished drawing.
3. Students copy the finished drawing onto their painting surface.
4. Students paint their drawing.
5. Take a break for lunch at the appropriate interval.

Artists' Lunch
Materials:
sparkling grape juice
plastic glasses
loaves of French
bread
variety of cheeses
cutting board
bread knife
selection of fresh
fruit

Make a Sun Hat

1. Be creative with recyclables. Call on parents, a school fund or purchase a straw hat for each student (these can sometimes be found for under two dollars).
2. With students' help, collect ribbons, flowers, bows, fishing lures (without hooks), feathers, bandanas, trinkets, medals, buttons, candy and other interesting items.
3. Provide glue, thin wire and a cool glue gun (if extra supervision is available).
4. Set up a table with all of these materials.
5. Allow students to create, make and take their own sun hat for the summer!

Variation: Round up painter caps or baseball caps and some fabric paints.

Dragon Boat Festival

PLACE: Taiwan

DATE: Held on the 5th day of the 5th moon—around the end of May or first part of June.

The Dragon Boat Festival is held in Taiwan, the beautiful, mountainous island in the South China Sea. This important festival commemorates the unsuccessful attempt to rescue Chu Yuan, a famous poet of ancient China, when he leaped into the Milo River. Exciting dragon boat races are the main event of the festival. Decorative heads and tails of dragons are attached to the boats during the races. On this day, children have charms in the shapes of hearts, peaches and tigers, and lotus-shaped sachets stuffed with dry scented herbs.

Create a dragon head design for a boat used in the races.

by Mary Ellen Switzer

Patriotic Party

Three cheers for the red, white and blue and for all the history these colors represent to the United States. In the months of April, May and June, there are three patriotic holidays–Armed Forces Day, Memorial Day and Flag Day.

Armed Forces Day honors the combined military, naval and air forces of the United States. It is celebrated on May 21.

Memorial Day (also known as Decoration Day) is a holiday for remembering those Americans who have been killed in war defending their country. It is observed on May 30.

Flag Day: The colonists wanted a flag as a symbol of the United States that declared its independence from Great Britain. Flag Day commemorates June 14, 1777, when the Continental Congress adopted the United States flag. The original flag is thought to have been made by Betsy Ross with 13 alternating stripes of red and white and 13 white stars arranged in a circle on a field of blue. As each state joined the Union, a star was added to the flag. Today there are 50 states that celebrate Flag Day.

Why not pick a special day to hold a patriotic party in your class complete with crafty decorations, fun food and games to play?

American Hand Kites

Before class, cut out the bottoms of plastic margarine tubs. Also cut six slits spaced around the outside of the tub. Thread equal lengths of red, white and blue crepe paper streamers into the slits and secure with tape or staples. Punch a hole on each side at the top to attach a chenille stem (pipe cleaner) for a handle. Decorate the tub with stickers, stars and flags.

Let the children march round the room carrying their hand kites. The streamers will dance in the air behind them.

by Tania Kourempis-Cowling

Revolutionary Soldier

Take a cardboard toilet paper tube and paint the bottom half blue. When dry, crisscross two white strips of vinyl or cloth adhesive tape across the bottom half of the tube. With markers, create a face on the upper half of the tube. Cut two small strips from blue construction paper and attach one to each side for arms. Make three 2½" curved strips from blue construction paper and staple together to make the soldier's three-cornered hat.

Woven Place Mats

Have the students do a paper weaving craft to make their party place mat. This mat will be a flag replica. Fold a white sheet of construction paper (9" x 12") in half lengthwise. Teachers need to draw straight lines about 2" from the cut edges. The children will cut a series of parallel slits from the folded edge to the teacher's guide line. Open the paper flat and proceed to weave red and white strips of paper in and out of the slits. Each strip will alternately go over and under the paper. Next, cut a blue square to be glued in the upper left corner. Use adhesive stars. Tape the ends of the woven strips down to secure.

Note: Betsy Ross' flag had 13 stars representing the 13 colonies. They were placed in a field of blue.

Noisemakers

Use clean aluminum soft drink cans. Place a handful of dried beans or popcorn kernels into the can; tape the opening shut. Completely cover each can with aluminum foil. Decorate with sticker stars and shake, shake, shake!

Sparkling Fireworks

Start with a sheet of black construction paper. With a hole punch, punch circles from different colors of construction paper. Glue circles in a cluster in the center of the black paper. Then use glue to draw lines leaving the circles in a swirl design. Sprinkle glitter over the paper, shaking off the excess. Now you have a picture to celebrate patriotic fireworks bursting in the night sky.

The Bell of Freedom

Hang a metal dinner bell or cowbell from the ceiling. Give the children six beanbags. Let them take turns tossing the bags, trying to ring the "bell of freedom." The player who rings the bell the most in six throws is the winner.

★ Colonial Muffins ★

Use your favorite muffin mix. Fold in fresh blueberries and chopped strawberries. Bake according to directions. Serve muffins with toothpick decorations.

Buy or make small flags. Adhere two flag stickers back to back with a toothpick in between. You can also use the same procedure with star stickers.

★ Perky Punch ★

Prior to serving, make a tray of ice cubes using several drops of red or blue food coloring in the water. Freeze. Serve apple juice or lemon-lime soda with the colorful ice cubes.

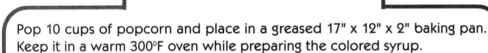

★ Patriotic Popcorn ★

Pop 10 cups of popcorn and place in a greased 17" x 12" x 2" baking pan. Keep it in a warm 300°F oven while preparing the colored syrup.

Grease the bottom and sides of a 2-quart saucepan. Combine 1 cup butter or margarine, 3/4 cup sugar, one 3-oz. package of Jell-O™ (red or blue), 3 tablespoons water and 1 tablespoon of light corn syrup. Use a candy thermometer; cook and stir over medium heat until the temperature reaches 225°F (hardball stage).

Pour the syrup over the popcorn and toss to coat. Bake this mixture in a 300°F oven for 10 minutes, stirring at least once during the baking time. Transfer this popcorn to another cool pan. (Makes one color; repeat for a second color.)

Cool completely breaking the popcorn into clusters. Proceed to make another batch in the other color. Serve the popcorn in class or make "doggie bags" to take home.

Red, White and Blue

See how many words you can make by combining letters from the phrase:

RED, WHITE AND BLUE.

Flag Trivia

Gather around the United States flag and answer the following questions:

1. How many red stripes does it have? _____

2. How many white stripes does it have? _____

3. How many stars does it have? _____

   How many stars are in each row? _____

   How many rows are in the blue section? _____

4. What is the shape of the flag? _____

5. What is the shape of the blue section in the upper left-hand corner? _____

6. What color is the top stripe? _____

7. What color is the bottom stripe? _____

Hooray for the 4th of July!

The United States celebrates the 4th of July (Indepedence Day) because of the signing of the Declaration of Independence by the Continental Congress on July 4, 1776. This important American holiday is celebrated with patriotic events and parades, as well as picnics and firework displays.

Let's plan a celebration! Plan a party for the 4th of July. What entertainment will you have? How will you decorate for the event? Tell about your special party. In the box, design an invitation for this event.

by Mary Ellen Switzer

Draw your own special fireworks display and color the picture.

Canadian Springtime Celebrations

Canada is a vast and beautiful land that stretches thousands of miles coast to coast. It is the second largest country in the world but one with the fewest people per square kilometer, with a population of just over 26 million. There are very sparse populations in the cold and icy far north, the mountainous west and the vast wheat plains in the center.

Canada is made up of 10 provinces and two territories. The official languages are French and English—that means it is a bilingual society. Canada is also a multicultural society—that means that people from all over the world live and share their language, religion, songs, celebrations, food and beliefs in Canada.

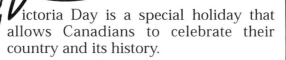

Victoria Day is a special holiday that allows Canadians to celebrate their country and its history.

On the Monday before May 24, Queen Victoria's birthday is celebrated in style. In the 19th century it was customary to officially celebrate the monarch's birthday. This queen ruled for so many years that Canadians kept this holiday even after she died! Today Victoria Day honors the present queen, Queen Elizabeth II, as well as Queen Victoria.

This holiday is celebrated across the country with Victorian picnics, boat races, games, contests, horse races, cultural festivities, food festivals, Maypole dancing, May Queen Balls, fireworks and planting ceremonies. In southern Canada, the Victoria Day weekend signals planting season and many families celebrate with seeds and hoes.

In the province of Quebec the holiday is called Fête de Dollard Des Ormeaux.

Canadians celebrate many special days including two important holidays–Canada Day and Victoria Day.

by Robynne Eagan

Canada Day

May Day

International Freedom Festival

The cities of Windsor, Ontario, and Detroit, Michigan, meet at the Canada/United States border. These two cities host the International Freedom Festival which celebrates both Canada Day (July 1) and Independence Day (July 4). Fireworks light up the sky on the night of July 2.

Canada and the United States have many close ties. Most of Canada's population lives in the southeast of the country near the border with the United States and many Canadian exports are sent south to the United States. Canada and the United States have formed a free-trade zone—imported and exported items can be traded without being taxed.

On July 1, a giant birthday party is celebrated all over Canada. It is the country's birthday! On this day Canadians celebrate the unity of their 10 provinces and two territories as one country. Originally called Dominion Day, this holiday was first celebrated in 1867 when a vote by the British House of Commons gave the Canadian Provinces the right to unite and form a confederation.

This holiday is celebrated in many ways by people of the various provinces, territories and ethnic origins. The country comes alive with parades, flotilla, sports events, street dances, folk festivals, outdoor concerts, contests, children's games, air shows, lobster dinners, fishing derbies, backyard barbecues and of course brilliant displays of fireworks.

May Day, traditionally celebrated on or near May 1 is sometimes mixed in with Victoria Day celebrations.

May Day has its roots in an ancient Celtic celebration (Beltane) held to welcome their summer which began on this day. Canadians of British descent carry this tradition–although summer does not arrive in Canada until June 21. This day is traditionally celebrated with a Maypole dance for freedom and the rights of all people. The pole symbolizes a tree and is decorated with colorful ribbons. Costumed dancers take the ribbon ends and perform dances that weave and unweave the ribbons.

Some Canadians harvest the first new shoots of spring for May Day feasts. The tender green leaves of dandelions are picked for salads and fiddleheads are sought for various dishes.

Today May Day is celebrated in many countries as an international worker's holiday.

Try This

Mark these Canadian holidays with a celebration of your own. Do students know any Canadians who might like to come and speak to your class on that day? Share some dandelion salad, fiddleheads or pancakes with Canadian maple syrup on that day. Make your own Maypole. Have a Victorian picnic—bring baskets, play Victorian games and dress for the occasion!

Learn more about Canada. Pin a map of Canada on the bulletin board. Have students do research and then print questions about Canada on one side of a card and answers on the other. Punch holes in the cards with a hole punch. Hang the completed cards with pins on the board around the map. Students will benefit from the research of others as they read the questions, try to answer and flip the cards.

Global neighbors. Twin your class with a class in Canada. Allow the students to exchange ideas, letters, information, photographs, local travel literature, class projects, a class set of coins, cassettes or videos of the school, the surrounding area, school concerts and celebrations; students' stories, songs and messages.

More Information About Canada

Parry, Caroline. *Let's Celebrate! Canada's Special Days.* Kids Can Press Ltd., Toronto, 1987.

Symbols of Nationhood. Department of the Secretary of State of Canada, 1991.

The Canadian Encyclopedia. Second edition, Edmonton: Hurtig Publishers, 1988.

The Canadian Global Almanac. Published annually by Global Press.

The Story of Canada. Janet Lunn and Christopher Moore, Lester Publishing, Key Porter Books, 1992.

999 Questions About Canada. John Robert Conombo, Doubleday Canada Ltd., 1989.

Flags ★ ★ ★ ★ ★ ★ ★ ★ ★ ★ ★

Flag Discussion

1. What is your first memory of your flag?
2. Has your flag always looked like it does now? Ask your grandparents what the flag looked like when they were children.
3. Do you know why the U.S. flag now has 50 stars and 13 stripes?

I salute a lovely flag
Of red and white and blue.
Around the world, other children
Are saluting, too.
The flags they honor may not look
Much like yours and mine.
No matter what the color,
They think their flag looks fine.
Some flags are green and white
    and orange;
And some are red and white;
Or other colors. But they all
Are exactly right.
For other children love their flags
The same as you and I.
We love to stand beneath our flags
And watch the colors fly.

Activities

1. Invite people from other countries to come in and show their flags, explaining what the symbols and colors mean. If there is an international institute or an ethnic organization in your area, they can help you with this.

2. Design a flag for your classroom or your home. What symbols will you put on it? What colors will you use? Share your ideas with your friends. Display your flags when they are finished.

The First U.S. Flags

The first U.S. flags were made in 1777. There were two different flags, each with 13 stars and 13 stripes.

A star and a stripe were added for each new state, but the flag became too big and hard to handle, so it was decided to revert to 13 stripes and add only stars for new states.

Can you imagine what the U.S. flag would look like if there were a stripe for every state?

Meaning of the Colors

The colors of the U.S. flag have meaning. Red stands for courage; white stands for purity and innocence; blue stands for justice, vigilance (being watchful and aware) and perseverance (sticking to a task until it is done). What do the colors of your flag mean?

The Stars and Stripes Symbols

The stars and stripes of the U.S. flag are symbols. Each star stands for a state. The flag the U.S. has now was first designed in 1959 when Hawaii became the 50th state. The 13 stripes stand for the first 13 states (then called colonies) who fought to be free from England in the Revolutionary War (1775-1783). If you have a different flag, what do the symbols on it mean?

by Mabel Duch

Resource

Flags of the Nations—video from Fusion Video, 100 Fusion Way, Country Club Hills, IL 60478-9906.

Flag Day in the United States

June 14

Every year on June 14th, the United States honors its country's flag. It was on June 14, 1777, that the Continental Congress decided what this country's flag would look like. The new flag would be red, white and blue with 13 stripes. It would have 13 stars to represent the 13 colonies. Now, there is a star for every state!

Design a flag to represent your family.

by Mary Ellen Switzer

Tell how this flag is representative of your family.

Happy St. Patrick's Day!

MARCH

Groundhog Day!

Happy Valentine's Day

Spring

Clip Art for Spring

It was great having you in my class!

Have a nice summer.

_____   _____
Date   **Teacher**

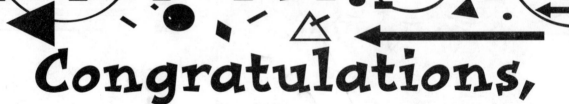

Congratulations,

_____

You're moving on!